PENGUIN CLASSICS

THE *MAYFLOWER* PAPERS

NATHANIEL PHILBRICK, a leading authority on the history of
Nantucket, is the author of the *New York Times* bestseller
Mayflower, the national bestseller *Sea of Glory*, and the National
Book Award winner for *In the Heart of the Sea*.

THOMAS PHILBRICK is a professor emeritus of English at the
University of Pittsburgh.

D1125252

WILLIAM BRADFORD, MARY ROWLANDSON, BENJAMIN CHURCH, AND OTHERS

The *Mayflower* Papers

SELECTED WRITINGS OF COLONIAL NEW ENGLAND

Edited with an Introduction and Notes by
NATHANIEL PHILBRICK *AND* THOMAS PHILBRICK

PENGUIN BOOKS

PENGUIN BOOKS

Published by the Penguin Group
Penguin Group (USA) Inc., 375 Hudson Street, New York, New York 10014, U.S.A.
Penguin Group (Canada), 90 Eglinton Avenue East, Suite 700, Toronto, Ontario, Canada M4P 2Y3
(a division of Pearson Penguin Canada Inc.)
Penguin Books Ltd, 80 Strand, London WC2R 0RL, England
Penguin Ireland, 25 St Stephen's Green, Dublin 2, Ireland (a division of Penguin Books Ltd)
Penguin Group (Australia), 250 Camberwell Road, Camberwell, Victoria 3124, Australia
(a division of Pearson Australia Group Pty Ltd)
Penguin Books India Pvt Ltd, 11 Community Centre, Panchsheel Park, New Delhi – 110 017, India
Penguin Group (NZ), 67 Apollo Drive, Mairangi Bay, Auckland 1311, New Zealand
(a division of Pearson New Zealand Ltd)
Penguin Books (South Africa) (Pty) Ltd, 24 Sturdee Avenue, Rosebank, Johannesburg 2196, South Africa

Penguin Books Ltd, Registered Offices:
80 Strand, London WC2R 0RL, England

First published in Penguin Books 2007

1 3 5 7 9 10 8 6 4 2

Introduction and selection copyright © Nathaniel Philbrick and Thomas Philbrick, 2007
All rights reserved

Map illustrations by Jeffrey L. Ward. Copyright © Penguin Group (USA) Inc., 2006

LIBRARY OF CONGRESS CATALOGING IN PUBLICATION DATA
Bradford, William, 1590–1657.
The Mayflower papers : selected writings of colonial New England / William Bradford,
Mary Rowlandson, Benjamin Church, and others ; edited with an introduction and notes by
Nathaniel Philbrick and Thomas Philbrick.
p.   cm.—(Penguin classics)
Includes bibliographical references.
ISBN 978-0-14-310498-8
1. New England—History—Colonial period, ca. 1600–1775   2. Massachusetts—History—Colonial
period, ca. 1600–1775.   3. Massachusetts—History—New Plymouth, 1620–1691.   4. Pilgrims
(New Plymouth Colony)—Early works to 1800.   5. New England—Description and travel—Early works
to 1800.   6. Massachusetts—Description and travel—Early works to 1800.   7. Indians of captivities—
Massachusetts.   9. King Philip's War, 1675–1676.   I. Rowlandson, Mary White, ca. 1635–1711.
II. Church, Benjamin, 1639–1718.   III. Philbrick, Nathaniel.   IV. Philbrick, Thomas.   V. Title.
F7.B757 2007
974'.02—dc22   2006052793

Printed in the United States of America
Set in Sabon

Contents

Introduction

In September of 1620, the people we refer to as the Pilgrims sailed from England to the New World. Hundreds of miles off course and months behind schedule, they stumbled on a harbor they named Plymouth. By the following spring they'd established an alliance with Massasoit, the leader of the Wampanoags. That fall they hosted what turned into a bicultural celebration now known as the First Thanksgiving. So ends the story many of us learned in elementary school: how America began with the voyage of the *Mayflower*.

Since the next significant event in American history—at least as taught in many of our schools—does not occur until more than 150 years later with the outbreak of the Revolution, it is not surprising that the Pilgrims have come to exist in a kind of mythic, ahistorical bubble. Then there is the Thanksgiving effect: an annual tidal wave of commercialism that only adds to the difficulty of understanding who the Pilgrims really were.

The best antidote to all this hype and nostalgia is to consult what may be the greatest book written in colonial America, William Bradford's *Of Plymouth Plantation*. In clear and evocative prose that resonates with the rhythms of the Bible, Bradford tells the story of how a group of Puritan Separatists came to found the first permanent settlement in New England. Their fiercely held spiritual beliefs were fundamental to their world view, but the Pilgrims also proved to be surprisingly flexible and pragmatic diplomats in their dealings with the Indians. Indeed, in reading Bradford's book, one is struck by the complexity and volatility of Indian-English relations, especially in the early years when the loyalties of the various Native groups were in near constant flux. Even several decades later, when the English servant Arthur Peach and some cohorts killed and robbed an Indian, all might have been lost if Governor Bradford had not insisted (despite considerable opposition) on trying and executing the malefactors for murder. It had been the Pilgrims' religious beliefs that had moved them to board the *Mayflower*, but it was their talent for negotiation and compromise that allowed them to survive and ultimately prosper in the New World.

Bradford's book is indispensable in tracking the course of Plymouth Colony during the first half of the seventeenth century, but there are other important texts from the period. Bradford and his fellow Pilgrim Edward Winslow coauthored an account of the first year in New England known as *Mourt's Relation*; soon after Winslow wrote *Good News from New England* in which he continued the Pilgrims' story through their controversial attack on the Massachusetts Indians at Wessagussett in the winter of 1623. These two books were written and published within months of the events they describe; as a consequence, they have an immediacy and level of detail not found in *Of Plymouth Plantation*, which Bradford began in the 1630s. To avoid repetition, *The Mayflower Papers* relies primarily on the earlier accounts to describe the Pilgrims' first eventful years in America while it looks to Bradford's history to tell what happened prior to their arrival in America and after the events recounted in *Good News from New England*.

Notably lacking from the historical record is a Native American account of what happened in New England during the seventeenth century. That is not to say that the Pilgrims' version of events has gone completely unchallenged. There is also Thomas Morton's wonderfully iconoclastic *New English Canaan* to remind us that Bradford and Winslow, as is true of all memorialists, told their story from their own and inevitably self-serving point of view. With Morton's help, we learn disturbing details about the Pilgrims' attack on the Indians at Wessagussett that Bradford and Winslow chose not to reveal. For those looking for other primary sources relating to the Pilgrims, there is a selection of additional readings at the end of this introduction.

If the true story of the Pilgrims was just getting started by the First Thanksgiving, there was, nonetheless, a culminating event that brought an abrupt and bloody end to what had been a remarkable half-century of peace in Plymouth Colony: the devastating fourteen-month conflagration known as King Philip's War. By the time Massasoit's son Philip was killed in August 1676 in a swamp near his ancestral home in modern Bristol, Rhode Island, more than a third of the towns in the region had been burned and abandoned. The English casualties were staggering (the male population of Plymouth Colony suffered losses of close to 8 percent—double the percentage of male casualties in the American Civil War), but the Indian losses were catastrophic. According to some estimates, the cumulative effects of war, disease, starvation, and slavery had inflicted losses of somewhere between 60 and 80 percent on the total Native population of New England. With King Philip's War, the story of the Pilgrims becomes something altogether different from the reassuring tale of multicultural cooperation taught in elementary school. Rather than being an exception to the long and tragic history of European-Native relations in the United States, the history of Plymouth Colony is very much in what William Carlos Williams called "the American Grain."

The two narratives that conclude this volume, Mary Rowlandson's *The Sovereignty and Goodness of God* and Benjamin Church's *Entertaining Passages Relating to Philip's War*, provide strikingly different but complementary perspectives on the conflict. Rowlandson's account, published within a few years of the war, tells of her four-month captivity by the Indians. Although she was a resident of Lancaster in Massachusetts Bay and her travels during her captivity took her far from Plymouth, her account has a special relevance to the history of the colony. As the wife of a well-known minister, she was recognized by the Indians as one of their more valuable captives. She also had a talent for knitting, and it was not long before she was brought before none other than Philip himself, who requested that she knit a cap for his young son. As a result, Rowlandson's narrative provides us with one of the few first-person accounts of the Wampanoag leader during the war. Upon its publication in 1683, *The Sovereignty and Goodness of God* became one of New England's first bestsellers and served as the model for what would become a new American genre: the Indian captivity narrative.

Unlike Rowlandson's account, which had been reprinted several times by the beginning of the eighteenth century, Benjamin Church's *Entertaining Passages Relating to Philip's War* did not appear until 1716, almost exactly forty years after the events it describes. Instead of a first-person account, it was written in the third person by Church's son Thomas, who wrote the narrative under his father's supervision. But *Entertaining Passages* is much more than a nostalgic "as-told-to" account. The extraordinary specificity and vividness of the narrative were made possible by the survival of Church's field notes from the war. As he says in his introduction, "having my minutes by me, my Son has taken the care and pains to Collect from them the Ensuing Narrative."

By the time Church's account appeared, there had been, in addition to Rowlandson's narrative, three published histories of the war, along with several extensive accounts published in London newspapers (see Suggestions for Further Reading). But except for a few descriptions of specific battles, there had been no account authored by an actual participant in the fighting. Church was, in many ways, the Forrest Gump of King Philip's War; he was there at a remarkable number of pivotal events. As tensions mounted in June of 1675, he spoke revealingly with two of the leading sachems in the colony, Awashonks and Weetamoo; he was present at the beginning of the fighting in Swansea; he and a small group of men held off a large number of Sakonnet Indians in the Pease Field Fight; he participated in the largest battle of the war, the Great Swamp Fight in modern Kingston, Rhode Island; he commanded the company of Indian and English soldiers who killed Philip; soon after, in what is one of the most memorable portions of the narrative, he captured Philip's "captain" Annawon.

Hundreds of letters, narratives, and poems were written during and after King Philip's War, but no other single source provides so many telling and provocative details about how the war was actually fought. Without Church's *Entertaining Passages*, we would not know that "friendly fire" injured and killed a significant number of English soldiers in several engagements; we would not have the same understanding of how the Plymouth authorities' callous treatment of potential Indian allies needlessly prolonged the war; and we'd know next to nothing about the circumstances of Philip's death. It is, perhaps, Church's account of how he persuaded a large number of captive Indian warriors to join his own ranks that is the most revealing, providing a fascinating and timeless portrait of how fear, frustration, and a leader's charisma can be used to change the tide of war.

As is true in many battle memoirs, Church is the hero of just about every tale he tells. But if the other published and unpublished accounts of King Philip's War are to be believed, he did, in fact, play an instrumental, if not crucial, role in securing an English victory. Even William Bradford's own son, William Jr., who had little patience with Church's reckless flamboyance, had to admit in a letter written to the minister John Cotton in July of 1676 that "without the Benjamin Forces, we had been either worsted or also lost many men."

Church's ability to irritate even his potential admirers persists to the present day. From the perspective of the twenty-first century, he displays an alarming lack of ethical consistency. Early in the war, he rails against the Plymouth authorities' decision to enslave a large group of Indians who surrendered at Dartmouth. By the end of the war, as he relentlessly pursues Philip through the swamps of Plymouth colony, he has become New England's premier slave catcher, providing hundreds of Indians, including Philip's wife and son, for shipment to the West Indies. I would maintain that Church personifies what would become a recurrent American type: the indignant critic of authority who, despite his best intentions, finds himself dragged remorselessly into moral compromise, violence, and tragedy.

Unlike the Puritan historians, who saw the virtual obliteration of their Native foes as inevitable and just, Church had his doubts, even as he remained proud of his own exploits in a conflict that had been sadly mismanaged from the start. Only Church would end his account of King Philip's War with a vignette about the capture of an Indian named Conscience and ruefully pronounce, "Then the war is over, for that was what they were searching for, it being much wanting."

Fifty-six years after the sailing of the *Mayflower*, Benjamin Church (a grandson of one of the original Pilgrims) had witnessed the blood-drenched and terrifying collapse of his forefathers' way of life. He had also seen the unsettling emergence of a new combative order that would become, in a little more than a century, the United States.

Suggestions for Further Reading

Bradford, William. *Letter Book*. Bedford, Mass.: Applewood Books, 2001.

Bradford, William, Jr. Letter to John Cotton, July 31, 1676, *Providence Journal*, January 15, 1876.

Drake, Samuel. *The Old Indian Chronicle*. 1867, rpt. Salem, Mass.: Higginson Book Company, 2004.

Easton, John. "A Relacion of the Indyan Warre." In Charles H. Lincoln, ed., *Narratives of the Indian Wars, 1675–1699*. New York, 1913.

Gookin, Daniel. *An Historical Account of the Doings and Sufferings of the Christian Indians in New England, in the Years 1675–1677*. 1677, rpt. New York: Arno Press, 1972.

Hubbard, William. *The Present-State of New-England Being a Narrative of the Troubles with the Indians*. 1676, rpt. Baltimore: Genealogical Publishing, 2002.

James, Sidney V., ed. *Three Visitors to Early Plymouth*. Bedford, Mass.: Applewood Books, 1997.

Mather, Increase. *The History of King Philip's War*. Samuel Drake, ed. Boston: Munsell, 1862.

Pratt, Phineas. *A Declaration of the Affairs of the English People that First Inhabited New England* (1662). MHS vol. IV, 4th Ser., 1858.

A Note on the Texts

The texts of the selections in this volume are drawn from the following sources:

Of Plymouth Plantation, from William T. Davis, ed., *Bradford's History of Plymouth Plantation* (New York: C. Scribner's Sons, 1908). A brief passage in the entry for 1642, omitted by Davis, is derived from Worthington. C. Ford, ed., *History of Plymouth Plantation, 1620–1647*, 2 vols. (Boston: The Massachusetts Historical Society, 1912), vol. 2.

Mourt's Relation and *Good News from New England*, from Edward Arber, ed., *The Story of the Pilgrim Fathers 1606–1623 A.D.* (London: Ward and Downey; Boston and New York: Houghton, Mifflin & Co., 1897).

New English Canaan, from Peter Force, ed. *Tracts and Other Papers Relating Principally to the Origin, Settlement, and Progress of the Colonies in North America*, 4 vols. (Washington, D.C.: P. Force, 1836–46), vol. 2.

The Sovereignty and Goodness of God, from Charles H. Lincoln, ed., *Narratives of the Indian Wars, 1675–1699* (New York: Charles Scribner's Sons, 1913).

Entertaining Passages Relating to Philip's War, from Henry Martyn Dexter, ed., *The History of King Philip's War* (Boston: John Kimball Wiggin, 1865).

Spellings have been modernized throughout the selections. To avoid confusion, this edition has adopted uniform spellings of the names of people and places. In the interest of readability, punctuation and paragraphing have been emended where necessary. Lastly, dates given in the old style have been converted to the new style.

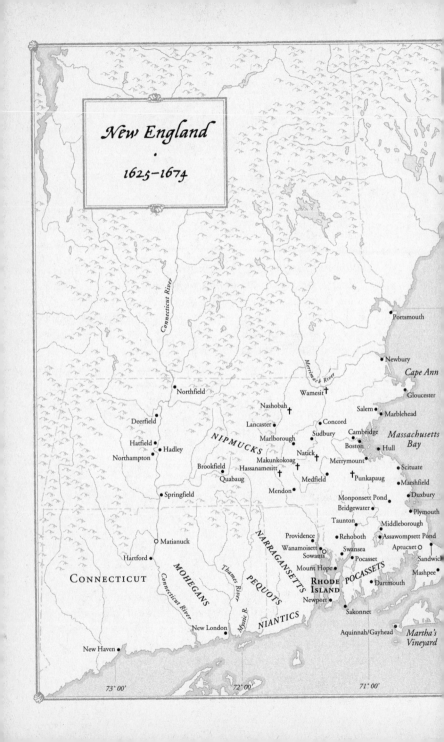

New England

·

1625–1674

Portsmouth

Newbury

Cape Ann

Gloucester

Northfield

Wamesit †

Nashobah †

Salem

Marblehead

Concord

Deerfield

Lancaster

Marlborough

Sudbury

Cambridge

Massachusetts Bay

Hatfield

Hadley

NIPMUCKS

Natick †

Boston

Hull

Northampton

Makunkokoag

Merrymount

Scituate

Brookfield

Hassanamesitt †

Medfield

† Punkapaug

Marshfield

Quabaug

Springfield

Mendon

Monponsett Pond

Bridgewater

Duxbury

Plymouth

Taunton

Middleborough

Matianuck

Providence

Rehoboth

Assawompsett Pond

Hartford

NARRAGANSETTS

Wanamoisett

Sowams

Swansea

Pocasset

Aptucxet

Sandwich

CONNECTICUT

MOHEGANS

Thames River

Mount Hope

RHODE ISLAND

POCASSETS

Mashpee

Connecticut River

PEQUOTS

Newport

Dartmouth

New London

Mystic R.

NIANTICS

Sakonnet

New Haven

Aquinnah/Gayhead

Martha's Vineyard

Connecticut River

Merrimack River

73° 00′   72° 00′   71° 00′

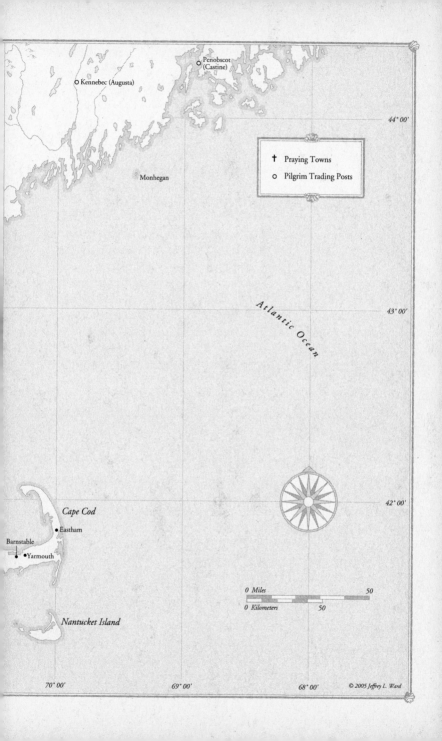

Penobscot
(Castine)

Kennebec (Augusta)

† Praying Towns

○ Pilgrim Trading Posts

Monhegan

Atlantic Ocean

44° 00'

43° 00'

42° 00'

Cape Cod

● Eastham

Barnstable

● Yarmouth

0 *Miles*   50

0 *Kilometers*   50

Nantucket Island

70° 00'   69° 00'   68° 00'   © 2005 Jeffrey L. Ward

The *Mayflower* Papers

From William Bradford,
Of Plymouth Plantation

*If ever there was the essential Pilgrim, it is William Brad-
ford. As the perennial governor and mainstay of Plymouth
Colony, he more than any other single person made possible the survival of his community. And surely no other
writer of his time affords the modern reader more imme-
diate access to the world of seventeenth-century New England and a better understanding of the mind and ways of
its white inhabitants. Begun in 1630 and completed a de-
cade before his death in 1657, Bradford's manuscript dis-
appeared from Boston after the British evacuation of that
city in 1776. A complete transcription did not find its way
into print until 1856, after it was discovered residing in, of
all places, the library of the Anglican Bishop of Oxford.*

*Bradford was born in 1588 into a farming community
in Yorkshire, England, where he began a lifelong process
of self-education through rigorous study and reading. As
a teenager he joined a congregation of Separatists—
extreme Protestants who believed that they must separate
themselves from the Church of England in order to recover the purity of authentic Christianity. When that
congregation moved to Holland to escape official perse-
cution in England, Bradford went with them, supporting
himself in Leyden by practicing the trade of weaver. The
following selections from his remarkable history of this
group, known ever after as the Pilgrims, tell the rest of
his story.*

THE FOURTH CHAPTER

Showing the reasons and causes of their removal.

After they had lived in [Leyden] about some eleven or twelve years (which is the more observable being the whole time of that famous truce[1] between that state and the Spaniards) and sundry of them were taken away by death, and many others began to be well-stricken in years, the grave mistress Experience having taught them many things, those prudent governors with sundry of the sagest members began both deeply to apprehend their present dangers and wisely to foresee the future, and think of timely remedy. In the agitation of their thoughts and much discourse of things hereabout, at length they began to incline to this conclusion, of removal to some other place. Not out of any newfangledness or other such like giddy humor by which men are oftentimes transported to their great hurt and danger, but for sundry weighty and solid reasons; some of the chief of which I will here briefly touch.

And first, they saw and found by experience the hardness of the place and country to be such as few in comparison would come to them, and fewer that would bide it out and continue with them. For many that came to them, and many more that desired to be with them, could not endure that great labor and hard fare with other inconveniences which they underwent and were contented with. But though they loved their persons, approved their cause, and honored their sufferings, yet they left them as it were weeping, as Orpah did her mother-in-law Naomi, or as those Romans Cato in Utica,[2] who desired to be excused and borne with, though they could not all be Catos. For many, though they desired to enjoy the ordinances of God in their purity and the liberty of the gospel with them, yet, alas, they admitted of bondage, with danger of conscience, rather than to endure these hardships; yea, some preferred and chose the prisons in England, rather than this liberty in Holland with these afflictions. But it was thought that if a better and easier place of living could be had, it would draw many and take away these discouragements. Yea, their pastor[3] would often say that many of those who both wrote and preached now against them, if they were in a place where they might have liberty and live comfortably, they would then practice as they did.

Secondly, they saw that though the people generally bore all these difficulties very cheerfully and with a resolute courage, being in the best and strength of their years, yet old age began to steal on many of them (and their great and continual labors, with other crosses and sorrows, hastened it before the time), so as it was not only probably thought, but apparently seen that within a few years more they would be in danger to scatter by necessities pressing them, or sink under their burdens, or both. And therefore according to the divine proverb, that a wise man seeth the plague when it cometh, and hideth himself, Proverbs 22:3, so they, like skilful and beaten[4] soldiers, were fearful either to be entrapped or surrounded by their enemies, so as they should neither be able to fight nor fly. And therefore thought it better to dislodge betimes to some place of better advantage and less danger, if any such could be found.

Thirdly, as necessity was a taskmaster over them, so they were forced to be such, not only to their servants, but in a sort, to their dearest children; the which as it did not a little wound the tender hearts of many a loving father and mother, so it produced likewise sundry sad and sorrowful effects. For many of their children that were of best dispositions and gracious inclinations, having learned to bear the yoke in their youth, and willing to bear part of their parents' burden, were often times so oppressed with their heavy labors, that though their minds were free and willing, yet their bodies bowed under the weight of the same and became decrepit in their early youth; the vigor of nature being consumed in the very bud as it were. But that which was more lamentable, and of all sorrows most heavy to be borne, was that many of their children by these occasions, and the great licentiousness of youth in that country, and the manifold temptations of the place, were drawn away by evil examples into extravagant and dangerous courses, getting the reins off their necks and departing from their parents. Some became soldiers, others took upon them far voyages by sea, and other[s] some worse courses, tending to dissoluteness and the danger of their souls, to the great grief of their parents and dishonor of God. So that they saw their posterity would be in danger to degenerate and be corrupted.

Lastly (and which was not least), a great hope and inward zeal they had of laying some good foundation, or at least to make some way thereunto, for the propagating and advancing the gospel of the kingdom of Christ in those remote parts of the world; yea, though they should be but even as stepping-stones unto others for the performing of so great a work. These, and some other like reasons, moved them to undertake this resolution of their removal; the which they afterward prosecuted with so great difficulties, as by the sequel will appear. The place they had thoughts on was some of those vast and unpeopled countries of America, which are fruitful and fit for habitation, being devoid of all civil inhabitants, where there are only savage and brutish men which range up and down, little otherwise than the wild beasts of the same.

This proposition being made public and coming to the scanning of all, it raised many variable opinions amongst men, and caused many fears and doubts amongst themselves. Some, from their reasons and hopes conceived, labored to stir up and encourage the rest to undertake and prosecute the same; others again, out of their fears, objected against it, and sought to divert from it, alleging many things, and those neither unreasonable nor unprobable; as that it was a great design and subject to many unconceivable perils and dangers; as, besides the casualties of the seas (which none can be freed from), the length of the voyage was such as the weak bodies of women and other persons worn out with age and travail (as many of them were) could never be able to endure. And yet if they should, the miseries of the land which they should be exposed unto would be too hard to be borne; and likely, some or all of them together to consume and utterly to ruinate them. For there they should be liable to famine, and nakedness, and the want, in a manner, of all things. The change of air, diet, and drinking of water would infect their bodies with sore sicknesses, and grievous diseases.

And also those which should escape or overcome these difficulties should yet be in continual danger of the savage people, who are cruel, barbarous, and most treacherous, being most furious in their rage and merciless where they overcome; not being content only to kill and take away life, but delight to torment men in the most bloody manner that may be; flaying some alive with the shells of fishes, cutting off the members and joints of others by piecemeal, and broiling on the coals, eat the collops of their flesh in their sight whilst they live; with other cruelties horrible to be related. And surely it could not be thought but the very hearing of these things could not but move the very bowels of men to grate within them, and make the weak to quake and tremble.

It was further objected, that it would require greater sums of money to furnish such a voyage, and to fit them with necessaries, than their consumed estates would amount to; and yet they must as well look to be seconded with supplies, as presently to be transported. Also many precedents of ill success and lamentable miseries befallen others in the like designs were easy to be found, and not forgotten to be alleged; besides their own experience, in their former troubles and hardships in their removal into Holland, and how hard a thing it was for them to live in that strange place, though it was a neighbor country and a civil and rich commonwealth.

It was answered that all great and honorable actions are accompanied with great difficulties, and must be both enterprised and overcome with answerable courages. It was granted the dangers were great, but not desperate; the difficulties were many, but not invincible. For though there were many of them likely, yet they were not certain; it might be sundry of the things feared might never befall; others by provident care and the use of good means might in a great measure be prevented; and all of them, through the help of God, by fortitude and patience might either be borne or overcome. True it was that such attempts were not to be made and undertaken without good ground and reason; not rashly or lightly as many have done for curiosity or hope of gain, etc. But their condition was not ordinary; their ends were good and honorable; their calling lawful and urgent; and therefore they might expect the blessing of God in their preceding. Yea, though they should lose their lives in this action, yet might they have comfort in the same, and their endeavors would be honorable. They lived here but as men in exile, and in a poor condition; and as great miseries might possibly befall them in this place, for the twelve years of truce were now out, and there was nothing but beating of drums and preparing for war, the events whereof are always uncertain. The Spaniard might prove as cruel as the savages of America, and the famine and pestilence as sore here as there, and their liberty less to look out for remedy. After many other particular things answered and alleged on both sides, it was fully concluded by the major part to put this design in execution and to prosecute it by the best means they could.

THE SEVENTH CHAPTER

Of their departure from Leyden, and other things thereabout, with their arrival at Southampton, where they all met together, and took in their provisions.

At length, after much travail and these debates, all things were got ready and provided. A small ship[1] was bought and fitted in Holland which was intended as to serve to help to transport them, so to stay in the country and attend upon fishing and such other affairs as might be for the good benefit of the colony when they came there. Another[2] was hired at London, of burden about nine score; and all other things got in readiness. So being ready to depart, they had a day of solemn humiliation, their pastor taking his text from Ezra 8:21. *And there at the river, by Ahava, I proclaimed a fast, that we might humble ourselves before our God, and seek of him a right way for us, and for our children, and for all our substance.* Upon which he spent a good part of the day very profitably, and suitable to their present occasion. The rest of the time was spent in pouring out praise to the Lord with great fervency, mixed with abundance of tears. And the time being come that they must depart, they were accompanied with most of their brethren out of the city unto a town sundry miles off called Delftshaven, where the ship lay ready to receive them. So they left that goodly and pleasant city which had been their resting place near twelve years; but they knew they were pilgrims[3] and looked not much on those things, but lifted up their eyes to the heavens, their dearest country, and quieted their spirits.

When they came to the place, they found the ship and all things ready; and such of their friends as could not come with them followed after them, and sundry also came from Amsterdam to see them shipped and to take their leave of them. That night was spent with little sleep by the most, but with friendly entertainment and Christian discourse and other real expressions of true Christian love. The next day, the wind being fair, they went aboard, and their friends with them, where truly doleful was the sight of that sad and mournful parting to see what sighs and sobs and prayers did sound amongst them, what tears did gush from every eye and pithy speeches pierced each heart; that sundry of the Dutch strangers that stood on the key as spectators could not refrain from tears. Yet comfortable and sweet it was to see such lively and true expressions of dear and unfeigned love. But the tide (which stays for no man) calling them away that were thus loath to depart, their Reverend pastor falling down on his knees (and they all with him), with watery cheeks commended them with most fervent prayers to the Lord and his blessing. And then with mutual embraces and many tears, they took their leaves one of another; which proved to be the last leave to many of them.

Thus hoisting sail, with a prosperous wind they came in short time to Southampton, where they found the bigger ship come from London, lying ready with all the rest of their company. After a joyful welcome and mutual congratulations, with other friendly entertainments, they fell to parley about their business, how to dispatch with the best expedition; as also with their agents about the alteration of the conditions. . . . All things being now ready, and every business dispatched, . . . they ordered and distributed their company for either ship, as they conceived for the best. And chose a Governor and two or three assistants for each ship to order the people by the way and see to the disposing of their provisions and such like affairs. All which was not only with the liking of the masters of the ships, but according to their desires. Which being done, they set sail from thence about the 5th of August; but what befell them further upon the coast of England will appear in the next chapter.

THE EIGHTH CHAPTER

Of the troubles that befell them on the coast, and at sea being forced, after much trouble, to leave one of their ships and some of their company behind them.

Being thus put to sea they had not gone far, but Mr. Reynolds, the master of the lesser ship, complained that he found his ship so leaky as he durst not put further to sea till she was mended. So the master of the bigger ship (called Mr. Jones[1]) being consulted with, they both resolved to put into Dartmouth and have her there searched and mended, which accordingly was done, to their great charge and loss of time and a fair wind. She was here thoroughly searched from stem to stern, some leaks were found and mended, and now it was conceived by the workmen and all that she was sufficient, and they might proceed without either fear or danger.

So with good hopes from hence, they put to sea again, conceiving they should go comfortably on, not looking for any more lets[2] of this kind; but it fell out otherwise, for after they were gone to sea again above 100 leagues without the Land's End, holding company together all this while, the master of the small ship complained his ship was so leaky as he must bear up or sink at sea, for they could scarce free her with much pumping. So they came to consultation again and resolved both ships to bear up back again and put into Plymouth, which accordingly was done. But no special leak could be found, but it was judged to be the general weakness of the ship, and that she would not prove sufficient for the voyage. Upon which it was resolved to dismiss her and part of the company and proceed with the other ship. The which (though it was grievous, and caused great discouragement) was put in execution.

So after they had took out such provision as the other ship could well stow, and concluded both what number and what persons to send back, they made another sad parting, the one ship going back for London, and the other was to proceed on her voyage. Those that went back were for the most part such as were willing so to do, either out of some discontent or fear they conceived of the ill success of the voyage, seeing so many crosses befall and the year time so far spent; but others, in regard of their own weakness and charge of many young children, were thought least useful and most unfit to bear the brunt of this hard adventure; unto which work of God and judgment of their brethren they were contented to submit. And thus, like Gideon's army,[3] this small number was divided, as if the Lord by this work of his providence thought these few too many for the great work he had to do.

But here by the way let me show how afterward it was found that the leakiness of this ship was partly by being overmasted and too much pressed with sails; for after she was sold and put into her old trim, she made many voyages and performed her service very sufficiently to the great profit of her owners. But more especially, by the cunning and deceit of the master and his company, who were hired to stay a whole year in the country, and now fancying dislike and fearing want of victuals, they plotted this stratagem to free themselves; as afterwards was known and by some of them confessed. For they apprehended that the greater ship; being of force, and in whom most of the provisions were stowed, she would retain enough for herself, whatsoever became of them or the passengers; and indeed such speeches had been cast out by some of them; and yet, besides other encouragements, the chief of them that came from Leyden went in this ship to give the master content. But so strong was self-love and his fears, as he forgot all duty and former kindnesses and dealt thus falsely with them, though he pretended otherwise. . . .

THE NINTH CHAPTER

*Of their voyage, and how they passed the sea,
and of their safe arrival at Cape Cod.*

September 6: These troubles being blown over, and now all being compact together in one ship, they put to sea again with a prosperous wind, which continued divers days together, which was some encouragement unto them; yet according to the usual manner, many were afflicted with seasickness. And I may not omit here a special work of God's providence. There was a proud and very profane young man, one of the seamen, of a lusty,[1] able body, which made him the more haughty. He would always be condemning the poor people in their sickness, and cursing them daily with grievous execrations, and did not let to tell them that he hoped to help to cast half of them overboard before they came to their journey's end and to make merry with what they had; and if he were by any gently reproved, he would curse and swear most bitterly. But it pleased God before they came half seas over, to smite this young man with a grievous disease of which he died in a desperate manner, and so was himself the first that was thrown overboard. Thus his curses lit on his own head; and it was an astonishment to all his fellows, for they noted it to be the just hand of God upon him.

After they had enjoyed fair winds and weather for a season, they were encountered many times with cross winds and met with many fierce storms, with which the ship was shroudly[2] shaken and her upper works made very leaky; and one of the main beams in the midships was bowed and cracked, which put them in some fear that the ship could not be able to perform the voyage. So some of the chief of the company, perceiving the mariners to fear the sufficiency of the ship, as appeared by their mutterings, they entered into serious consultation with the master and other officers of the ship to consider in time of the danger, and rather to return than to cast themselves into a desperate and inevitable peril. And truly there was great distraction and difference of opinion amongst the mariners themselves; fain would they do what could be done for their wages' sake (being now half the seas over), and on the other hand they were loath to hazard their lives too desperately.

But in examining of all opinions, the master and others affirmed they knew the ship to be strong and firm under water; and for the buckling of the main beam, there was a great iron screw the passengers brought out of Holland which would raise the beam into his place; the which being done, the carpenter and master affirmed that with a post put under it, set firm in the lower deck and otherways bound, he would make it sufficient. And as for the decks and upper works, they would caulk them as well as they could, and though with the working of the ship they would not long keep staunch, yet there would otherwise be no great danger, if they did not overpress her with sails. So they committed themselves to the will of God and resolved to proceed.

In sundry of these storms the winds were so fierce and the seas so high as they could not bear a knot of sail, but were forced to hull[3] for divers days together. And in one of them, as they thus lay at hull in a mighty storm, a lusty young man (called John Howland), coming upon some occasion above the gratings, was with a seel[4] of the ship thrown into sea; but it pleased God that he caught hold of the topsail halyards, which hung overboard and ran out at length; yet he held his hold (though he was sundry fathoms under water) till he was hauled up by the same rope to the brim of the water and then with a boat hook and other means got into the ship again and his life saved; and though he was something ill with it, yet he lived many years after and became a profitable member both in church and commonwealth. In all this voyage there died but one of the passengers, which was William Butten, a youth, servant to Samuel Fuller, when they drew near the coast.

But to omit other things (that I may be brief), after long beating at sea, they fell with that land which is called Cape Cod; the which being made and certainly known to be it, they were not a little joyful. After some deliberation had amongst themselves and with them of the ship, they tacked about and resolved to stand for the southward (the wind and weather being fair) to find some place about Hudson's river for their habitation. But after they had sailed that course about half the day, they fell amongst dangerous shoals and roaring breakers, and they were so far entangled therewith as they conceived themselves in great danger; and the wind shrinking upon them withal, they resolved to bear up again for the Cape, and thought themselves happy to get out of those dangers before night overtook them, as by God's providence they did. And the next day they got into the Cape harbor[5] where they rode in safety. . . .

Being thus arrived in a good harbor and brought safe to land, they fell upon their knees and blessed the God of heaven, who had brought them over the vast and furious ocean, and delivered them from all the perils and miseries thereof again to set their feet on the firm and stable earth, their proper element. And no marvel if they were thus joyful, seeing wise Seneca was so affected with sailing a few miles on the coast of his own Italy, as he affirmed that he had rather remain twenty years on his way by land than pass by sea to any place in a short time; so tedious and dreadful was the same unto him.[6]

But here I cannot but stay and make a pause, and stand half amazed at this poor people's present condition; and so I think will the reader too, when he well considers the same. Being thus passed the vast ocean and a sea of troubles before in their preparation (as may be remembered by that which went before), they had now no friends to welcome them, nor inns to entertain or refresh their weatherbeaten bodies, no houses or much less towns to repair to, to seek for succor. It is recorded in scripture[7] as a mercy to the apostle and his shipwrecked company, that the barbarians showed them no small kindness in refreshing them, but these savage barbarians, when they met with them (as after will appear) were readier to fill their sides full of arrows than otherwise.

And for the season it was winter, and they that know the winters of that country know them to be sharp and violent and subject to cruel and fierce storms, dangerous to travel to known places, much more to search an unknown coast. Besides, what could they see but a hideous and desolate wilderness, full of wild beasts and wild men, and what multitudes there might be of them they knew not. Neither could they, as it were, go up to the top of Pisgah[8] to view from this wilderness a more goodly country to feed their hopes; for which way soever they turned their eyes (save upward to the heavens), they could have little solace or content in respect of any outward objects. For summer being done, all things stand upon them with a weatherbeaten face; and the whole country, full of woods and thickets, represented a wild and savage hue.

If they looked behind them, there was the mighty ocean

which they had passed, and was now as a main bar and gulf to separate them from all the civil parts of the world. If it be said they had a ship to succor them, it is true; but what heard they daily from the master and company but that with speed they should look out a place with their shallop,⁹ where they would be at some near distance; for the season was such as he would not stir from thence till a safe harbor was discovered by them where they would be, and he might go, without danger; and that victuals consumed apace, but he must and would keep sufficient for themselves and their return. Yea, it was muttered by some that if they got not a place in time, they would turn them and their goods ashore and leave them.

Let it also be considered what weak hopes of supply and succor they left behind them that might bear up their minds in this sad condition and trials they were under; and they could not but be very small. It is true, indeed, the affections and love of their brethren at Leyden was cordial and entire towards them, but they had little power to help them, or themselves; and how the case stood between them and the merchants at their coming away hath already been declared.¹⁰ What could now sustain them but the spirit of God and his grace? May not and ought not the children of these fathers rightly say: *Our fathers were Englishmen which came over this great ocean, and were ready to perish in this wilderness; but they cried unto the Lord, and he heard their voice, and looked on their adversity,¹¹ etc. Let them therefore praise the Lord, because he is good, and his mercies endure forever. Yea, let them which have been redeemed of the Lord, show how he hath delivered them from the hand of the oppressor. When they wandered in the desert wilderness out of the way, and found no city to dwell in, both hungry and thirsty, their soul was overwhelmed in them. Let them confess before the Lord his lovingkindness, and his wonderful works before the sons of men.¹²*

THE REMAINDER OF ANNO 1620

The rest of this History (if God give me life, and opportunity) I shall, for brevity's sake, handle by way of annals, noting only the heads of principal things and passages as they fell in order of time and may seem to be profitable to know, or to make use of. . . .

[After exploring alternative sites on Cape Cod, the Pilgrims decided on Plymouth as their place of settlement and landed there in late December.] I shall a little return back and begin with a combination[1] made by them before they came ashore, being the first foundation of their government in this place; occasioned partly by the discontented and mutinous speeches that some of the strangers[2] amongst them had let fall from them in the ship—That when they came ashore they would use their own liberty; for none had power to command them, the patent they had being for Virginia and not for New England, which belonged to another Government,[3] with which the Virginia Company had nothing to do. And partly that such an act by them done (this their condition considered) might be as firm as any patent, and in some respects more sure. The form was as followeth:

In the name of God, Amen. We whose names are underwritten, the loyal subjects of our dread sovereign Lord, King James, by the grace of God, of Great Britain, France, and Ireland king, defender of the faith, etc., having undertaken, for the glory of God, and advancement of the Christian faith, and honor of our king and country, a voyage to plant the first colony in the Northern parts of Virginia, do by these presents solemnly and mutually in the presence of God, and one of another, covenant and combine ourselves together into a civil body politic, for our better ordering and preservation and furtherance of the ends aforesaid; and by virtue hereof to enact, constitute, and frame such just and equal laws, ordinances, acts, constitutions, and offices, from time to time, as shall be thought most meet and convenient for the general good of the Colony, unto which we promise all due submission and obedience. In witness whereof we have hereunder subscribed our names at Cape Cod the 11th of November, in the year of the reign of our sovereign lord, King James, of England, France, and Ireland the eighteenth, and of Scotland the fifty-fourth. Anno Domini 1620.

After this they chose, or rather confirmed, Mr. John Carver[4] (a man godly and well approved amongst them) their Governor for that year. And after they had provided a place for their goods or common store (which were long in unlading for want of boats, foulness of winter weather, and sickness of divers), and begun some small cottages for their habitation, as time would admit they met and consulted of laws and orders, both for their civil and military Government, as the necessity of their condition did require, still adding thereunto as urgent occasion in several times, and as cases did require.

In these hard and difficult beginnings they found some dis-contents and murmurings arise amongst some, and mutinous speeches and carriages in other; but they were soon quelled and overcome by the wisdom, patience, and just and equal carriage of things by the Governor and better part, which cleaved faith-fully together in the main. But that which was most sad and lamentable was that in two or three months' time half of their company died, especially in January and February, being the depth of winter, and wanting houses and other comforts; being infected with the scurvy and other diseases, which this long voyage and their inaccommodate condition had brought upon them; so as there died sometimes two or three of a day in the foresaid time, that of 100 and odd persons scarce fifty re-mained.

And of these in the time of most distress, there was but six or seven sound persons, who, to their great commendations be it spoken, spared no pains, night nor day, but with abundance of toil and hazard of their own health, fetched them wood, made them fires, dressed them meat, made their beds, washed their loathsome clothes, clothed and unclothed them; in a word, did all the homely and necessary offices for them which dainty and queasy stomachs cannot endure to hear named; and all this willingly and cheerfully, without any grudging in the least, showing herein their true love unto their friends and brethren, a rare example and worthy to be remembered.

Two of these seven were Mr. William Brewster, their rev-erend Elder,[5] and Miles Standish,[6] their Captain and military commander, unto whom myself, and many others, were much beholden in our low and sick condition. And yet the Lord so upheld these persons, as in this general calamity they were not at all infected either with sickness or lameness. And what I have said of these, I may say of many others who died in this general visitation, and others yet living, that whilst they had health, yea, or any strength continuing, they were not wanting to any that had need of them. And I doubt not but their recompense is with the Lord.

But I may not here pass by another remarkable passage not to be forgotten. As this calamity fell among the passengers that were to be left here to plant, and were hasted ashore and made to drink water, that the seamen might have the more beer, and one in his sickness desiring but a small can of beer, it was answered that if he were their own father he should have none. The disease began to fall amongst them also, so as almost half of their company died before they went away, and many of their officers and lustiest men, as the boatswain, gunner, three quartermasters, the cook, and others. At which the master was something stricken and sent to the sick ashore and told the Governor he should send for beer for them that had need of it, though he drunk water homeward bound.

But now amongst his company there was far another kind of carriage in this misery than amongst the passengers; for they that before had been boon companions in drinking and jollity in the time of their health and welfare, began now to desert one another in this calamity, saying they would not hazard their lives for them, they should be infected by coming to help them in their cabins, and so, after they came to die by it, would do little or nothing for them, but if they died let them die. But such of the passengers as were yet aboard showed them what mercy they could, which made some of their hearts relent, as the boatswain (and some others), who was a proud young man and would often curse and scoff at the passengers; but when he grew weak, they had compassion on him and helped him. Then he confessed he did not deserve it at their hands, he had abused them in word and deed. "Oh!" saith he, "you, I now see, show your love like Christians indeed one to another, but we let one another lie and die like dogs."

Another lay cursing his wife, saying if it had not been for her he had never come this unlucky voyage, and anon cursing his fellows, saying he had done this and that for some of them, he had spent so much, and so much, amongst them, and they were now weary of him, and did not help him, having need. Another gave his companion all he had, if he died, to help him in his weakness; he went and got a little spice and made him a mess of meat once or twice, and because he died not so soon as he expected, he went amongst his fellows and swore the rogue would cozen him, he would see him choked before he made him any more meat; and yet the poor fellow died before morning. . . .

The spring now approaching, it pleased God the mortality began to cease amongst them, and the sick and lame recovered apace, which put as it were new life into them; though they had borne their sad affliction with much patience and contentedness, as I think any people could do. But it was the Lord which upheld them, and had beforehand prepared them; many having long borne the yoke, yea from their youth. And being now come to the 25th of March, I shall begin the year 1621.[7]

ANNO 1621

They now began to dispatch the ship away which brought them over, which lay till about this time, or the beginning of April. The reason on their parts why she stayed so long was the necessity and danger that lay upon them, for it was well towards the end of December before she could land anything here, or they able to receive anything ashore. Afterwards, the 14th of January, the house which they had made for a general rendezvous by casualty fell afire, and some were fain to retire aboard for shelter. Then the sickness began to fall sore amongst them, and the weather so bad as they could not make much sooner any dispatch. Again, the Governor and chief of them, seeing so many die and fall down sick daily, thought it no wisdom to send away the ship, their condition considered and the danger they stood in from the Indians, till they could procure some shelter; and therefore thought it better to draw some more charge upon themselves and friends than hazard all. The master and seamen likewise, though before they hasted the passengers ashore to be gone, now many of their men being dead and of the ablest of them (as is before noted) and of the rest many lay sick and weak, the master durst not put to sea, till he saw his men begin to recover and the heart of winter over.

Afterwards they (as many as were able) began to plant their corn, in which service Squanto[1] stood them in great stead, showing them both the manner how to set[2] it, and after how to dress and tend it. Also he told them except they got fish and set with it (in these old grounds) it would come to nothing, and he showed them that in the middle of April they should have store enough come up the brook by which they began to build, and taught them how to take it, and where to get other provisions necessary for them; all which they found true by trial and experience. Some English seed they sowed, as wheat and peas, but it came not to good, either by the badness of the seed or lateness of the season, or both, or some other defect.

In this month of April whilst they were busy about their seed, their Governor (Mr. John Carver) came out of the field very sick, it being a hot day. He complained greatly of his head, and lay down, and within a few hours his senses failed, so as he never spoke more till he died, which was within a few days after. Whose death was much lamented, and caused great heaviness amongst them, as there was cause. He was buried in the best manner they could, with some volleys of shot by all that bore arms; and his wife, being a weak woman, died within five or six weeks after him.

Shortly after William Bradford was chosen Governor in his stead, and being not yet recovered of his illness, in which he had been near the point of death, Isaac Allerton[3] was chosen to be an Assistant unto him, who, by renewed election every year, continued sundry years together, which I here note once for all.

May 12th was the first marriage in this place, which, according to the laudable custom of the Low-Countries in which they had lived, was thought most requisite to be performed by the magistrate, as being a civil thing, upon which many questions about inheritances do depend, with other things most proper to their cognizance, and most consonant to the scriptures, Ruth 4, and nowhere found in the gospel to be laid on the ministers as a part of their office. . . . And this practice hath continued amongst not only them, but hath been followed by all the famous churches of Christ in these parts to this time, Anno 1646.

Having in some sort ordered their business at home, it was thought meet to send some abroad to see their new friend Massasoit,[4] and to bestow upon him some gratuity to bind him the faster unto them; as also that hereby they might view the country, and see in what manner he lived, what strength he had about him, and how the ways were to his place, if at any time they should have occasion. So the second of July they sent Mr. Edward Winslow and Mr. Hopkins,[5] with the foresaid Squanto for their guide, who gave him a suit of clothes, and a horseman's coat, with some other small things, which were kindly accepted; but they found but short commons,[6] and came both weary and hungry home. For the Indians used then to have nothing so much corn as they have since the English have stored them with their hoes, and seen their Industry in breaking up new grounds therewith.

They found his place[7] to be forty miles from hence, the soil good, and the people not many, being dead and abundantly wasted in the late great mortality which fell in all these parts about three years before the coming of the English, wherein thousands of them died. They not being able to bury one another; their skulls and bones were found in many places lying still above ground, where their houses and dwellings had been; a very sad spectacle to behold. But they brought word that the Narragansetts lived but on the other side of that great bay and were a strong people and many in number, living compact together, and had not been at all touched with this wasting plague.

About the latter end of this month, one John Billington lost himself in the woods, and wandered up and down some five days, living on berries and what he could find. At length he lit on an Indian plantation, twenty miles south of this place, called Manomet.[8] They conveyed him further off to Nauset,[9] among those people that had before set upon the English when they were coasting, whilst the ship lay at the Cape. . . . But the Governor caused him to be inquired for among the Indians, and at length Massasoit sent word where he was, and the Governor sent a shallop for him and had him delivered. Those people also came and made their peace; and they gave full satisfaction to those whose corn they had found and taken when they were at Cape Cod.

Thus their peace and acquaintance was pretty well established with the natives about them; and there was another Indian called Hobbamock come to live amongst them, a proper lusty man, and a man of account for his valor and parts amongst the Indians, and continued very faithful and constant to the English till he died. He and Squanto being gone upon business among the Indians, at their return (whether it was out of envy to them or malice to the English) there was a Sachem called Corbitant, allied to Massasoit but never any good friend to the English to this day, met with them at an Indian town called Nemasket[10] fourteen miles to the west of this place, and began to quarrel with them, and offered to stab Hobbamock; but being a lusty man, he cleared himself of him, and came running away all sweating and told the Governor what had befallen him, and he feared they had killed Squanto, for they threatened them both, and for no other cause but because they were friends to the English and serviceable unto them.

Upon this the Governor taking counsel, it was conceived not fit to be borne; for if they should suffer their friends and messengers thus to be wronged, they should have none would cleave unto them, or give them any intelligence, or do them service afterwards; but next they would fall upon themselves. Whereupon it was resolved to send the Captain and fourteen men well armed and to go and fall upon them in the night; and if they found that Squanto was killed, to cut off Corbitant's head, but not to hurt any but those that had a hand in it.

Hobbamock was asked if he would go and be their guide and bring them there before day. He said he would and bring them to the house where the man lay and show them which was he. So they set forth the 14th of August and beset the house round; the Captain, giving charge to let none pass out, entered the house to search for him. But he was gone away that day, so they missed him but understood that Squanto was alive, and that he had only threatened to kill him, and made an offer to stab him but did not. So they withheld and did no more hurt, and the people came trembling and brought them the best provisions they had, after they were acquainted by Hobbamock what was only intended. There was three sore wounded which broke out of the house and assayed to pass through the guard. These they brought home with them, and they had their wounds dressed and cured and sent home. After this they had many gratulations from divers sachems and much firmer peace; yea, those of the Isles of Capawack[11] sent to make friendship; and this Corbitant himself used the mediation of Massasoit to make his peace, but was shy to come near them a long while after.

After this, the 18th of September, they sent out their shallop to the Massachusetts, with ten men and Squanto for their guide and interpreter, to discover and view that bay and trade with the natives; the which they performed and found kind entertainment. The people were much afraid of the Tarentines,[12] a people to the eastward which used to come in harvest time and take away their corn and many times kill their persons. They returned in safety and brought home a good quantity of beaver and made report of the place, wishing they had been there seated (but it seems the Lord, who assigns to all men the bounds of their habitations,[13] had appointed it for another use). And thus they found the Lord to be with them in all their ways, and to bless their outgoings and incomings, for which let his holy name have the praise forever, to all posterity.

They began now to gather in the small harvest they had, and to fit up their houses and dwellings against winter, being well recovered in health and strength, and had all things good plenty; for as some were thus employed in affairs abroad, others were exercised in fishing about cod and bass and other fish, of which they took good store, of which every family had their portion. All the summer there was no want. And now began to come in store of fowl as winter approached, of which this place did abound when they came first (but afterward decreased by degrees). And besides water fowl, there was great store of wild

Turkeys, of which they took many, besides venison, etc. Besides they had about a peck a meal a week to a person, or now, since harvest, Indian corn to that proportion. Which made many afterwards write so largely of their plenty here to their friends in England, which were not feigned, but true reports.

In November, about that time twelfth month that themselves came, there came in a small ship to them unexpected or looked for in which came Mr. Cushman[14] . . . and with him thirty-five persons to remain and live in the plantation; which did not a little rejoice them. And they, when they came ashore and found all well and saw plenty of victuals in every house, were no less glad. For most of them were lusty young men and many of them wild enough, who little considered whither or about what they went, till they came into the harbor at Cape Cod and there saw nothing but a naked barren place. They then began to think what should become of them, if the people here were dead or cut off by the Indians. They began to consult (upon some speeches that some of the seamen had cast out) to take the sails from the yard lest the ship should get away and leave them there. But the master, hearing of it, gave them good words and told them if anything but well should have befallen the people here, he hoped he had victuals enough to carry them to Virginia, and whilst he had a bit, they should have their part; which gave them good satisfaction.

So they were all landed; but there was not so much as biscuit-cake or any other victuals for them, neither had they any bedding but some sorry things they had in their cabins, nor pot nor pan to dress any meat in; nor over many clothes, for many of them had brushed away their coats and cloaks at Plymouth [England] as they came. But there was sent over some Birching-Lane[15] suits in the ship, out of which they were supplied. The plantation was glad of this addition of strength, but could have wished that many of them had been of better condition, and all of them better furnished with provisions; but that could not now be helped. . . .

After the departure of this ship (which stayed not above fourteen days), the Governor and his assistant having disposed these late comers into several families, as they best could, took an exact account of all their provisions in store and proportioned the same to the number of persons, and found that it would not hold out above six months at half allowance, and hardly that. And they could not well give less this winter time till fish came in again. So they were presently put to half allowance, one as well as another, which began to be hard, but they bore it patiently under hope of supply.

Soon after this ship's departure, the great people of the Narragansetts, in a braving manner, sent a messenger unto them with a bundle of arrows tied about with a great snakeskin; which their interpreters told them was a threatening and a challenge. Upon which the Governor, with the advice of others sent them a round answer that if they had rather have war than peace, they might begin when they would; they had done them no wrong, neither did they fear them, or should they find them unprovided. And by another messenger sent the snakeskin back with bullets in it; but they would not receive it, but sent it back again. . . . And it is like the reason was their own ambition, who (since the death of so many of the Indians), thought to domineer and lord it over the rest, and conceived the English would be a bar in their way, and saw that Massasoit took shelter already under their wings.

But this made them the more carefully to look to themselves, so as they agreed to enclose their dwellings with a good strong pale, and make flankers[16] in convenient places, with gates to shut, which were every night locked, and a watch kept and when need required there was also warding in the day time. And the company was by the Captain's and the Governor's advice divided into four squadrons, and every one had their quarter appointed them unto which they were to repair upon any sudden alarm. And if there should be any cry of fire, a company were appointed for a guard with muskets, whilst others quenched the same, to prevent Indian treachery. This was accomplished very cheerfully, and the town impaled round by the beginning of March, in which every family had a pretty garden plot secured. And herewith I shall end this year.

Only I shall remember one passage more, rather of mirth than of weight. On the day called Christmas Day, the Governor called them out to work (as was used), but the most of this new-company excused themselves and said it went against their consciences to work on that day. So the Governor told them that if they made it matter of conscience, he would spare them till they were better informed. So he led away the rest and left them; but when they came home at noon from their work, he found them in the street at play, openly; some pitching the bar and some at stool-ball,[17] and such like sports.

So he went to them, and took away their implements, and told them that was against his conscience, that they should play and others work. If they made the keeping of it matter of devotion, let them keep their houses, but there should be no gaming or reveling in the streets. Since which time nothing hath been attempted that way, at least openly.

ANNO 1622

At the spring of the year they had appointed the Massachusetts to come again and trade with them, and began now to prepare for that voyage about the latter end of March. But upon some rumors heard, Hobbamock, their Indian, told them upon some jealousies[1] he had; he feared they were joined with the Narragansetts and might betray them if they were not careful. He intimated also some jealousy of Squanto by what he gathered from some private whisperings between him and other Indians. But they resolved to proceed and sent out their shallop with ten of their chief men about the beginning of April, and both Squanto and Hobbamock with them, in regard of the jealousy between them.

But they had not been gone long but an Indian belonging to Squanto's family came running in seeming great fear, and told them that many of the Narragansetts, with Corbitant and he thought also Massasoit, were coming against them; and he got away to tell them, not without danger. And being examined by the Governor, he made as if they were at hand and would still be looking back, as if they were at his heels. At which the Governor caused them to take arms and stand on their guard, and supposing the boat to be still within hearing (by reason it was calm), caused a warning piece or two to be shot off, the which they heard and came in. But no Indians appeared; watch was kept all night, but nothing was seen. Hobbamock was confident for Massasoit and thought all was false; yet the Governor caused him to send his wife privately to see what she could observe (pretending other occasions), but there was nothing found, but all was quiet. After this they proceeded on their voyage to the Massachusetts and had good trade and returned in safety, blessed be God.

But by the former passages and other things of like nature, they began to see that Squanto sought his own ends and played his own game by putting the Indians in fear and drawing gifts from them to enrich himself; making them believe he could stir up war against whom he would, and make peace for whom he would. Yea, he made them believe they kept the plague buried in the ground and could send it amongst whom they would, which did much terrify the Indians and made them depend more on him and seek more to him than to Massasoit, which procured him envy and had like to have cost him his life. For after the discovery of his practices, Massasoit sought it both privately and openly; which caused him to stick close to the English, and never durst go from them till he died. They also made good use of the emulation that grew between Hobbamock and him, which made them carry more squarely. And the Governor seemed to countenance the one, and the Captain the other, by which they had better intelligence and made them both more diligent.

Now in a manner their provisions were wholly spent, and they looked hard for supply, but none came. But about the latter end of May, they spied a boat at sea which at first they thought had been some Frenchman; but it proved a shallop which came from a ship which Mr. Weston[2] and another had set out a-fishing, at a place called Damariscove,[3] forty leagues to the eastward of them, where were that year many more ships come a-fishing. This boat brought seven passengers and some letters, but no victuals, nor any hope of any. . . .

Now the welcome time of harvest approached, in which all

had their hungry bellies filled. But it arose but to a little in comparison of a full year's supply; partly by reason they were not yet well acquainted with the manner of Indian corn (and they had no other), also their many other employments, but chiefly their weakness for want of food to tend it as they should have done. Also much was stolen both by night and day before it became scarce eatable, and much more afterward. And though many were well whipped (when they were taken) for a few ears of corn, yet hunger made others (whom conscience did not restrain) to venture. So as it well appeared that famine must still ensue the next year also if not some way prevented, or supply should fail, to which they durst not trust. Markets there was none to go to, but only the Indians, and they had no trading commodities.

Behold now another providence of God; a ship comes into the harbor, one Captain Jones being chief therein. They were set out by some merchants to discover all the harbors between this and Virginia, and the shoals of Cape Cod, and to trade along the coast where they could. This ship had store of English-beads (which were then good trade) and some knives, but would sell none but at dear rates, and also a good quantity together. Yet they were glad of the occasion, and fain to buy at any rate; they were fain to give after the rate of cent per cent, if not more, and yet pay away coat-beaver at three shillings per pound, which in a few years after yielded twenty shillings. By this means they were fitted again to trade for beaver and other things, and intended to buy what corn they could. . . .

Shortly after harvest, Mr. Weston's people, who were now seated at the Massachusetts[4] and by disorder (as it seems) had made havoc of their provisions, began now to perceive that want would come upon them. And hearing that they here had bought trading commodities and intended to trade for corn, they wrote to the Governor and desired they might join with them, and they would employ their small ship in the service; and further requested either to lend or sell them so much of their trading commodities as their part might come to, and they would undertake to make payment when Mr. Weston or their supply, should come. The Governor condescended upon equal terms of agreement, thinking to go about the Cape to the south-ward with the ship, where some store of corn might be got.

All things being provided, Captain Standish was appointed to go with them, and Squanto for a guide and interpreter, about the latter end of September; but the winds put them in again, and putting out the second time, he fell sick of a fever, so the Governor went himself. But they could not get about the shoal of Cape Cod for flats and breakers, neither could Squanto direct them better, nor the master durst venture any further, so they put into Manamoyick Bay[5] and got [what] they could there. In this place Squanto fell sick of an Indian fever, bleeding much at the nose (which the Indians take for a symptom of death), and within a few days died there; desiring the Governor to pray for him, that he might go to the Englishmen's God in heaven, and bequeathed sundry of his things to sundry of his English friends, as remembrances of his love; of whom they had a great loss.

They got in this voyage in one place and other about twenty-six or twenty-eight hogsheads of corn and beans, which was more than the Indians could well spare in these parts, for they set but a little till they got English hoes. And so were fain to return, being sorry they could not get about the Cape, to have been better laden. Afterward the Governor took a few men and went to the inland places, to get what he could, and to fetch it home at the spring, which did help them something.

After these things, in February a messenger came from John Sanders, who was left chief over Mr. Weston's men in the bay of Massachusetts, who brought a letter showing the great wants they were fallen into; and he would have borrowed a hogshead of corn of the Indians, but they would lend him none. He desired advice whether he might not take it from them by force to succor his men till he came from the eastward, whither he was going. The Governor and rest dissuaded him by all means from it, for it might so exasperate the Indians as might endanger their safety, and all of us might smart for it; for they had already heard how they had so wronged the Indians by stealing their corn, etc. as they were much incensed against them. Yea, so base were some of their own company, as they went and told the Indians that their Governor was purposed to come and take their corn by force. The which with other things made them enter into a conspiracy against the English, of which more in the next. Herewith I end this year.

ANNO DOMINI 1623

It may be thought strange that these people [belonging to Weston's plantation] should fall to these extremities in so short a time, being left competently provided when the ship left them, and had an addition by that moiety of corn that was got by trade, besides much they got of the Indians where they lived, by one means and other. It must needs be their great disorder, for they spent excessively whilst they had, or could get it; and, it may be, wasted part away among the Indians (for he that was their chief was taxed by some amongst them for keeping Indian women, how truly I know not).

And after they began to come into wants, many sold away their clothes and bed coverings; others (so base were they) became servants to the Indians and would cut them wood and fetch them water for a capful of corn; others fell to plain stealing both night and day from the Indians, of which they grievously complained. In the end, they came to that misery that some starved and died with cold and hunger. One in gathering shellfish was so weak as he stuck fast in the mud, and was found dead in the place. At last most of them left their dwellings and scattered up and down in the woods and by the watersides, where they could find ground nuts[1] and clams, here six and there ten.

By which their carriages they became condemned and scorned of the Indians, and they began greatly to insult over them in a most insolent manner; insomuch many times as they lay thus scattered abroad and had set on a pot with ground nuts or shellfish, when it was ready the Indians would come and eat it up; and when night came, whereas some of them had a sorry blanket or such like to lap themselves in, the Indians would take it and let the other lie all night in the cold; so as their condition was very lamentable. Yea, in the end they were fain to hang one of their men, whom they could not reclaim from stealing, to give the Indians content.

Whilst things went in this manner with them, the Governor and people here had notice that Massasoit, their friend, was sick and near unto death. They sent to visit him, and withal sent him such comfortable things as gave him great content, and was a means of his recovery; upon which occasion he discovers[2] the conspiracy of these Indians, how they were resolved to cut off Mr. Weston's people for the continual injuries they did them, and would now take opportunity of their weakness to do it; and for that end had conspired with other Indians, their neighbors thereabout. And thinking the people here would revenge their death, they therefore thought to do the like by them, and had solicited him to join with them. He advised them therefore to prevent it and that speedily by taking of some of the chief of them before it was too late, for he assured them of the truth hereof.

This did much trouble them, and they took it into serious deliberation, and found upon examination other evidence to give light here unto, too long here to relate. In the meantime, came one of them from the Massachusetts with a small pack at his back; and though he knew not a foot of the way, yet he got safe hither, but lost his way, which was well for him, for he was pursued and so was missed. He told them here how all things stood amongst them, and that he durst stay no longer, he apprehended they (by what he observed) would be all knocked in the head shortly.

This made them make the more haste, and dispatched a boat away with Captain Standish and some men, who found them in a miserable condition, out of which he rescued them and helped them to some relief, cut off some few of the chief conspirators, and, according to his order, offered to bring them all hither if they thought good; and they should fare no worse than themselves, till Mr. Weston or some supply came to them. Or, if any other course liked them better, he was to do them any helpfulness he could.

They thanked him and the rest. But most of them desired he

would help them with some corn, and they would go with their small ship to the eastward, where haply they might hear of Mr. Weston, or some supply from him, seeing the time of the year was for fishing ships to be in the land. If not, they would work among the fishermen for their living, and get their passage into England, if they heard nothing from Mr. Weston in time. So they shipped what they had of any worth, and he got them all the corn he could (scarce leaving [enough] to bring him home), and saw them well out of the bay, under sail at sea, and so came home, not taking the worth of a penny of anything that was theirs. . . .

This was the end of these that some time boasted of their strength (being all able lusty men), and what they would do and bring to pass in comparison of the people here, who had many women and children and weak ones amongst them; and said at their first arrival, when they saw the wants here, that they would take another course and not to fall into such a condition as this simple people were come to. But a man's way is not in his own power; God can make the weak to stand; let him also that standeth take heed lest he fall.[3]

Shortly after, Mr. Weston came over with some of the fishermen under another name and the disguise of a blacksmith, where he heard of the ruin and dissolution of his colony. He got a boat and with a man or two came to see how things were. But by the way, for want of skill, in a storm he cast away his shallop in the bottom of the bay between Merrimac river and Piscataqua,[4] and hardly escaped with life, and afterwards fell into the hands of the Indians, who pillaged him of all he saved from the sea, and stripped him out of all his clothes to his shirt. At last he got to Piscataqua and borrowed a suit of clothes, and got means to come to Plymouth. A strange alteration there was in him to such as had seen and known him in his former flourishing condition; so uncertain are the mutable things of this unstable world. And yet men set their hearts upon them, though they daily see the vanity thereof.

After many passages, and much discourse (former things boiling in his mind, but bit in[5] as was discerned), he desired to borrow some beaver of them; and told them he had hope of a ship and good supply to come to him, and then they should have anything for it they stood in need of. They gave little credit to his supply, but pitied his case and remembered former courtesies. They told him he saw their wants, and they knew not when they should have any supply; also how the case stood between them and their adventurers.[6] He well knew they had not much beaver, and if they should let him have it, it were enough to make a mutiny among the people, seeing there was no other means to procure them food which they so much wanted, and clothes also. Yet they told him they would help him, considering his necessity, but must do it secretly for the former reasons. So they let him have 100 beaver skins, which weighed 170-odd pounds. Thus they helped him when all the world failed him, and with this means he went again to the ships, and stayed his small ship and some of his men, and bought provisions and fitted himself; and it was the only foundation of his after course.

But he requited them ill, for he proved after a bitter enemy unto them upon all occasions, and never repaid them anything for it to this day, but reproaches and evil words. Yea, he divulged it to some that were none of their best friends, whilst he yet had the beaver in his boat, that he could now set them all together by the ears, because they had done more than they could answer in letting him have this beaver, and he did not spare to do what he could. But his malice could not prevail.

All this while no supply was heard of, neither knew they when they might expect any. So they began to think how they might raise as much corn as they could, and obtain a better crop than they had done, that they might not still thus languish in misery. At length, after much debate of things, the Governor (with the advice of the chiefest amongst them) gave way that they should set corn every man for his own particular,[7] and in that regard trust to themselves; in all other things to go on in the general way as before. And so assigned to every family a parcel of land according to the proportion of their number for that end, only for present use (but made no division for inheritance), and ranged all boys and youth under some family.

This had very good success; for it made all hands very industrious, so as much more corn was planted than otherwise would have been by any means the Governor or any other could use, and saved him a great deal of trouble, and gave far better content. The women now went willingly into the field and took their little ones with them to set corn, which before would allege weakness and inability; whom to have compelled would have been thought great tyranny and oppression.

The experience that was had in this common course and condition, tried sundry years, and that amongst godly and sober men, may well evince the vanity of that conceit of Plato's and other ancients, applauded by some of later times; that the taking away of property and bringing in community into a commonwealth would make them happy and flourishing; as if they were wiser than God. For this community (so far as it was) was found to breed much confusion and discontent, and retard much employment that would have been to their benefit and comfort.

For the young-men that were most able and fit for labor and service did repine that they should spend their time and strength to work for other men's wives and children without any recompense. The strong, or man of parts, had no more in division of victuals and clothes than he that was weak and not able to do a quarter the other could; this was thought injustice. The aged and graver men to be ranked and equalized in labors, and victuals, clothes, etc., with the meaner and younger sort, thought it some indignity and disrespect unto them. And for men's wives to be commanded to do service for other men, as dressing their meat, washing their clothes, etc., they deemed it a kind of slavery, neither could many husbands well brook it.

Upon the point all being to have alike, and all to do alike, they thought themselves in the like condition, and one as good as another; and so, if it did not cut off those relations that God hath set amongst men, yet it did at least much diminish and take off the mutual respects that should be preserved amongst them. And would have been worse if they had been men of another condition. Let none object this is men's corruption, and nothing to the course itself. I answer, seeing all men have this corruption in them, God in his wisdom saw another course fitter for them.

But to return. After this course settled, and by that their corn was planted, all their victuals were spent, and they were only to rest on God's providence; at night not many times knowing where to have a bit of anything the next day. And so, as one well observed, [they] had need to pray that God would give them their daily bread, above all people in the world. Yet they bore these wants with great patience and alacrity of spirit, and that for so long a time as for the most part of two years. . . .

They having but one boat left and she not over well fitted, they were divided into several companies, six or seven to a gang or company, and so went out with a net they had bought, to take bass and such like fish, by course,[8] every company knowing their turn. No sooner was the boat discharged of what she brought, but the next company took her and went out with her. Neither did they return till they had caught something, though it were five or six days before, for they knew there was nothing at home, and to go home empty would be a great discouragement to the rest. Yea, they strive who should do best. If she stayed long or got little, then all went to seeking of shellfish, which at low-water they digged out of the sands. And this was their living in the summertime, till God sent them better; and in winter they were helped with ground nuts and fowl. Also in the summer they got now and then a deer; for one or two of the fittest was appointed to range the woods for that end, and what was got that way was divided amongst them. . . .

[In early July a ship arrived] called the *Anne*, whereof Mr. William Peirce was master, and about a week or ten days after came in the pinnace[9] which in foul weather they lost at sea, a fine new vessel of about forty-four tons, which the company had built to stay in the country. They brought about sixty persons for the general, some of them being very useful persons, and became good members to the body, and some were the wives and children of such as were here already. And some were so bad, as they were fain to be at charge to send them home again the next year. Also, besides these there came a company that did not belong to the general body, but came on their particular, and were to have lands assigned them, and be for themselves, yet to be subject to the general Government; which caused some difference and disturbance amongst them, as will after appear. . . .

These passengers, when they saw their low and poor condition ashore, were much daunted and dismayed, and according to their divers humors were diversely affected; some wished themselves in England again; others fell a-weeping, fancying their own misery in what they saw now in others; other some pitying the distress they saw their friends had been long in, and still were under; in a word, all were full of sadness. Only some of their old friends rejoiced to see them, and that it was no worse with them, for they could not expect it should be better, and now hoped they should enjoy better days together.

And truly it was no marvel they should be thus affected, for they were in a very low condition, many were ragged in apparel, and some little better than half naked; though some that were well stored before were well enough in this regard. But for food they were all alike, save some that had got a few peas of the ship that was last here. The best dish they could present their friends with was a lobster, or a piece of fish, without bread or anything else but a cup of fair spring water. And the long continuance of this diet and their labors abroad had something abated the freshness of their former complexion. But God gave them health and strength in a good measure; and showed them by experience the truth of that word, Deuteronomy 8:3, *That man liveth not by bread only, but by every word that proceedeth out of the mouth of the Lord doth a man live.* . . .

On the other hand the old planters were afraid that their corn, when it was ripe, should be imparted to the newcomers, whose provisions which they brought with them they feared would fall short before the year went about (as indeed it did). They came to the Governor and besought him that as it was before agreed that they should set corn for their particular, and accordingly they had taken extraordinary pains thereabout, that they might freely enjoy the same, and they would not have a bit of the victuals now come, but wait till harvest for their own, and let the newcomers enjoy what they had brought; they would have none of it, except they could purchase any of it of them by bargain or exchange. Their request was granted them, for it gave both sides good content; for the newcomers were as much afraid that the hungry planters would have ate up the provisions brought, and they should have fallen into the like condition.

This ship was in a short time laden with clapboard, by the help of many hands. Also they sent in her all the beaver and other furs they had, and Mr. Winslow was sent over with her to inform of all things, and procure such things as were thought needful for their present condition. By this time harvest was come, and instead of famine, now God gave them plenty, and the face of things was changed, to the rejoicing of the hearts of many, for which they blessed God. And the effect of their particular planting was well seen, for all had, one way and other, pretty well to bring the year about, and some of the abler sort and more industrious had to spare and sell to others, so as any general want or famine hath not been amongst them since to this day. . . .

It rests now that I speak a word about the pinnace . . . which was sent by the adventurers to be employed in the country. She was a fine vessel, and bravely set out, and I fear the adventurers did overpride themselves in her, for she had ill success. However, they erred grossly in two things about her; first, though she had a sufficient master, yet she was rudely manned, and all her men were upon shares, and none was to have any wages but the master. Secondly, whereas they mainly looked at trade, they had sent nothing of any value to trade with. When the men came here, and met with ill counsel from Mr. Weston and his crew with others of the same stamp, neither master nor Governor could scarce rule them, for they exclaimed that they were abused and deceived, for they were told they should go for a man of war, and take I know not whom, French and Spaniards, etc. They would neither trade nor fish, except they had wages; in fine, they would obey no command of the master's. So it was apprehended they would either run away with the vessel, or get away with the ships and leave her; so as Mr. Peirce and others of their friends persuaded the Governor to change their condition, and give them wages; which was accordingly done.

And she was sent about the Cape to the Narragansetts to trade, but they made but a poor voyage of it. Some corn and beaver they got, but the Dutch used to furnish them with cloth and better commodities, they having only a few beads and knives, which were not there much esteemed. Also, in her return home, at the very entrance into their own harbor, she had like to have been cast away in a storm, and was forced to cut her mainmast by the board to save herself from driving on the flats that lie without, called Brown's Islands, the force of the wind being so great as made her anchors give way and she drive right upon them; but her mast and tackling being gone, they held her till the wind shifted.

ANNO DOMINI 1624

. . . They having with some trouble and charge new-masted and rigged their pinnace, in the beginning of March they sent her well victualed to the eastward on fishing. She arrived safely at a place near Damariscove, and was there well harbored in a place where ships used to ride, there being also some ships already arrived out of England. But shortly after there arose such a violent and extraordinary storm, as the seas broke over such places in the harbor as was never seen before, and drove her against great rocks, which beat such a hole in her bulk, as a horse and cart might have gone in, and after drove her into deep-water, where she lay sunk. The master was drowned, the rest of the men, all save one, saved their lives with much ado; all her provision, salt, and what else was in her, was lost. And here I must leave her to lie till afterward. . . .

Shortly after, Mr. Winslow came over, and brought a pretty good supply, and the ship came on fishing, a thing fatal to this plantation. He brought three heifers and a bull, the first beginning of any cattle of that kind in the land, with some clothing and other necessaries, as will further appear; but withal the report of a strong faction amongst the adventurers against them, and especially against the coming of the rest from Leyden, and with what difficulty this supply was procured, and how, by their strong and long opposition, business was so retarded as not only they were now fallen too late for the fishing season, but the best men were taken up of the fishermen in the west country, and he was forced to take such a master and company for that employment as he could procure upon the present. . . .

They began now highly to prize corn as more precious than silver, and those that had some to spare began to trade one with another for small things, by the quart, pottle,[1] and peck, etc.; for money they had none, and if any had, corn was preferred before it. That they might therefore increase their tillage to better advantage, they made suit to the Governor to have some portion of land given them for continuance, and not by yearly lot, for by that means, that which the more industrious had brought into good culture (by much pains) one year, came to leave it the next, and often another might enjoy it; so as the dressing of their lands were the more slighted over, and to less profit. Which being well considered, their request was granted. And to every person was given only one acre of land, to them and theirs, as near the town as might be, and they had no more till the seven years were expired. The reason was that they might be kept close together both for more safety and defense, and the better improvement of the general employments. . . .

The ship which brought this supply was speedily discharged, and with her master and company sent to Cape Ann . . . on fishing, and because the season was so far spent some of the planters were sent to help to build their stage,[2] to their own hindrance. But partly by the lateness of the year, and more especially by the baseness of the master, one Baker, they made a poor voyage of it. He proved a very drunken beast, and did nothing (in a manner) but drink, and guzzle, and consume away the time and his victuals; and most of his company followed his example; and though Mr. William Peirce was to oversee the business, and to be master of the ship home, yet he could do no good amongst them, so as the loss was great, and would have been more to them, but that they kept one a-trading there, which in those times got some store of skins, which was some help unto them.

The ship carpenter that was sent them was an honest and very

industrious man, and followed his labor very diligently, and
made all that were employed with him do the like. He quickly
built them two very good and strong shallops (which after did
them great service), and a great and strong lighter, and had
hewn timber for two ketches; but that was lost, for he fell into
a fever in the hot season of the year, and though he had the best
means the place could afford, yet he died; of whom they had a
very great loss, and were very sorry for his death.

But he whom they sent to make salt was an ignorant, foolish,
self-willed fellow. He bore them in hand he could do great matters in making salt-works, so he was sent to seek out fit ground
for his purpose; and after some search he told the Governor
that he had found a sufficient place, with a good bottom to hold
water and otherwise very convenient, which he doubted not but
in a short time to bring to good perfection, and to yield them
great profit; but he must have eight or ten men to be constantly
employed. He was wished to be sure that the ground was good,
and other things answerable, and that he could bring it to perfection; otherwise he would bring upon them a great charge by
employing himself and so many men. But he was, after some
trial, so confident as he caused them to send carpenters to rear
a great frame for a large house to receive the salt and such other
uses. But in the end all proved vain. Then he laid fault of the
ground, in which he was deceived; but if he might have the
lighter to carry clay, he was sure then he could do it.

Now though the Governor and some other[s] foresaw that
this would come to little, yet they had so many malignant spirits amongst them that would have laid it upon them in their letters of complaint to the adventurers as to be their fault that
would not suffer him to go on to bring his work to perfection;
for as he by his bold confidence and large promises deceived
them in England that sent him, so he had wound himself into
these men's high esteem here, so as they were fain to let him go
on till all men saw his vanity. For he could not do anything but
boil salt in pans, and yet would make them that were joined
with him believe there was so great a mystery in it as was not
easy to be attained, and made them do many unnecessary things
to blind their eyes, till they discerned his subtlety. The next year

he was sent to Cape Ann, and the pans were set up there where the fishing was; but before summer was out, he burnt the house, and the fire was so vehement as it spoiled the pans, at least some of them, and this was the end of that chargeable business.

The third eminent person . . . was the minister which they sent over, by name Mr. John Lyford, of whom and whose doing I must be more large, though I shall abridge things as much as I can. When this man first came ashore, he saluted them with that reverence and humility as is seldom to be seen, and indeed made them ashamed, he so bowed and cringed unto them, and would have kissed their hands if they would have suffered him; yea, he wept and shed many tears, blessing God that had brought him to see their faces, and admiring the things they had done in their wants, etc. as if he had been made all of love, and the humblest person in the world. . . .

They gave him the best entertainment they could (in all simplicity) and a larger allowance of food out of the store than any other had, and as the Governor had used in all weighty affairs to consult with their Elder, Mr. Brewster (together with his assistants), so now he called Mr. Lyford also to counsel with them in their weightiest businesses. After some short time he desired to join himself a member to the church here, and was accordingly received. He made a large confession of his faith, and an acknowledgment of his former disorderly walking, and his being entangled with many corruptions, which had been a burden to his conscience, and blessed God for this opportunity of freedom and liberty to enjoy the ordinances of God in purity among his people, with many more such like expressions.

I must here speak a word also of Mr. John Oldham, who was a co-partner with him in his after courses. He had been a chief stickler in the former faction among the particulars, and an intelligencer to those in England. But now, since the coming of this ship and he saw the supply that came, he took occasion to open his mind to some of the chief amongst them here, and confessed he had done them wrong both by word and deed and writing into England; but he now saw the eminent hand of God to be with them, and his blessing upon them, which made his heart smite him, neither should those in England ever use him as an instrument any longer against them in anything. He also desired former things might be forgotten, and that they would look upon him as one that desired to close with them in all things, with such like expressions. Now whether this was in hypocrisy, or out of some sudden pang of conviction (which I rather think), God only knows. Upon it they show all readiness to embrace his love, and carry towards him in all friendliness, and called him to counsel with them in all chief affairs, as the other, without any distrust at all.

Thus all things seemed to go very comfortably and smoothly on amongst them, at which they did much rejoice; but this lasted not long, for both Oldham and he grew very perverse, and showed a spirit of great malignancy, drawing as many into faction as they could. Were they never so vile or profane, they did nourish and back them in all their doings; so they would but cleave to them and speak against the church here; so as there was nothing but private meetings and whisperings amongst them; they feeding themselves and others with what they should bring to pass in England by the faction of their friends there, which brought others as well as themselves into a fool's paradise. Yet they could not carry so closely but much of both their doings and sayings were discovered, yet outwardly they still set a fair face of things.

At length when the ship was ready to go, it was observed Lyford was long in writing, and sent many letters, and could not forbear to communicate to his intimates such things as made them laugh in their sleeves, and thought he had done their errand sufficiently. The Governor and some other of his friends, knowing how things stood in England and what hurt these things might do, took a shallop and went out with the ship a league or two to sea, and called for all Lyford's and Oldham's letters. Mr. William Peirce being master of the ship (and knew well their evil dealing both in England and here) afforded him all the assistance he could. He found above twenty of Lyford's letters, many of them large, and full of slanders and false accusations, tending not only to their prejudice but to their ruin and utter subversion. Most of the letters they let pass, only took copies of them, but some of the most material they sent true copies of them, and kept the originals, least he should deny them, and that they might produce his own hand against him. . . .

This ship went out towards evening, and in the night the Governor returned. They were somewhat blank at it, but after some weeks, when they heard nothing, they then were as brisk as ever, thinking nothing had been known, but all was gone current, and that the Governor went but to dispatch his own letters. The reason why the Governor and rest concealed these things the longer was to let things ripen, that they might the better discover their intents and see who were their adherents. . . .

For Oldham, few of his letters were found (for he was so bad a scribe as his hand was scarce legible), yet he was as deep in the mischief as the other. And thinking they were now strong enough, they began to pick quarrels at everything. Oldham being called to watch (according to order) refused to come, fell out with the Captain, called him rascal, and beggarly rascal, and resisted him, drew his knife at him though he offered him no wrong, nor gave him no ill terms, but with all fairness required him to do his duty. The Governor, hearing the tumult, sent to quiet it, but he ramped more like a furious beast than a man, and called them all traitors and rebels, and other such foul language as I am ashamed to remember; but after he was clapped up awhile, he came to himself, and with some slight punishment was let go upon his behavior for further censure.

But to cut things short, at length it grew to this issue, that Lyford with his accomplices, without ever speaking one word either to the Governor, Church, or Elder, withdrew themselves and set up a public meeting apart on the Lord's day; with sundry such insolent carriages too long here to relate, beginning now publicly to act what privately they had been long plotting.

It was now thought high time (to prevent further mischief) to call them to account; so the Governor called a court and summoned the whole company to appear. And then charged Lyford and Oldham with such things as they were guilty of. But they were stiff, and stood resolutely upon the denial of most things, and required proof. . . . Lyford denied that he had anything to do with them in England, or knew of their courses, and made other things as strange that he was charged with. Then his letters were produced and some of them read, at which he was struck mute. But Oldham began to rage furiously, because they had intercepted and opened his letters, threatening them in very high language, and in a most audacious and mutinous manner stood up and called upon the people, saying, "My masters, where is your hearts? Now show your courage, you have oft complained to me so and so; now is the time, if you will do anything, I will stand by you, etc." Thinking that every one (knowing his humor) that had soothed and flattered him, or otherwise in their discontent uttered anything unto him, would now side with him in open rebellion. But he was deceived, for not a man opened his mouth, but all were silent, being struck with the injustice of the thing.

Then the Governor turned his speech to Mr. Lyford, and asked him if he thought they had done evil to open his letters; but he was silent, and would not say a word, well knowing what they might reply. Then the Governor showed the people he did it as a magistrate, and was bound to it by his place, to prevent the mischief and ruin that this conspiracy and plots of theirs would bring on this poor colony. But he, besides his evil dealing here, had dealt treacherously with his friends that trusted him, and stole their letters and opened them, and sent copies of them, with disgraceful annotations, to his friends in England. And then the Governor produced them and his other letters under his own hand (which he could not deny), and caused them to be read before all the people; at which all his friends were blank, and had not a word to say. . . .

After the reading of his letters before the whole company, he was demanded what he could say to these things. But all the answer he made was, that Billington and some others had informed him of many things, and made sundry complaints, which they now denied. He was again asked if that was a sufficient ground for him thus to accuse and traduce them by his letters, and never say word to them, considering the many bonds between them. And so they went on from point to point; and wished him, or any of his friends and confederates, not to spare them in anything. If he or they had any proof or witness of any corrupt or evil dealing of theirs, his or their evidence must needs be there present, for there was the whole company and sundry strangers. He said he had been abused by others in their informations (as he now well saw), and so had abused them. And this was all the answer they could have, for none would take his part in any thing but Billington, and any whom he named denied the things, and protested he wronged them, and would have drawn them to such and such things which they could not consent to, though they were sometimes drawn to his meetings.

Then they dealt with him about his dissembling with them about the church, and that he professed to concur with them in all things, and what a large confession he made at his admittance, and that he held not himself a minister till he had a new calling, etc. And yet now he contested against them, and drew a company apart, and sequestered himself; and would go minister the sacraments (by his Episcopal calling) without ever speaking a word unto them, either as magistrates or brethren. In conclusion, he was fully convicted, and burst out into tears, and confessed he feared he was a reprobate, his sins were so great that he doubted God would not pardon them, he was unsavory salt, etc.; and that he had so wronged them as he could never make them amends, confessing all he had written against them was false and naught, both for matter and manner. And all this he did with as much fullness as words and tears could express.

After their trial and conviction, the court censured them to be expelled the place; Oldham presently, though his wife and family had liberty to stay all winter, or longer, till he could make provision to remove them comfortably. Lyford had liberty to stay six months. It was, indeed, with some eye to his release, if he carried himself well in the meantime, and that his repentance proved sound. Lyford acknowledged his censure was far less than he deserved.

Afterwards, he confessed his sin publicly in the church, with tears more largely than before. . . . So as they began again to conceive good thoughts of him upon this his repentance, and admitted him to teach amongst them as before; and Samuel Fuller (a deacon amongst them) and some other tenderhearted men amongst them were so taken with his signs of sorrow and repentance, as they professed they would fall upon their knees to have his censure released.

But that which made them all stand amazed in the end, and may do all others that shall come to hear the same (for a rarer precedent can scarce be shown) was that after a month or two notwithstanding all his former confessions, convictions, and public acknowledgments, both in the face of the church and whole company, with so many tears and sad censures of himself before God and men, he should go again to justify what he had done. For secretly he wrote a second letter to the adventurers in England, in which he justified all his former writings. . . .

The pinnace that was left sunk and cast away near Damariscove, as is before showed, some of the fishing masters said it was a pity so fine a vessel should be lost, and sent them word that, if they would be at the cost, they would both direct them how to weigh her, and let them have their carpenters to mend her. They thanked them, and sent men about it, and beaver to defray the charge (without which all had been in vain). So they got coopers to trim I know not how many tun of cask, and being made tight and fastened to her at low-water, they buoyed her up; and then with many hands hauled her on shore in a convenient place where she might be wrought upon; and then hired sundry carpenters to work upon her, and other to saw planks, and at last fitted her and got her home. But she cost a great deal of money in thus recovering her, and buying rigging and sails for her, both now and when before she lost her mast; so as she proved a chargeable vessel to the poor plantation. So they sent her home, and with her Lyford sent his last letter, in great secrecy; but the party entrusted with it gave it the Governor.

The winter was passed over in their ordinary affairs, without any special matter worth noting; saving that many who before stood something off from the church, now seeing Lyford's unrighteous dealing, and malignity against the church, now tendered themselves to the church, and were joined to the same; professing that it was not out of the dislike of anything that they had stood off so long, but a desire to fit themselves better for such a state, and they saw now the Lord called for their help. And so these troubles produced a quite contrary effect in sundry here, than these adversaries hoped for. Which was looked at as a great work of God, to draw on men by unlikely means; and that in reason which might rather have set them further off. And thus I shall end this year.

ANNO DOMINI 1625

At the spring of the year, about the time of their Election Court,[1] Oldham came again amongst them; and though it was a part of his censure for his former mutiny and miscarriage not to return without leave first obtained, yet in his daring spirit he presumed without any leave at all, being also set on and hardened by the ill counsel of others. And not only so, but suffered his unruly passion to run beyond the limits of all reason and modesty; in so much that some strangers which came with him were ashamed of his outrage and rebuked him; but all reproofs were but as oil to the fire, and made the flame of his choler greater. He called them all to naught, in this his mad fury, and a hundred rebels and traitors, and I know not what. But in conclusion they committed him till he was tamer, and then appointed a guard of musketeers which he was to pass through, and everyone was ordered to give him a thump on the breech with the butt end of his musket, and then was conveyed to the waterside, where a boat was ready to carry him away. Then they bid him go and mend his manners.

Whilst this was a doing, Mr. William Peirce and Mr. Winslow came up from the waterside, being come from England; but they were so busy with Oldham, as they never saw them till they came thus upon them. They bid them not spare either him or Lyford, for they had played the villains with them. But that I may here make an end with him, I shall here once for all relate what befell concerning him in the future, and that briefly.

After the removal of his family from hence, he fell into some straits (as some others did), and about a year or more afterwards, towards winter, he intended a voyage for Virginia; but it so

pleased God that the bark that carried him and many other passengers was in that danger as they despaired of life; so as many of
them, as they fell to prayer, so also did they begin to examine
their consciences and confess such sins as did most burden them.
And Mr. Oldham did make a free and large confession of the
wrongs and hurt he had done to the people and church here in
many particulars, that as he had sought their ruin, so God had
now met with him and might destroy him; yea, he feared they all
fared the worse for his sake; he prayed God to forgive him, and
made vows that, if the Lord spared his life, he would become otherwise, and the like. This I had from some of good credit, yet living in the Bay, and were themselves partners in the same dangers
on the shoals of Cape Cod, and heard it from his own mouth. It
pleased God to spare their lives, though they lost their voyage;
and in time afterwards, Oldham carried himself fairly towards
them, and acknowledged the hand of God to be with them, and
seemed to have an honorable respect of them; and so far made
his peace with them as he in aftertime had liberty to go and come,
and converse with them at his pleasure.

He went after this to Virginia, and had there a great sickness,
but recovered and came back again to his family in the Bay, and
there lived till some store of people came over. At length going
a-trading in a small vessel among the Indians, and being weakly
manned, upon some quarrel they knocked him on the head
with a hatchet, so as he fell down dead and never spoke word
more. Two little boys that were his kinsmen were saved, but
had some hurt, and the vessel was strangely recovered from the
Indians by another that belonged to the Bay of Massachusetts;
and this his death was one ground of the Pequot war which followed.

I am now come to Mr. Lyford. His time being now expired,
his censure was to take place. He was so far from answering
their hopes by amendment in the time, as he had doubled his
evil, as is before noted. But first behold the hand of God concerning him, wherein that of the Psalmist is verified, Psalm
7:15: "He hath made a pit, and digged it, and is fallen into the
pit he made." He thought to bring shame and disgrace upon
them, but instead thereof opens his own to all the world. For

when he was dealt with all about his second letter, his wife was so affected with his doings, as she could no longer conceal her grief and sorrow of mind, but opens the same to one of their deacons and some other of her friends, and after uttered the same to Mr. Peirce upon his arrival. Which was to this purpose, that she feared some great judgment of God would fall upon them, and upon her, for her husband's cause; now that they were to remove, she feared to fall into the Indians' hands, and to be defiled by them, as he had defiled other women; or some such like judgment, as God had threatened David, 2 Samuel 12:11: "I will raise up evil against thee, and will take thy wives and give them, etc."

And upon it showed how he had wronged her, as first he had a bastard by another before they were married, and she having some inkling of some ill carriage that way, when he was a suitor to her, she told him what she heard, and denied him; but she not certainly knowing the thing otherwise than by some dark and secret mutterings, he not only stiffly denied it, but to satisfy her took a solemn oath there was no such matter. Upon which she gave consent, and married with him; but afterwards it was found true, and the bastard brought home to them. She then charged him with his oath, but he prayed pardon, and said he should else not have had her. And yet afterwards she could keep no maids but he would be meddling with them, and some time she hath taken him in the manner, as they lay at their beds' feet with such other circumstances as I am ashamed to relate.

The woman being a grave matron and of good carriage all the while she was here, and spoke these things out of the sorrow of her heart, sparingly, and yet with some further intimations. And that which did most seem to affect her (as they conceived) was to see his former carriage in his repentance, not only here with the church, but formerly about these things; shedding tears and using great and sad expressions, and yet eftsoon fall into the like things.

Another thing of the same nature did strangely concur herewith. When Mr. Winslow and Mr. Peirce were come over, Mr. Winslow informed them that they had had the like bickering with Lyford's friends in England, as they had with himself and his friends here, about his letters and accusations in them. And many meetings and much clamor was made by his friends thereabout, crying out, a minister, a man so godly, to be so esteemed and taxed they held a great scandal, and threatened to prosecute law against them for it. But things being referred to a further meeting of most of the adventurers to hear the case and decide the matters, they agreed to chose two eminent men for moderators in the business. Lyford's faction chose Mr. White, a counselor at law, the other part chose Reverend Mr. Hooker,[2] the minister, and many friends on both sides were brought in, so as there was a great assembly.

In the meantime, God in his providence had detected Lyford's evil carriage in Ireland to some friends amongst the company, who made it known to Mr. Winslow, and directed him to two godly and grave witnesses, who would testify the same (if called thereunto) upon their oath. The thing was this; he being got into Ireland, had wound himself into the esteem of sundry godly and zealous professors in those parts, who, having been burdened with the ceremonies in England, found there some more liberty to their consciences; amongst whom were these two men, which gave this evidence.

Amongst the rest of [Lyford's] hearers, there was a godly young man that intended to marry, and cast his affection on a maid which lived there about; but desiring to choose in the Lord, and preferred the fear of God before all other things, before he suffered his affection to run too far, he resolved to take Mr. Lyford's advice and judgment of this maid (being the minister of the place), and so broke the matter unto him; and he promised faithfully to inform him, but would first take better knowledge of her, and have private conference with her; and so had sundry times; and in conclusion commended her highly to the young man as a very fit wife for him.

So they were married together; but some time after marriage the woman was much troubled in mind and afflicted in conscience, and did nothing but weep and mourn, and long it was before her husband could get of her what was the cause. But at length she discovered the thing, and prayed him to forgive her, for Lyford had overcome her and defiled her body before marriage, after he had commended him unto her for a husband, and she resolved to have him, when he came to her in that private way. The circumstances I forbear, for they would offend chaste ears to hear them related (for though he satisfied his lust on her, yet he endeavored to hinder conception.). These things being thus discovered, the woman's husband took some godly friends with him to deal with Lyford for this evil. At length he confessed it, with a great deal of seeming sorrow and repentance, but was forced to leave Ireland upon it, partly for shame, and partly for fear of further punishment, for the godly withdrew themselves from him upon it; and so coming into England unhappily he was lit upon and sent hither.

But in this great assembly and before the moderators, in handling the former matters about the letters, upon provocation in some heat of reply to some of Lyford's defenders, Mr. Winslow let fall these words, that "he had dealt knavishly." Upon which one of his friends took hold and called for witnesses, that he called a minister of the gospel knave, and would prosecute law upon it, which made a great tumult. Upon which (to be short) this matter broke out, and the witnesses were produced, whose persons were so grave, and evidence so plain, and the fact so foul, yet delivered in such modest and chaste terms, and with such circumstances, as struck all his friends mute, and made them all ashamed. Insomuch as the moderators with great gravity declared that the former matters gave them cause enough to refuse him and to deal with him as they had done, but these made him unmeet forever to bear ministry any more, what repentance soever he should pretend; with much more to like effect, and so wished his friends to rest quiet. Thus was this matter ended.

From hence Lyford went to Nantasket in the Bay of the Massachusetts with some other of his friends with him, where Oldham also lived. From thence he removed to Naumkeag, since called Salem. But after there came some people over, whether for hope of greater profit, or what ends else I know not, he left his friends that followed him, and went from thence to Virginia, where he shortly after died, and so I leave him to the Lord. His wife afterwards returned again to this country, and thus much of this matter.

This storm being thus blown over, yet sundry sad effects followed the same; for the Company of Adventurers broke in pieces here upon; and the greatest part wholly deserted the colony in regard of any further supply, or care of their subsistence. And not only so, but some of Lyford's and Oldham's friends and their adherents set out a ship on fishing on their own account, and getting the start of the ships that came to the plantation, they took away their stage and other necessary provisions that they had made for fishing at Cape Ann the year before at their great charge, and would not restore the same except they would fight for it. But the Governor sent some of the planters to help the fishermen to build a new one, and so let them keep it. This ship also brought them some small supply of little value; but they made so poor a business of their fishing (neither could these men make them any return for the supply sent), so as, after this year, they never looked more after them. . . .

Captain Standish from the plantation [was sent over to England] with letters and instructions, both to their friends of the company which still cleaved to them, and also to the Honorable Council of New England. . . . But he came in a very bad time, for the State was full of trouble, and the plague very hot in London, so as no business could be done; yet he spoke with some of the Honored Council, who promised all helpfulness to the plantation which lay in them. And sundry of their friends the adventurers were so weakened with their losses the last year, . . . as, though their wills were good, yet their power was little. And there died such multitudes weekly of the plague, as all trade was dead, and little money stirring. Yet with much ado he took up £150 (and spent a good deal of it in expenses) at 50 per cent, which he bestowed in trading goods and such other most needful commodities as he knew requisite for their use; and so returned passenger in a fishing ship, having prepared a good way for the composition[3] that was afterward made.

In the meantime it pleased the Lord to give the plantation peace and health and contented minds, and so to bless their labors, as they had corn sufficient (and some to spare to others) with other food; neither ever had they any supply of food but what they first brought with them. After harvest this year, they sent out a boat's load of corn forty or fifty leagues to the eastward, up a river called Kennebec; it being one of those two shallops which their carpenter had built them the year before; for bigger vessel had they none. They had laid a little deck over her midships to keep the corn dry, but the men were fain to stand it out all weathers without shelter; and that time of the year begins to grow tempestuous. But God preserved them, and gave them good success, for they brought home 700 pounds of beaver, besides some other furs, having little or nothing else but this corn which themselves had raised out of the earth. This voyage was made by Mr. Winslow and some of the old standers,[4] for seamen they had none.

ANNO DOMINI 1626

About the beginning of April they heard of Captain Standish's arrival, and sent a boat to fetch him home, and the things he had brought. Welcome he was, but the news he brought was sad in many regards; not only in regard of the former losses, before related, which their friends had suffered, by which some in a manner were undone, others much disabled from doing any further help, and some dead of the plague, but also that Mr. Robinson, their pastor, was dead, which struck them with much sorrow and sadness, as they had cause. His and their adversaries had been long and continually plotting how they might hinder his coming hither, but the Lord had appointed him a better place. . . .

He further brought them notice of the death of their ancient friend, Mr. Cushman, whom the Lord took away also this year, and about this time, who was as their right hand with their friends the adventurers, and for divers years had done and agitated all their business with them to their great advantage. He had written to the Governor but some few months before of the sore sickness of Mr. James Sherley,[1] who was a chief friend to the plantation, and lay at the point of death, declaring his love and helpfulness in all things; and much bemoaned the loss they should have of him, if God should now take him away, as being the stay and life of the whole business. As also his own purpose this year to come over, and spend his days with them. But he that thus wrote of another's sickness knew not that his own death was so near. It shows also that a man's ways are not in his own power, but in his hands who hath the issues of life and death. Man may purpose, but God doth dispose.

Their other friends from Leyden wrote many letters to them full of sad laments for their heavy loss; and though their wills were good to come to them, yet they saw no probability of means how it might be effected, but concluded (as it were) that all their hopes were cut off; and many, being aged, began to drop away by death.

All which things (before related) being well weighed and laid together, it could not but strike them with great perplexity; and to look humanly on the state of things as they presented themselves at this time, it is a marvel it did not wholly discourage them and sink them. But they gathered up their spirits, and the Lord so helped them, whose work they had in hand, as now when they were at lowest they began to rise again, and being stripped (in a manner) of all human helps and hopes, he brought things about otherwise, in his divine providence as they were not only upheld and sustained, but their proceedings both honored and imitated by others; as by the sequel will more appear, if the Lord spare me life and time to declare the same.

Having now no fishing business, or other things to intend, but only their trading and planting, they set themselves to follow the same with the best industry they could. The Planters finding their corn, what they could spare from their necessities, to be a commodity (for they sold it at six shillings a bushel), used great diligence in planting the same. And Governor and such as were designed to manage the trade (for it was retained for the general good, and none were to trade in particular), they followed it to the best advantage they could; and wanting trading goods, they understood that a plantation which was at Monhegan, and belonged to the merchants of Plymouth [England] was to break up, and divers useful goods was there to be sold; the Governor and Mr. Winslow took a boat and some hands and went thither.

But Mr. David Thompson, who lived at Piscataqua, under-standing their purpose, took opportunity to go with them, which was some hindrance to them both; for they, perceiving their joint desires to buy, held their goods at higher rates; and not only so, but would not sell a parcel of their trading goods except they sold all. So, lest they should further prejudice one another, they agreed to buy all, and divide them equally be-tween them. They bought also a parcel of goats, which they dis-tributed at home as they saw need and occasion, and took corn for them of the people, which gave them good content. Their moiety of the goods came to above £400 sterling.

There was also that spring a French ship cast away at Sagada-hoc,[2] in which were many Biscay rugs and other commodities, which were fallen into these men's hands, and some other fisher-men at Damariscove, which were also bought in partnership, and made their part arise to above £500. This they made shift to pay for, for the most part, with the beaver and commodities they had got the winter before, and what they had gathered up that summer. Mr. Thompson having something overcharged himself, desired they would take some of his, but they refused except he would let them have his French goods only; and the merchant (who was one of Bristol) would take their bill for to be paid the next year. They were both willing, so they became engaged for them and took them.

By which means they became very well furnished for trade; and took of thereby some other engagements which lay upon them, as the money taken up by Captain Standish and the re-mains of former debts. With these goods and their corn after harvest, they got good store of trade, so as they were enabled to pay their engagements against the time, and to get some cloth-ing for the people, and had some commodities beforehand. But now they began to be envied, and others went and filled the In-dians with corn and beat down the price, giving them twice as much as they had done, and undertraded them in other com-modities also.

This year they sent Mr. Allerton into England and gave him order to make a composition with the adventurers upon as good terms as he could (unto which some way had been made

the year before by Captain Standish); but yet enjoined him not
to conclude absolutely till they knew the terms and had well
considered of them; but to drive it to as good an issue as he
could and refer the conclusion to them. Also they gave him a
commission under their hands and seals to take up some money,
provided it exceeded not such a sum specified for which they
engaged themselves, and gave him order how to lay out the
same for the use of the plantation.

And finding they ran a great hazard to go so long voyages in
a small open boat, especially the winter season, they began to
think how they might get a small pinnace; as for the reason
aforesaid, so also because others had raised the price with the
Indians above the half of what they had formerly given, so as in
such a boat they could not carry a quantity sufficient to answer
their ends. They had no ship carpenter amongst them, neither
knew how to get one at present; but they having an ingenious
man that was a house carpenter, who also had wrought with
the ship carpenter (that was dead) when he built their boats, at
their request he put forth himself to make a trial that way of his
skill; and took one of the biggest of their shallops and sawed
her in the middle, and so lengthened her some five or six feet,
and strengthened her with timbers, and so built her up, and laid
a deck on her; and so made her a convenient and wholesome
vessel, very fit and comfortable for their use, which did them
service seven years after; and they got her finished, and fitted
with sails and anchors, the ensuing year. And thus passed the
affairs of this year.

ANNO DOMINI 1627

At the usual season of the coming of ships Mr. Allerton returned, and brought some useful goods with him, according
to the order given him. For upon his commission he took up
£200 which he now got at 30 per cent. The which goods they
got safely home and well conditioned, which was much to the
comfort and content of the plantation. He declared unto them,
also, how, with much ado and no small trouble, he had made a

composition with the adventurers by the help of sundry of their faithful friends there, who had also took much pains there about. . . .

There is one thing that fell out in the beginning of the winter before, which I have referred to this place, that I may handle the whole matter together. There was a ship, with many passengers in her and sundry goods, bound for Virginia. They had lost themselves at sea, either by the insufficiency of the master, or his illness; for he was sick and lame of the scurvy, so that he could but lie in the cabin door and give direction; and it should seem was badly assisted either with mate or mariners; or else the fear and unruliness of the passengers were such as they made them steer a course between the southwest and the northwest, that they might fall with some land, whatsoever it was they cared not. For they had been six weeks at sea, and had no water, nor beer, nor any wood left, but had burnt up all their empty cask; only one of the company had a hogshead of wine or two which was also almost spent. So as they feared they should be starved at sea, or consumed with diseases, which made them run this desperate course.

But it pleased God that though they came so near the shoals of Cape Cod or else ran stumbling over them in the night, they knew not how, they came right before a small blind harbor that lies about the middle of Manamoyick Bay to the southward of Cape Cod, with a small gale of wind; and about high water touched upon a bar of sand that lies before it, but had no hurt, the sea being smooth; so they laid out an anchor. But towards the evening the wind sprung up at sea and was so rough as broke their cable and beat them over the bar into the harbor, where they saved their lives and goods, though much were hurt with salt water; for with beating they had sprung the butt end of a plank or two, and beat out their oakum.[1] But they were soon over, and ran on a dry flat within the harbor, close by a beach; so at low water they got out their goods on dry shore, and dried those that were wet, and saved most of their things without any great loss; neither was the ship much hurt, but she might be mended, and made serviceable again.

But though they were not a little glad that they had thus

saved their lives, yet when they had a little refreshed themselves, and began to think on their condition, not knowing where they were, nor what they should do, they began to be stricken with sadness. But shortly after they saw some Indians come to them in canoes, which made them stand upon their guard. But when they heard some of the Indians speak English unto them, they were not a little revived, especially when they heard them demand if they were the Governor of Plymouth's men, or friends: and that they would bring them to the English houses, or carry their letters.

They feasted these Indians, and gave them many gifts; and sent two men and a letter with them to the Governor, and did entreat him to send a boat unto them, with some pitch and oakum, and spikes, with divers other necessaries for the mending of their ship (which was recoverable). Also they besought him to help them with some corn and sundry other things they wanted to enable them to make their voyage to Virginia; and they should be much bound to him, and would make satisfaction for anything they had, in any commodities they had aboard. After the Governor was well informed by the messengers of their condition, he caused a boat to be made ready, and such things to be provided as they wrote for; and because others were abroad upon trading and such other affairs as had been fit to send unto them, he went himself, and also carried some trading commodities to buy them corn of the Indians.

It was no season of the year to go without the Cape, but understanding where the ship lay, he went into the bottom of the bay on the inside, and put into a creek called Namskaket,[2] where it is not much above two mile overland to the bay where they were, where he had the Indians ready to carry over anything to them. Of his arrival they were very glad, and received the things to mend their ship, and other necessaries. Also he bought them as much corn as they would have; and whereas some of their seamen were run away among the Indians, he procured their return to the ship, and so left them well furnished and contented, being very thankful for the courtesies they received.

But after the Governor thus left them, he went into some

other harbors thereabout and loaded his boat with corn, which he traded, and so went home. But he had not been at home many days, but he had notice from them, that by the violence of a great storm, and the bad mooring of their ship (after she was mended) she was put ashore, and so beaten and shaken as she was now wholly unfit to go to sea. And so their request was that they might have leave to repair to them and sojourn with them till they could have means to convey themselves to Virginia; and that they might have means to transport their goods, and they would pay for the same or anything else wherewith the plantation should relieve them. Considering their distress, their requests were granted, and all helpfulness done unto them; their goods transported, and themselves and goods sheltered in their houses as well as they could.

The chief amongst these people was one Mr. Fells and Mr. Sibsey, which had many servants[3] belonging unto them, many of them being Irish. Some others there were that had a servant or two apiece; but the most were servants, and such as were engaged to the former persons, who also had the most goods. After they were hither come, and something settled, the masters desired some ground to employ their servants upon; seeing it was like to be the latter end of the year before they could have passage for Virginia, and they had now the winter before them, they might clear some ground, and plant a crop (seeing they had tools, and necessaries for the same) to help to bear their charge, and keep their servants in employment; and if they had opportunity to depart before the same was ripe, they would sell it on the ground. So they had ground appointed them in convenient places, and Fells and some other of them raised a great deal of corn, which they sold at their departure.

This Fells, amongst his other servants, had a maidservant which kept his house and did his household affairs, and by the intimation of some that belonged unto him, he was suspected to keep her as his concubine; and both of them were examined thereupon, but nothing could be proved, and they stood upon their justification; so with admonition they were dismissed. But afterward it appeared she was with child, so he got a small boat, and ran away with her, for fear of punishment. First he went to Cape Ann, and after into the bay of the Massachusetts, but could get no passage and had like to have been cast away; and was forced to come again and submit himself; but they packed him away and those that belonged unto him by the first opportunity, and dismissed all the rest as soon as could, being many untoward people amongst them; though there were also some that carried themselves very orderly all the time they stayed.

And the plantation had some benefit by them, in selling them corn and other provisions of food for clothing; for they had of diverse kinds, as cloth, perpetuanes,[4] and other stuffs, besides hose, and shoes, and such like commodities as the planters stood in need of. So they both did good, and received good one from another; and a couple of barks carried them away at the latter end of summer. And sundry of them have acknowledged their thankfulness since from Virginia.

ANNO DOMINI 1628

This year the Dutch sent again unto them from their plantation both kind letters and also divers commodities, as sugar, linen cloth, Holland finer and coarser stuffs, etc. They came up with their bark to Manomet to their house there, in which came their Secretary Rasieres; who was accompanied with a noise of trumpeters and some other attendants; and desired that they would send a boat for him, for he could not travel so far overland. So they sent a boat to Scusset,[1] and brought him to the plantation with the chief of his company. And after some few days' entertainment, he returned to his bark, and some of them went with him, and bought sundry of his goods; after which beginning thus made, they sent oftentimes to the same place, and had intercourse together for divers years; and amongst other commodities, they vended much tobacco for linen cloth, stuffs, etc., which was a good benefit to the people till the Virginians found out their plantation.

But that which turned most to their profit in time was an entrance into the trade of Wampumpeag,[2] for they now bought about £50 worth of it of [the Dutch]; and they told them how vendible it was at their fort Orania;[3] and did persuade them they would find it so at Kennebec; and so it came to pass in time, though at first it stuck, and it was two years before they could put off this small quantity, till the inland people knew of it; and afterwards they could scarce ever get enough for them for many years together. And so this, with their other provisions, cut off their trade quite from the fishermen, and in great part from other of the straggling planters.

And strange it was to see the great alteration it made in a few years among the Indians themselves; for all the Indians of these parts and the Massachusetts had none or very little of it but the sachems and some special persons that wore a little of it for ornament. Only it was made and kept among the Narragansetts and Pequots, which grew rich and potent by it, and these people were poor and beggarly, and had no use of it. Neither did the English of this plantation or any other in the land, till now that they had knowledge of it from the Dutch, so much as know what it was, much less that it was a commodity of that worth and value. But after it grew thus to be a commodity in these parts, these Indians fell into it also, and to learn how to make it; for the Narragansetts do gather the shells of which they make it from their shores. And it hath now continued a current commodity about this twenty years, and it may prove a drug in time.

In the meantime it makes the Indians of these parts rich and powerful and also proud thereby and fills them with pieces, powder, and shot, which no laws can restrain, by reason of the baseness of sundry unworthy persons, both English, Dutch, and French, which may turn to the ruin of many. Hitherto the Indians of these parts had no pieces nor other arms but their bows and arrows, nor of many years after; neither durst they scarce handle a gun, so much were they afraid of them; and the very sight of one (though out of kilter) was a terror unto them. But those Indians to the east parts, which had commerce with the French, got pieces of them, and they in the end made a common trade of it; and in time our English fishermen, led with the like covetousness, followed their example for their own gain; but upon complaint against them, it pleased the king's majesty to prohibit the same by a strict proclamation, commanding that no sort of arms or munition should by any of his subjects be traded with them.

About some three or four years before this time, there came over one Captain Wollaston (a man of pretty parts) and with him three or four more of some eminency, who brought with them a great many servants with provisions and other implements for to begin a plantation; and pitched themselves in a place within the Massachusetts, which they called, after their Captain's name, Mount Wollaston.[4] Amongst whom was one Mr. Morton,[5] who, it should seem, had some small adventure (of his own or other men's) amongst them; but had little respect amongst them and was slighted by the meanest servants.

Having continued there some time, and not finding things to answer their expectations, nor profit to arise as they looked for, Captain Wollaston takes a great part of the servants and transports them to Virginia, where he puts them off at good rates, selling their time to other men; and writes back to one Mr. Rasdall, one of his chief partners and accounted their merchant, to bring another part of them to Virginia likewise, intending to put them off there as he had done the rest. And he, with the consent of the said Rasdall, appointed one Fitcher to be his Lieutenant and govern the remains of the plantation till he or Rasdall returned to take further order thereabout.

But this Morton abovesaid, having more craft than honesty (who had been a kind of pettifogger of Furnival's Inn[6]), in the others' absence, watches an opportunity (commons being but hard amongst them), and got some strong drink and other junkets, and made them a feast; and after they were merry, he began to tell them, he would give them good counsel. "You see (saith he) that many of your fellows are carried to Virginia; and if you stay till this Rasdall return, you will also be carried away and sold for slaves with the rest. Therefore I would advise you to thrust out this Lieutenant Fitcher; and I, having a part in the plantation, will receive you as my partners and consociates;[7] so may you be free from service, and we will converse, trade, plant, and live together as equals, and support and protect one another," or to like effect. This counsel was easily received; so they took opportunity and thrust Lieutenant Fitcher out of doors, and would suffer him to come no more amongst them, but forced him to seek bread to eat and other relief from his neighbors, till he could get passage for England.

After this they fell to great licentiousness and led a dissolute life, pouring out themselves into all profaneness. And Morton became lord of misrule, and maintained (as it were) a school of Atheism. And after they had got some good[s] into their hands, and got much by trading with the Indians, they spent it as vainly in quaffing and drinking both wine and strong waters in great excess, and, as some reported, £10 worth in a morning. They also set up a Maypole, drinking and dancing about it many days together, inviting the Indian women for their consorts, dancing and frisking together (like so many fairies, or furies rather) and worse practices, as if they had anew revived and celebrated the feasts of the Roman Goddess Flora, or the beastly practices of the mad Bacchanalians. Morton likewise (to show his poetry) composed sundry rhymes and verses, some tending to lasciviousness, and others to the detraction and scandal of some persons, which he affixed to this idle or idol Maypole. They changed also the name of their place, and instead of calling it Mount Wollaston, they call it Merrymount, as if this jollity would have lasted ever.

But this continued not long, for after Morton was sent for England (as follows to be declared), shortly after came over that worthy gentleman, Mr. John Endecott,[8] who brought over a patent under the broad seal,[9] for the government of the Massachusetts, who, visiting those parts, caused that Maypole to be cut down and rebuked them for their profaneness, and admonished them to look there should be better walking; so they now, or others, changed the name of their place again, and called it Mount Dagon.[10]

Now to maintain this riotous prodigality and profuse excess, Morton, thinking himself lawless, and hearing what gain the French and fishermen made by trading of pieces, powder, and shot to the Indians, he, as the head of this consortship, began the practice of the same in these parts; and first he taught them how to use them, to charge and discharge, and what proportion of powder to give the piece according to the size or bigness of the same; and what shot to use for fowl and what for deer. And having thus instructed them, he employed some of them to hunt and fowl for him, so as they became far more active in that employment than any of the English by reason of their swiftness of foot and nimbleness of body, being also quick-sighted, and by continual exercise well knowing the haunts of all sorts of game. So as when they saw the execution that a piece would do, and the benefit that might come by the same, they became mad, as it were, after them and would not stick to give any price they could attain to for them; accounting their bows and arrows but babies in comparison of them.

And here I may take occasion to bewail the mischief that this wicked man began in these parts, and which since base covetousness prevailing in men that should know better, has now at length got the upper hand, and made this thing common, notwithstanding any laws to the contrary; so as the Indians are full of pieces all over, both fowling pieces, muskets, pistols, etc. They have also their moulds to make shot of all sorts, as musket bullets, pistol bullets, swan and goose shot, and of smaller sorts; yea, some have seen them have their screw-plates[11] to make screw-pins themselves when they want them, with sundry other implements wherewith they are ordinarily better fitted and furnished than the English themselves.

Yea, it is well known that they will have powder and shot, when the English want it nor cannot get it; and that in a time of war or danger, as experience hath manifested, that when lead hath been scarce, and men for their own defense would gladly have given a groat[12] a pound, which is dear enough, yet hath it been bought up and sent to other places, and sold to such as trade it with the Indians at twelvepence the pound; and it is like they give three or four shillings the pound, for they will have it at any rate. And these things have been done in the same times, when some of their neighbors and friends are daily killed by the Indians, or are in danger thereof, and live but at the Indians' mercy. Yea, some (as they have acquainted them with all other things) have told them how gunpowder is made, and all the

own private benefit; which was more than any man had
herto attempted. But because he had otherwise done them
service, and also he sold them among the people at the
tion, by which their wants were supplied, and he alleged
the love of Mr. Sherley and some other friends that would
trust him with some goods, conceiving it might do him
ood, and none hurt, it was not much looked at, but passed
But this year he brought over a greater quantity, and they
o intermixed with the goods of the general, as they knew
hich were theirs, and which was his, being packed up to-
; so as they well saw that, if any casualty had befallen at
e might have laid the whole on them, if he would; for
was no distinction. Also what was most vendible, and
yield present pay, usually that was his; and he now began
o sell abroad to others of foreign places, which, consider-
eir common course, they began to dislike.

because love thinks no evil, nor is suspicious, they took
ir words for excuse and resolved to send him again this
or England; considering how well he had done the former
ess, and what good acceptation he had with their friends
as also seeing sundry of their friends from Leyden were
or, which would or might be much furthered by his
.....

they gave him instructions and sent him for England this
again. And in his instructions bound him to bring over
oods on their account but £50 in hose and shoes and
linen cloth (as they were bound by covenant when they
the trade), also some trading goods to such a value; and
case to exceed his instructions, nor run them into any
er charge, he well knowing how their state stood. Also
e should so provide that their trading goods came over
es, and whatsoever was sent on their account should be
d up by itself, marked with their mark, and no other
s to be mixed with theirs. For so he prayed them to give
uch instructions as they saw good, and he would follow
to prevent any jealousy or farther offence upon the for-
orementioned dislikes. And thus they conceived they had
provided for all things.

materials in it, and that they are to be had in their own land;
and I am confident, could they attain to make saltpeter, they
would teach them to make powder.

Oh, the horribleness of this villainy! how many both Dutch
and English have been lately slain by those Indians, thus furnished; and no remedy provided, nay, the evil more increased,
and the blood of their brethren sold for gain, as is to be feared;
and in what danger all these colonies are in is too well known.
Oh! that princes and parliaments would take some timely order
to prevent this mischief, and at length to suppress it by some ex-
emplary punishment upon some of these gain-thirsty murderers
(for they deserve no better title) before their colonies in these
parts be overthrown by these barbarous savages, thus armed
with their own weapons by these evil instruments and traitors
to their neighbors and country.

But I have forgot myself, and have been too long in this di-
gression; but now to return. This Morton having thus taught
them the use of pieces, he sold them all he could spare; and he
and his consorts determined to send for many out of England,
and had by some of the ships sent for above a score. The which
being known, and his neighbors meeting the Indians in the
woods armed with guns in this sort, it was a terror unto them
who lived stragglingly and were of no strength in any place.
And other places (though more remote) saw this mischief would
quietly spread over all, if not prevented. Besides, they saw they
should keep no servants, for Morton would entertain any, how
vile soever, and all the scum of the country, or any discontents,
would flock to him from all places if this nest was not broken;
and they should stand in more fear of their lives and goods (in
short time) from this wicked and debauched crew than from
the savages themselves.

So sundry of the chief of the straggling plantations, meeting
together, agreed by mutual consent to solicit those of Plymouth
(who were then of more strength than them all) to join with
them to prevent the further growth of this mischief, and suppress Morton and his consorts before they grew to further head
and strength. Those that joined in this action (and after contributed to the charge of sending him for England) were from

Piscataqua, Naumkeag, Winnisimmet,[13] Wessagussett, Nantasket and other places where any English were seated. Those of Plymouth, being thus sought to by their messengers and letters and weighing both their reasons and the common danger, were willing to afford them their help; though themselves had least cause of fear or hurt.

So, to be short, they first resolved jointly to write to him, and in a friendly and neighborly way to admonish him to forbear these courses, and sent a messenger with their letters to bring his answer. But he was so high as he scorned all advice, and asked who had to do with him; he had and would trade pieces with the Indians in despite of all, with many other scurrilous terms full of disdain. They sent to him a second time, and bade him be better advised and more temperate in his terms, for the country could not bear the injury he did; it was against their common safety, and against the king's proclamation. He answered in high terms as before, and that the king's proclamation was no law; demanding what penalty was upon it. It was answered, more than he could bear, his majesty's displeasure. But insolently he persisted, and said the king was dead and his displeasure with him, and many the like things; and threatened withal that if any came to molest him, let them look to themselves, for he would prepare for them.

Upon which they saw there was no way but to take him by force; and having so far proceeded, now to give over would make him far more haughty and insolent. So they mutually resolved to proceed, and obtained of the Governor of Plymouth to send Captain Standish and some other aid with him to take Morton by force. The which accordingly was done; but they found him to stand stiffly in his defense, having made fast his doors, armed his consorts, set divers dishes of powder and bullets ready on the table; and if they had not been over-armed with drink, more hurt might have been done.

They summoned him to yield, but he kept his house, and they could get nothing but scoffs and scorns from him; but at length, fearing they would do some violence to the house, he and some of his crew came out, but not to yield, but to shoot; but they

were so steeled with drink as their pieces
them; himself with a carbine (over-charg
filled with powder and shot, as was after f
have shot Captain Standish; but he steppe
his piece, and took him. Neither was there
of either side, save that one was so drunk
nose upon the point of a sword that one h
entered the house; but he lost but a little o

Morton they brought away to Plymouth
till a ship went from the Isle of Shoals for
he was sent to the Council of New Englan
to give them information of his course an
one was sent at their common charge to i
more particularly, and to prosecute agains
off the messenger after he was gone from h
went for England, yet nothing was done to
rebuke, for ought was heard; but returned
of the worst of the company were disperse
more modest kept the house till he should
I have been too long about so unworthy a
cause.

This year Mr. Allerton brought over a yo
ister to the people here, whether upon his
motion of some friends there, I well know n
out the church's sending; for they had been s
ford as they desired to know the person well
invite amongst them. His name was Mr. R
ceived upon some trial that he was crazed i
were fain to be at further charge to send h
next year, and lose all the charge that wa
hither bringing, which was not small by Mr.
in provisions, apparel, bedding, etc. After
quite distracted, and Mr. Allerton was mu
would bring such a man over, they having ch
wise.

Mr. Allerton, in the years before, had b
small quantity of goods upon his own particu

for hi
yet hi
good
plant
it wa
needs
some
over.
were
not v
gethe
sea,
there
woul
also
ing t

Ye
his f
year
busi
there
sent
mea

Sc
year
no g
som
took
in n
furt
that
beti
pack
goo
him
ther
mer
well

ANNO DOMINI 1629

Mr. Allerton safely arriving in England, and delivering his letters to their friends there, and acquainting them with his instructions, found good acceptation with them, and they were
very forward and willing to join with them in the partnership of
trade, and in the charge to send over the Leyden people; a company whereof were already come out of Holland and prepared
to come over, and so were sent away before Mr. Allerton could
be ready to come. They had passage with the ships that came to
Salem, that brought over many godly persons to begin the plantations and churches of Christ there and in the Bay of Massachusetts. So their long stay and keeping back was recompensed
by the Lord to their friends here with a double blessing, in that
they not only enjoyed them now beyond their late expectation
(when all their hopes seemed to be cut off), but with them
many more godly friends and Christian brethren as the beginning of a larger harvest unto the Lord in the increase of his
churches and people in these parts, to the admiration of many,
and almost wonder of the world; that of so small beginnings so
great things should ensue, as time after manifested; and that
here should be a resting place for so many of the Lord's people,
when so sharp a scourge came upon their own nation. But it
was the Lord's doing, and it ought to be marvelous in our
eyes. . . .

Mr. Allerton gave them great and just offense in this (which I
had omitted and almost forgotten) in bringing over this year
for base gain, that unworthy man and instrument of mischief,
Morton, who was sent home but the year before for his misdemeanors. He not only brought him over, but to the town (as it
were to nose[1] them), and lodged him at his own house, and for a
while used him as a scribe to do his business, till he was caused to
pack him away. So he went to his old nest in the Massachusetts,
where it was not long but by his miscarriage he gave them just
occasion to lay hands on him; and he was by them again sent
prisoner into England, where he lay a good while in Exeter Jail.
For besides his miscarriage here, he was vehemently suspected for

the murder of a man that had adventured moneys with him, when he came first into New England. And a warrant was sent from the Lord Chief Justice to apprehend him, by virtue whereof he was by the Governor of the Massachusetts sent into England; and for other his misdemeanors amongst them, they demolished his house, that it might be no longer a roost for such unclean birds to nestle in.

Yet he got free again, and wrote an infamous and scurrilous book against many godly and chief men of the country; full of lies and slanders, and fraught with profane calumnies against their names and persons, and the ways of God. After sundry years, when the wars were hot in England, he came again into the country, and was imprisoned at Boston for this book and other things, being grown old in wickedness.

Concerning the rest of Mr. Allerton's instructions in which they strictly enjoined him not to exceed above that £50 in the goods before mentioned, not to bring any but trading commodities, he followed them not at all but did the quite contrary; bringing over many other sorts of retail goods, selling what he could by the way on his own account, and delivering the rest, which he said to be theirs, into the store; and for trading goods brought but little in comparison. . . . These things did much trouble them here, but they well knew not how to help it, being loath to make any breach or contention here about. . . . Another more secret cause was herewith concurrent; Mr. Allerton had married the daughter of their Reverend Elder, Mr. Brewster (a man beloved and honored amongst them, and who took great pains in teaching and dispensing the word of God unto them), whom they were loath to grieve or any way offend, so as they bore with much in that respect. . . .

ANNO DOMINI 1630

. . . This year John Billington the elder (one that came over with the first) was arraigned, and both by grand and petty jury found guilty of willful murder by plain and notorious evidence. And was for the same accordingly executed. This, as it was the first execution amongst them, so was it a matter of great sadness unto them. They used all due means about his trial, and took the advice of Mr. Winthrop[1] and other the ablest gentlemen in the Bay of the Massachusetts that were then newly come over, who concurred with them that he ought to die, and the land to be purged from blood. He and some of his had been often punished for miscarriages before, being one of the profanest families amongst them. They came from London, and I know not by what friends shuffled into their company. His fact was, that he waylaid a young man, one John Newcomen (about a former quarrel), and shot him with a gun, whereof he died. . . .

ANNO DOMINI 1631

. . . Concerning Mr. Allerton's accounts, they were so large and intricate, as they could not well understand them, much less examine and correct them, without a great deal of time and help and his own presence, which was now hard to get amongst them; and it was two or three years before they could bring them to any good pass, but never make them perfect. . . . Yea, he screwed up his poor old father-in-law's account to above £200 and brought it on the general account, and to befriend him made most of it to arise out of those goods taken up by him at Bristol, at 50 per cent, because he knew they would never let it lie on the old man, when, alas! he, poor man, never dreamt of any such thing, nor that what he had could arise near that value; but thought that many of them had been freely bestowed on him and his children by Mr. Allerton. . . .

Into these deep sums had Mr. Allerton run them in two years, for in the later end of the year 1628 all their debts did not amount to much above £400, as was then noted, and now come to so many thousands. . . . And to mend the matter, Mr. Allerton doth in a sort wholly now desert them; having brought them into the briers, he leaves them to get out as they can.

But God crossed him mightily, for he having hired the ship of Mr. Sherley at £30 a month, he set forth again with a most wicked and drunken crew, and for covetousness' sake did so overlade her, not only filling her hold, but so stuffed her between decks, as she was walte,[1] and could not bear sail, and they had like to have been cast away at sea, and were forced to put for Milford Haven and new stow her, and put some of their ordnance and more heavy goods in the bottom; which lost them time, and made them come late into the country, lose their season, and made a worse voyage than the year before.

But being come into the country, he sells trading commodities to any that will buy, to the great prejudice of the plantation here; but that which is worse, what he could not sell, he trusts; and sets up a company of base fellows and makes them traders, to run into every hole and into the river of Kennebec to glean away the trade from the house there. . . . Yea, not only this, but he furnishes a company, and joins with some consorts, . . . and sets up a trading house beyond Penobscot to cut off the trade from thence also. But the French perceiving that that would be greatly to their damage also, they came in their beginning before they were well settled and displanted them, slew two of their men, and took all their goods to a good value, the loss being most, if not all, Mr. Allerton's; for though some of them should have been his partners, yet he trusted them for their parts; the rest of the men were sent into France, and this was the end of that project.

The rest of those he trusted, being loose and drunken fellows, did for the most part but cozen and cheat him of all they got into their hands; that howsoever he did his friends some hurt hereby for the present, yet he got little good but went by the loss by God's just hand. After in time, when he came to Plymouth, the church called him to account for these and other his gross miscarriages. He confessed his fault and promised better walking, and that he would wind himself out of these courses as soon as he could, etc. . . .

This year their house at Penobscot was robbed by the French, and all their goods of any worth they carried away, to the value of £400 or £500; . . . in beaver 300 pounds' weight; and the rest in trading goods, as coats, rugs, blanket, biscuit, etc. It was in this manner. The master of the house and part of the company with him were come with their vessel to the westward to fetch a supply of goods which was brought over for them. In the meantime comes a small French ship into the harbor (and amongst the company was a false Scot). They pretended they were newly come from the sea, and knew not where they were, and that their vessel was very leaky, and desired they might haul her ashore and stop their leaks. And many French compliments they used, and congés[2] they made; and in the end, seeing but three or four simple men that were servants, and by this Scotchman understanding that the master and the rest of the company were gone from home, they fell of commending their guns and muskets that lay upon racks by the wall side, and took them down to look on them, asking if they were charged. And when they were possessed of them, one presents a piece ready charged against the servants, and another a pistol; and bid them not stir, but quietly deliver them their goods, and carries some of the men aboard, and made the other help to carry away the goods. And when they had took what they pleased, they set them at liberty, and went their way with this mock, bidding them tell their master when he came that some of the Ile of Rey gentlemen[3] had been there.

This year one Sir Christopher Gardiner, being, as himself said, descended of that house that the Bishop of Winchester came of (who was so great a persecutor of God's saints in Queen Mary's days), and being a great traveler, received his first honor of knighthood at Jerusalem, being made Knight of the Sepulcher there. He came into these parts under pretence of forsaking the world and to live a private life in a godly course, not unwilling to put himself upon any mean employments and take any pains for his living; and sometime offered himself to join to the churches in sundry places. He brought over with him a servant or two and a comely young woman whom he called his cousin, but it was suspected, she (after the Italian manner) was his concubine.

Living at the Massachusetts, for some miscarriages which he should have answered, he fled away from authority, and got among the Indians of these parts. They sent after him but could not get him, and promised some reward to those that should find him. The Indians came to the Governor here and told where he was, and asked if they might kill him. He told them no, by no means, but if they could take him and bring him hither, they should be paid for their pains. They said he had a gun and a rapier, and he would kill them if they went about it; and the Massachusett Indians said they might kill him. But the Governor told them no, they should not kill him, but watch their opportunity and take him.

And so they did, for when they light of him by a river side, he got into a canoe to get from them, and when they came near him, whilst he presented his piece at them to keep them off, the stream carried the canoe against a rock and tumbled both him and his piece and rapier into the water; yet he got out, and having a little dagger by his side, they durst not close with him, but getting long poles they soon beat his dagger out of his hand, so he was glad to yield; and they brought him to the Governor. But his hands and arms were swollen and very sore with the blows they had given him. So he used him kindly and sent him to a lodging where his arms were bathed and anointed, and he was quickly well again, and blamed the Indians for beating him so much. They said that they did but a little whip him with sticks.

In his lodging, those that made his bed found a little notebook that by accident had slipped out of his pocket, or some private place, in which was a memorial what day he was reconciled to the pope and church of Rome, and in what university he took his scapular,[4] and such and such degrees. It being brought to the Governor, he kept it, and sent the Governor of the Massachusetts word of his taking, who sent for him. So the Governor sent him and these notes to the Governor there, who took it very thankfully; but after he got for England he showed his malice, but God prevented him.[5] . . .

ANNO DOMINI 1632

. . . The people of the plantation began to grow in their outward estates, by reason of the flowing of many people into the country, especially into the Bay of the Massachusetts; by which means corn and cattle rose to a great price by which many were much enriched and commodities grew plentiful; and yet in other regards this benefit turned to their hurt, and this accession of strength to their weakness. For now as their stocks increased, and the increase vendible, there was no longer any holding them together, but now they must of necessity go to their great lots; they could not otherwise keep their cattle; and having oxen grown, they must have land for plowing and tillage. And no man now thought he could live, except he had cattle and a great deal of ground to keep them; all striving to increase their stocks. By which means they were scattered all over the bay quickly, and the town, in which they lived compactly till now, was left very thin and in a short time almost desolate.

And if this had been all, it had been less, though too much; but the church must also be divided, and those that had lived so long together in Christian and comfortable fellowship must now part and suffer many divisions. First, those that lived on their lots on the other side of the bay (called Duxbury) they could not long bring their wives and children to the public worship and church meetings here but with such burden as, growing to some competent number, they sued to be dismissed and become a body of themselves; and so they were dismissed (about this time), though very unwillingly.

But to touch this sad matter and handle things together that fell out afterward: to prevent any further scattering from this place, and weakening of the same, it was thought best to give out some good farms to special persons that would promise to live at Plymouth and likely to be helpful to the church or commonwealth, and so tie the lands to Plymouth as farms for the same; and there they might keep their cattle and tillage by some servants and retain their dwellings here. And so some special lands were granted at a place general called Green's Harbor,[1] where no allotments had been in the former division, a place very well meadowed and fit to keep and rear cattle, good store.

But alas! this remedy proved worse than the disease; for within a few years those that had thus got footing there rent themselves away, partly by force, and partly wearing the rest with importunity and pleas of necessity, so as they must either suffer them to go or live in continual opposition and contention.

And others still, as they conceived themselves straitened, or to want accommodation, broke away under one pretence or other, thinking their own conceived necessity and the example of others a warrant sufficient for them. And this, I fear, will be the ruin of New England, at least of the churches of God there, and will provoke the Lord's displeasure against them. . . .

ANNO DOMINI 1633

This year Mr. Edward Winslow was chosen Governor.[1] . . .

Mr. Roger Williams (a man godly and zealous, having many precious parts, but very unsettled in judgment) came over first to the Massachusetts, but upon some discontent left that place,[2] and came hither (where he was friendly entertained, according to their poor ability) and exercised his gifts amongst them, and after some time was admitted a member of the church; and his teaching well approved, for the benefit whereof I still bless God, and am thankful to him, even for his sharpest admonitions and reproofs, so far as they agreed with truth. He this year began to fall into some strange opinions, and from opinion to practice; which caused some controversy between the church and him, and in the end some discontent on his part, by occasion whereof he left them something abruptly. Yet afterwards sued for his dismission to the church of Salem, which was granted, with some caution to them concerning him, and what care they ought to have of him.

But he soon fell into more things there, both to their and the government's trouble and disturbance. I shall not need to name particulars, they are too well known now to all, though for a time the church here went under some hard censure by his occasion from some that afterwards smarted themselves. But he is to be pitied and prayed for, and so I shall leave the matter, and desire the Lord to show him his errors, and reduce him into the way of truth, and give him a settled judgment and constancy in the same; for I hope he belongs to the Lord, and that he will show him mercy.

Having had formerly converse and familiarity with the Dutch

(as is before remembered), they, seeing them seated here in a barren quarter, told them of a river called by them the Fresh River, but now is known by the name of Connecticut River, which they often commended unto them for a fine place both for plantation and trade, and wished them to make use of it. But their hands being full otherwise, they let it pass. But afterwards there coming a company of banished Indians into these parts that were driven out from thence by the potency of the Pequots, which usurped upon them and drove them from thence, they often solicited them to go thither, and they should have much trade, especially if they would keep a house there.

And having now good store of commodities, and also need to look out where they could advantage themselves to help them out of their great engagements, they now began to send that way to discover the same, and trade with the natives. They found it to be a fine place, but had no great store of trade; but the Indians excused the same in regard of the season, and the fear the Indians were in of their enemies. So they tried divers times, not without profit, but saw the most certainty would be by keeping a house there to receive the trade when it came down out of the inland. These Indians, not seeing them very forward to build there, solicited them of the Massachusetts in like sort (for their end was to be restored to their country again); but they in the Bay being but lately come, were not fit for the same; but some of their chief made a motion to join with the partners here to trade jointly with them in that river, the which they were willing to embrace, and so they should have built and put in equal stock together.

A time of meeting was appointed at the Massachusetts, and some of the chief here was appointed to treat with them and went accordingly; but they cast many fears of danger and loss and the like, which was perceived to be the main obstacles, though they alleged they were not provided of trading goods. But those here offered at present to put in sufficient for both, provided they would become engaged for the half and prepare against the next year. They confessed more could not be offered, but thanked them, and told them they had no mind to it. They then answered they hoped it would be no offence unto them, if themselves went on without them, if they saw it meet. They said there was no reason they should; and thus this treaty broke off, and those here took convenient time to make a beginning there; and were the first English that both discovered that place and built in the same, though they were little better than thrust out of it afterward as may appear.

But the Dutch began now to repent, and hearing of their purpose and preparation, endeavored to prevent them, and got in a little before them, and made a slight fort,[3] and planted two pieces of ordnance, threatening to stop their passage. But they having made a small frame of a house ready, and having a great new bark, they stowed their frame in her hold, and boards to cover and finish it, having nails and all other provisions fitting for their use. This they did the rather that they might have a present defense against the Indians, who were much offended that they brought home and restored the right Sachem of the place (called Natawanute); so as they were to encounter with a double danger in this attempt, both the Dutch and the Indians.

When they came up the river, the Dutch demanded what they intended and whither they would go; they answered, "Up the river to trade" (now their order was to go and seat above them). They bid them strike and stay, or else they would shoot them; and stood by their ordnance ready fitted. They answered they had commission from the Governor of Plymouth to go up the river to such a place, and if they did shoot, they must obey their order and proceed; they would not molest them, but would go on. So they passed along, and though the Dutch threatened them hard, yet they shot not. Coming to their place,[4] they clapped up their house quickly, and landed their provisions, and left the company appointed, and sent the bark home; and afterwards palisaded their house about, and fortified themselves better.

The Dutch sent word home to the Manhattan what was done; and in process of time, they sent a band of about seventy men in warlike manner with colors displayed to assault them; but seeing them strengthened, and that it would cost blood, they came to parley, and returned in peace. And this was their entrance there, who deserved to have held it, and not by friends to have been thrust out,[5] as in a sort they were. . . . They did the Dutch no wrong, for they took not a foot of any land they bought, but went to the place above them, and bought that tract of land which belonged to these Indians which they carried with them and their friends, with whom the Dutch had nothing to do. . . .

It pleased the Lord to visit them this year with an infectious fever of which many fell very sick, and upward of twenty persons died, men and women, besides children, and sundry of them of their ancient friends which had lived in Holland; as Thomas Blossom, Richard Masterson, with sundry others, and in the end (after he had much helped others) Samuel Fuller, who was their surgeon and physician, and had been a great help and comfort unto them; as in his faculty, so otherwise, being a deacon of the church, a man godly and forward to do good, being much missed after his death; and he and the rest of their brethren much lamented by them, and caused much sadness and mourning amongst them; which caused them to humble themselves, and seek the Lord; and towards winter it pleased the Lord the sickness ceased.

This disease also swept away many of the Indians from all the places near adjoining; and the spring before, especially all the month of May, there was such a quantity of a great sort of flies,[6] like (for bigness) to wasps, or bumblebees, which came out of holes in the ground, and replenished all the woods, and ate the green things, and made such a constant yelling noise, as made all the woods ring of them, and ready to deafen the hearers. They have not by the English been heard or seen before or since. But the Indians told them that sickness would follow, and so it did in June, July, August, and the chief heat of summer.

It pleased the Lord to enable them this year to send home a great quantity of beaver, besides paying all their charges and debts at home, which good return did much encourage their friends in England. They sent in beaver 3,366 pounds weight, and much of it coat beaver, which yielded twenty shillings per pound, and some of it above; and of otter-skins 346, sold also at a good price. And thus much of the affairs of this year.

ANNO DOMINI 1634

This year Mr. Thomas Prence was chosen Governor.[1] . . .

This year (in the forepart of the same) they sent forth a bark to trade at the Dutch Plantation; and they met there with one Captain Stone, that had lived in Christopher's, one of the West India Islands, and now had been some time in Virginia, and came from thence into these parts. He kept company with the Dutch Governor, and, I know not in what drunken fit, he got leave of the Governor to seize on their bark when they were ready to come away, and had done their market, having the value of £500 worth of goods aboard her; having no occasion at all, or any color of ground for such a thing, but having made the Governor drunk, so as he could scarce speak a right word; and when he urged him hereabout, he answered him, "*Als 't u beleeft.*"[2]

So he got aboard (the chief of their men and merchant being ashore), and with some of his own men, made the rest of theirs weigh anchor, set sail, and carry her away towards Virginia. But divers of the Dutch seamen, which had been often at Plymouth, and kindly entertained there, said one to another, "Shall we suffer our friends to be thus abused, and have their goods carried away, before our faces, whilst our Governor is drunk?" They vowed they would never suffer it; and so got a vessel or two and pursued him, and brought him in again; and delivered them their bark and goods again.

Afterwards Stone came into the Massachusetts, and they sent and commenced suit against him for this fact; but by mediation of friends it was taken up, and the suit let fall. And in the company of some other gentlemen Stone came afterwards to Plymouth, and had friendly and civil entertainment amongst them, with the rest; but revenge boiled within his breast (though concealed), for some conceived he had a purpose (at one time) to have stabbed the Governor, and put his hand to his dagger for that end, but by God's providence and the vigilance of some was prevented.

He afterward returned to Virginia in a pinnace with one

Captain Norton and some others; and, I know not for what occasion, they would needs go up Connecticut River; and how they carried themselves I know not, but the Indians knocked him in the head as he lay in his cabin and had thrown the covering over his face (whether out of fear or desperation is uncertain); this was his end. They likewise killed all the rest, but Captain Norton defended himself a long time against them all in the cook-room, till by accident the gunpowder took fire, which (for readiness) he had set in an open thing before him, which did so burn and scald him, and blind his eyes, as he could make no longer resistance, but was slain also by them, though they much commended his valor. And having killed the men, they made a prey of what they had, and chaffered away some of their things to the Dutch that lived there. But it was not long before a quarrel fell between the Dutch and them, and they would have cut off their bark; but they slew the chief sachem with the shot of a murderer.[3]

I am now to relate some strange and remarkable passages. There was a company of people[4] lived in the country, up above in the river of Connecticut, a great way from their trading house there, and were enemies to those Indians which lived about them, and of whom they stood in some fear (being a stout people). About a thousand of them had enclosed themselves in a fort, which they had strongly palisaded about. Three or four Dutchmen went up in the beginning of winter to live with them, to get their trade and prevent them for bringing it to the English, or to fall into amity with them; but at spring to bring all down to their place. But their enterprise failed, for it pleased God to visit these Indians with a great sickness, and such a mortality that of a thousand, above nine and a half hundred of them died, and many of them did rot above ground for want of burial, and the Dutchmen almost starved before they could get away, for ice and snow. But about February they got with much difficulty to their trading house; whom they kindly relieved, being almost spent with hunger and cold. Being thus refreshed by them divers days, they got to their own place, and the Dutch were very thankful for this kindness.

This spring, also, those Indians that lived about their trading house there fell sick of the small pox, and died most miserably; for a sorer disease cannot befall them. They fear it more than the plague; for usually they that have this disease have them in abundance, and for want of bedding and linen and other helps, they fall into a lamentable condition, as they lie on their hard mats, the pox breaking and mattering, and running one into another, their skin cleaving (by reason thereof) to the mats they lie on; when they turn them, a whole side will flay off at once (as it were), and they will be all of a gore-blood, most fearful to behold; and then being very sore, what with cold and other distempers, they die like rotten sheep. The condition of this people was so lamentable, and they fell down so generally of this disease, as they were (in the end) not able to help one another; no, not to make a fire, nor to fetch a little water to drink, nor any to bury the dead; but would strive as long as they could, and when they could procure no other means to make fire, they would burn the wooden trays and dishes they ate their meat in, and their very bows and arrows; and some would crawl out on all four to get a little water, and sometimes die by the way, and not be able to get in again.

But those of the English house (though at first they were afraid of the infection), yet seeing their woeful and sad condition, and hearing their pitiful cries and lamentations, they had compassion of them, and daily fetched them wood and water, and made them fires, got them victuals whilst they lived, and buried them when they died. For very few of them escaped, notwithstanding they did what they could for them to the hazard of themselves. The chief Sachem himself now died, and almost all his friends and kindred. But by the marvelous goodness and providence of God not one of the English was so much as sick, or in the least measure tainted with this disease, though they daily did these offices for them for many weeks together. And this mercy which they showed them was kindly taken, and thankfully acknowledged of all the Indians that knew or heard of the same; and their master here did much commend and reward them for the same.

ANNO DOMINI 1635

. . . This year, the 14th or 15th of August (being Saturday) was such a mighty storm of wind and rain, as none living in these parts, either English or Indians, ever saw. Being like (for the time it continued) to those Hurricanes and Typhoons that writers make mention of in the Indies. It began in the morning, a little before day, and grew not by degrees, but came with violence in the beginning, to the great amazement of many. It blew down sundry houses and uncovered others; divers vessels were lost at sea, and many more in extreme danger. It caused the sea to swell (to the southward of this place) above twenty foot, right up and down, and made many of the Indians to climb into trees for their safety. It took off the boarded roof of a house which belonged to the plantation at Manomet, and floated it to another place, the posts still standing in the ground; and if it had continued long without the shifting of the wind, it is like it would have drowned some part of the country.

It blew down many hundred thousands of trees, turning up the stronger by the roots, and breaking the higher pine trees off in the middle, and the tall young oaks and walnut trees of good bigness were wound like a withe, very strange and fearful to behold. It began in the southeast, and parted toward the south and east, and veered sundry ways; but the greatest force of it here was from the former quarters. It continued not (in the extremity) above five or six hours, but the violence began to abate. The signs and marks of it will remain this hundred years in these parts where it was sorest. The moon suffered a great eclipse the second night after it. . . .

ANNO DOMINI 1636

. . . In the year 1634, the Pequots (a stout and warlike people), who had made wars with sundry of their neighbors, and puffed up with many victories, grew now at variance with the Narragansetts, a great people bordering upon them. These

Narragansetts held correspondence and terms of friendship with the English of the Massachusetts. Now the Pequots, being conscious of the guilt of Captain Stone's death, whom they knew to be an Englishman, as also those that were with him, and being fallen out with the Dutch, lest they should have overmany enemies at once, sought to make friendship with the English of the Massachusetts; and for that end sent both messengers and gifts unto them. . . .

After these things, and, as I take, this year, John Oldham (of whom much is spoken before), being now an inhabitant of the Massachusetts, went with a small vessel and slenderly manned a-trading into these south parts, and upon a quarrel between him and the Indians was cut off by them (as hath been before noted) at an island called by the Indians Munisses, but since by the English Block Island. This, with the former about the death of Stone, and the baffling of the Pequots with the English of the Massachusetts, moved them to set out some to take revenge, and require satisfaction for these wrongs; but it was done so superficially, and without their acquainting of those of Connecticut and other neighbors with the same, as they did little good.

But their neighbors had more hurt done, for some of the murderers of Oldham fled to the Pequots, and though the English went to the Pequots and had some parley with them, yet they did but delude them, and the English returned without doing anything to purpose, being frustrated of their opportunity by the others' deceit. After the English were returned, the Pequots took their time and opportunity to cut off some of the English as they passed in boats and went on fowling, and assaulted them the next spring at their habitations, as will appear in its place. I do but touch these things, because I make no question they will be more fully and distinctly handled by themselves, who had more exact knowledge of them, and whom they did more properly concern. . . .

ANNO DOMINI 1637

In the fore part of this year, the Pequots fell openly upon the English at Connecticut in the lower parts of the river, and slew sundry of them (as they were at work in the fields), both men and women, to the great terror of the rest; and went away in great pride and triumph, with many high threats. They also assaulted a fort at the river's mouth, though strong and well defended; and though they did not there prevail, yet it struck them with much fear and astonishment to see their bold attempts in the face of danger; which made them in all places to stand upon their guard, and to prepare for resistance, and earnestly to solicit their friends and confederates in the Bay of Massachusetts to send them speedy aid, for they looked for more forcible assaults. Mr. Vane,[1] being then Governor, wrote from their General Court to them here to join with them in this war; to which they were cordially willing. . . .

In the meantime, the Pequots, especially in the winter before, sought to make peace with the Narragansetts, and used very pernicious arguments to move them thereunto: as that the English were strangers and began to overspread their country, and would deprive them thereof in time, if they were suffered to grow and increase; and if the Narragansetts did assist the English to subdue them, they did but make way for their own overthrow, for if they were rooted out, the English would soon take occasion to subjugate them. And if they would harken to them, they should not need to fear the strength of the English; for they would not come to open battle with them, but fire their houses, kill their cattle, and lie in ambush for them as they went abroad upon their occasions; and all this they might easily do without any or little danger to themselves.

The which course being held, they well saw the English could not long subsist, but they would either be starved with hunger, or be forced to forsake the country; with many the like things; insomuch that the Narragansetts were once wavering, and were half-minded to have made peace with them, and joined against the English. But again when they considered how much wrong they had received from the Pequots, and what an opportunity they now had by the help of the English to right themselves, revenge was so sweet unto them as it prevailed above all the rest; so as they resolved to join with the English against them, and did.

The Court here agreed forthwith to send fifty men at their own charge; and with as much speed as possibly they could, got them armed, and had made them ready under sufficient leaders, and provided a bark to carry them provisions and tend upon them for all occasions; but when they were ready to march (with a supply from the Bay) they had word to stay, for the enemy was as good as vanquished, and there would be no need.

I shall not take upon me exactly to describe their proceedings in these things, because I expect it will be fully done by themselves, who best know the carriage and circumstances of things; I shall therefore but touch them in general. From Connecticut (who were most sensible of the hurt sustained, and the present danger), they set out a party of men, and another party met them from [Massachusetts] Bay, at the Narragansetts, who were to join with them. The Narragansetts were earnest to be gone before the English were well rested and refreshed, especially some of them which came last. It should seem their desire was to come upon the enemy suddenly, and undiscovered. There was a bark of this place newly put in there, which was come from Connecticut, who did encourage them to lay hold of the Indians' forwardness, and to show as great forwardness as they, for it would encourage them, and expedition might prove to their great advantage.

So they went on, and so ordered their march as the Indians brought them to a fort of the enemy's (in which most of their chief men were) before day. They approached the same with great silence, and surrounded it both with English and Indians, that they might not break out; and so assaulted them with great courage, shooting amongst them, and entered the fort with all speed. And those that first entered found sharp resistance from the enemy, who both shot at and grappled with them; others ran into their houses, and brought out fire, and set them on fire, which soon took in their mats, and, standing close together, with the wind, all was quickly on a flame, and thereby more were burnt to death than was otherwise slain; it burnt their bowstrings, and made them unserviceable. Those that escaped the fire were slain with the sword; some hewed to pieces, others run through with their rapiers, so as they were quickly dispatched, and very few escaped.

It was conceived they thus destroyed about 400 at this time. It was a fearful sight to see them thus frying in the fire, and the streams of blood quenching the same, and horrible was the stink and scent thereof; but the victory seemed a sweet sacrifice,[2] and they gave the praise thereof to God, who had wrought so wonderfully for them, thus to enclose their enemies in their hands, and give them so speedy a victory over so proud and insulting an enemy.

The Narragansett Indians, all this while, stood round about, but aloof from all danger, and left the whole execution to the English, except it were the stopping of any that broke away, insulting over their enemies in this their ruin and misery, when they saw them dancing in the flames, calling them by a word in their own language, signifying, "Oh brave Pequots!" which they used familiarly among themselves in their own praise, in songs of triumph after their victories.

After this service was thus happily accomplished, they marched to the waterside, where they met with some of their vessels, by which they had refreshing with victuals and other necessaries. But in their march the rest of the Pequots drew into a body, and accosted them, thinking to have some advantage against them by reason of a neck of land; but when they saw the English prepare for them, they kept aloof, so as they neither did hurt, nor could receive any. After their refreshing and repair together for further counsel and directions, they resolved to pursue their victory, and follow the war against the rest, but the Narragansett Indians most of them forsook them, and such of them as they had with them for guides, or otherwise, they found them very cold and backward in the business, either out of envy, or that they saw the English would make more profit of the victory than they were willing they should, or else deprive them of such advantage as themselves desired by having them become tributaries unto them, or the like.

For the rest of this business, I shall only relate the same as it is in a letter which came from Mr. Winthrop to the Governor here, as followeth:

Worthy Sir:

I received your loving letter, and am much provoked to express my affections towards you, but straitness of time forbids me; for my desire is to acquaint you with the Lord's great mercies towards us, in our prevailing against his and our enemies; that you may rejoice and praise his name with us. About eighty of our men, having coasted along towards the Dutch plantation (sometimes by water, but most by land), met here and there with some Pequots, whom they slew or took prisoners. Two sachems they took, and beheaded; and not hearing of Sassacus (the chief sachem), they gave a prisoner his life to go and find him out. He went and brought them word where he was, but Sassacus, suspecting him to be a spy, after he was gone, fled away with some twenty more to the Mohawks,[3] so our men missed of him.

Yet, dividing themselves and ranging up and down, as the providence of God guided them (for the Indians were all gone, save three or four, and they knew not whither to guide them, or else would not), upon the 13th of this month, they lighted upon a great company of them, viz. eighty strong men, and 200 women and children, in a small Indian town, fast by a hideous swamp, which they all slipped into before our men could get to them. Our captains were not then come together, but there was Mr. Ludlow and Captain Mason, with some ten of their men, and Captain Patrick with some twenty or more of his, who shooting at the Indians, Captain Trask with fifty more came soon in at the noise.

Then they gave order to surround the swamp, it being about a mile about; but Lieutenant Davenport and some twelve more, not hearing that command, fell into the swamp among the Indians. The swamp was so thick with shrub-wood, and so boggy withal, that some of them stuck fast, and received many shot. Lieutenant Davenport was dangerously wounded about his armhole, and another shot in the head, so as, fainting, they were in great danger to have been taken by the Indians. But Sergeant Riggs, and Jeffery, and two or more, rescued them, and slew divers of the Indians with their swords.

After they were drawn out, the Indians desired parley, and were offered (by Thomas Stanton, our interpreter) that, if they would come out, and yield themselves, they should have their lives, all that had not their hands in the English blood. Whereupon the sachem of the place came forth, and an old man or two and their wives and children, and after that some other women and children, and so they spake two hours, till it was night. Then Thomas Stanton was sent into them again, to call them forth; but they said they would sell their lives there, and so shot at him so thick as, if he had not cried out and been presently rescued, they had slain him. Then our men cut off a place of the swamp with their swords, and cooped the Indians into so narrow a compass, as they could easier kill them through the thickets. So they continued all the night, standing about twelve foot one from another, and the Indians, coming close up to our men, shot their arrows so thick, as they pierced their hat brims, and their sleeves, and stockings, and other parts of their clothes, yet so miraculously did the Lord preserve them as not one of them was wounded, save those three who rashly went into the swamp. When it was near day, it grew very dark, so as those of them which were left dropped away between our men, though they stood but twelve or fourteen foot asunder; but were presently discovered, and some killed in the pursuit.

Upon searching of the swamp the next morning, they found nine slain, and some they pulled up, whom the Indians had buried in the mire, so as they do think that, of all this company, not twenty did escape, for they after found some who died in their flight of their wounds received. The prisoners were divided, some to those of the river, and the rest to us. Of these we sent the male children to Bermuda,[4] by Mr. William Peirce, and the women and maid children are disposed about in the towns. There have been now slain and taken, in all, about 700. The rest are dispersed, and the Indians in all quarters so terrified as all their friends are afraid to receive them. Two of the sachems of Long Island came to Mr. Stoughton and tendered themselves to be tributaries under our protection. And two of the Nipmuck sachems have been with me to seek our friendship.

Among the prisoners we have the wife and children of Mononoto, a woman of a very modest countenance and behavior. It was by her mediation that the two English maids were spared from death, and were kindly used by her; so that I have taken charge of her. One of her first requests was that the English would not abuse her body, and that her children might not be taken from her. Those which were wounded were fetched off soon by John Gallup, who came with his shallop in a happy hour to bring them victuals and to carry their wounded men to the pinnace, where our chief surgeon was, with Mr. Wilson, being about eight leagues off. Our people are all in health (the Lord be praised), and although they had marched in their arms all the day, and had been in fight all the night, yet they professed they found themselves so fresh as they could willingly have gone to such another business. This is the substance of that which I received, though I am forced to omit many considerable circumstances. So, being in much straitness of time (the ships being to depart within this four days, and in them the Lord Lee and Mr. Vane), I here break off, and with hearty salutes to, etc., I rest,

    Yours assured,

    The 28th of the 5th month, 1637.   John Winthrop

    The captains report we have slain thirteen sachems; but Sassacus and Mononoto are yet living.

That I may make an end of this matter: this Sassacus (the Pequots' chief sachem) being fled to the Mohawks, they cut off his head with some other of the chief of them, whether to satisfy the English, or rather the Narragansetts (who, as I have since heard, hired them to do it), or for their own advantage, I well know not; but thus this war took end. The rest of the Pequots were wholly driven from their place, and some of them submitted themselves to the Narragansetts, and lived under them; others of them betook themselves to the Mohegans under Uncas,[5] their sachem, with the approbation of the English of Connecticut, under whose protection Uncas lived, and he and his men had been faithful to them in this war, and done them very good service. But this did so vex the Narragansetts, that they had not the whole sway over them, as they have never ceased plotting and contriving how to bring them under, and because they cannot attain their ends, because of the English who have protected them, they have sought to raise a general conspiracy against the English, as will appear in another place. . . .

ANNO DOMINI 1638

This year Mr. Thomas Prence was chosen Governor. Amongst other enormities that fell out amongst them, this year three men were (after due trial) executed for robbery and murder which they had committed; their names were these, Arthur Peach, Thomas Jackson, and Richard Stinnings; there was a fourth, Daniel Cross, who was also guilty, but he escaped away and could not be found.

This Arthur Peach was the chief of them, and the ringleader of all the rest. He was a lusty and a desperate young man, and had been one of the soldiers in the Pequot war, and had done as good service as the most there, and one of the forwardest in any attempts. And being now out of means, and loath to work, and falling to idle courses and company, he intended to go to the Dutch plantation; and had allured these three, being other men's servants and apprentices, to go with him. But another cause there was also of his secret going away in this manner; he was not only run into debt, but he had got a maid with child (which was not known till after his death), a man's servant in the town, and fear of punishment made him get away. The other three, complotting with him, ran away from their masters in the night, and could not be heard of, for they went not the ordinary way but shaped such a course as they thought to avoid the pursuit of any.

But falling into the way that lyeth between the Bay of Massachusetts and the Narragansetts, and being disposed to rest themselves, struck fire, and took tobacco, a little out of the way, by the wayside. At length there came a Narragansett Indian by, who had been in the Bay a-trading, and had both cloth and beads about him. (They had met him the day before, and he was now returning.) Peach called him to drink tobacco[1] with them, and he came and sat down with them. Peach told the others he would kill him, and take what he had from him. But they were something afraid; but he said, "Hang him, rogue," he had killed many of them.

So they let him alone to do as he would; and when he saw his time, he took a rapier and ran him through the body once or twice, and took from him five fathom of wampum, and three coats of cloth, and went their way, leaving him for dead. But he scrabbled away, when they were gone and made shift to get home (but died within a few days after), by which means they were discovered; and by subtlety the Indians took them. For they desiring a canoe to set them over a water (not thinking their fact had been known), by the sachem's command they were carried to Aquidneck Island,[2] and there accused of the murder, and were examined and committed upon it by the English there.

The Indians sent for Mr. Williams and made a grievous complaint; his friends and kindred were ready to rise in arms, and provoke the rest thereunto, some conceiving they should now find the Pequots' words true: that the English would fall upon them. But Mr. Williams pacified them, and told them they should see justice done upon the offenders; and went to the man, and took Mr. James, a physician, with him. The man told him who did it, and in what manner it was done; but the physician found his wounds mortal, and that he could not live (as he after testified upon oath, before the jury in open court), and so he died shortly after, as both Mr. Williams, Mr. James, and some Indians testified in court.

The Government in the Bay were acquainted with it, but referred it hither, because it was done in this jurisdiction; but pressed by all means that justice might be done in it; or else the country must rise and see justice done, otherwise it would raise a war. Yet some of the rude and ignorant sort murmured that any English should be put to death for the Indians. So at last they of the island brought them hither, and being often examined, and the evidence produced, they all in the end freely confessed in effect all that the Indian accused them of, and that they had done it in the manner aforesaid; and so, upon the forementioned evidence, were cast[3] by the jury, and condemned, and executed for the same. And some of the Narragansett Indians, and of the party's friends, were present when it was done, which gave them and all the country good satisfaction. But it was a matter of much sadness to them here, and was the second execution which they had since they came; being both for willful murder, as hath been before related. Thus much of this matter. . . .

This year, about the 1st or 2nd of June, was a great fearful earthquake; it was in this place heard before it was felt. It came with a rumbling noise, or low murmur like unto remote thunder; it came from the northward, and passed southward. As the noise approached nearer, the earth began to shake, and came at length with that violence as caused platters, dishes, and such like things as stood upon shelves, to clatter and fall down; yea, persons were afraid of the houses themselves.

It so fell out that at the same time divers of the chief of this town were met together at one house, conferring with some of their friends that were upon removal from the place (as if the Lord would hereby show the signs of his displeasure, in their shaking a-pieces and removals one from another). However it was very terrible for the time, and as the men were set talking in the house, some women and others were without the doors, and the earth shook with that violence as they could not stand without catching hold of the posts and pales that stood next them; but the violence lasted not long. And about half an hour or less came another noise and shaking, but neither so loud nor strong; as the former, but quickly passed over; and so it ceased.

It was not only on the sea coast, but the Indians felt it within land; and some ships that were upon the coast were shaken by it. So powerful is the mighty hand of the Lord, as to make both the earth and sea to shake, and the mountains to tremble before him, when he pleases; and who can stay his hand?[4] It was observed that the summers, for divers years together after this earthquake, were not so hot and seasonable for the ripening of corn and other fruits as formerly, but more cold and moist and subject to early and untimely frosts, by which, many times, much Indian corn came not to maturity; but whether this was any cause, I leave it to naturalists to judge. . . .

ANNO DOMINI 1642

Marvelous it may be to see and consider how some kind of wickedness did grow and break forth here, in a land where the same was so much witnessed against, and so narrowly looked unto, and severely punished when it was known, as in no place more, or so much, that I have known or heard of; insomuch as they have been somewhat censured, even by moderate and good men, for their severity in punishments. And yet all this could not suppress the breaking out of sundry notorious sins (as this year, besides other[s], gives us too many sad precedents and instances), especially drunkenness and uncleanness; not only incontinency between persons unmarried, for which many both men and women have been punished sharply enough, but some married persons also. But that which is worse, even sodomy and buggery (things fearful to name) have broke forth in this land, oftener than once. I say it may justly be marveled at, and cause us to fear and tremble at the consideration of our corrupt natures, which are so hardly bridled, subdued, and mortified; nay, cannot by any other means but the powerful work and grace of God's spirit.

But (besides this) one reason may be, that the Devil may carry a greater spite against the churches of Christ and the gospel here, by how much the more they endeavor to preserve holiness and purity amongst them, and strictly punisheth the contrary when it ariseth either in church or commonwealth; that he might cast a blemish and stain upon them in the eyes of [the] world, who use to be rash in judgment. I would rather think thus than that Satan hath more power in these heathen lands, as some have thought, than in more Christian nations, especially over God's servants in them.

2. Another reason may be, that it may be in this case as it is with waters when their streams are stopped or dammed up, when they get passage they flow with more violence and make more noise and disturbance than when they are suffered to run quietly in their own channels. So wickedness being here more stopped by strict laws, and the same more nearly looked unto, so as it cannot run in a common road of liberty as it would and is inclined, it searches everywhere and at last breaks out where it gets vent.

3. A third reason may be, here (as I am verily persuaded) is

not more evils in this kind nor nothing near so many by proportion as in other places; but they are here more discovered and seen and made public by due search, inquisition, and due punishment; for the churches look narrowly to their members, and the magistrates over all more strictly than in other places. Besides, here the people are but few in comparison of other places, which are full and populous and lie hid, as it were, in a wood or thicket, and many horrible evils by that means are never seen nor known; whereas here, they are, as it were, brought into the light, and set in the plain field, or rather on a hill, made conspicuous to the view of all. . . .

[There] befell a very sad accident of the like foul nature in this government, this very year, which I shall now relate. There was a youth whose name was Thomas Granger; he was servant to an honest man of Duxbury, being about sixteen or seventeen years of age. (His father and mother lived at the same time at Scituate.[1]) He was this year detected of buggery (and indicted for the same) with a mare, a cow, two goats, five sheep, two calves, and a turkey. Horrible it is to mention, but the truth of the history requires it. He was first discovered by one that accidentally saw his lewd practice towards the mare. (I forbear particulars.)

Being upon it examined and committed, in the end he not only confessed the fact with that beast at that time but sundry times before, and at several times with all the rest of the forenamed in his indictment; and this his free-confession was not only in private to the magistrates (though at first he strived to deny it), but to sundry, both ministers and others, and afterwards, upon his indictment, to the whole court and jury; and confirmed it at his execution. And whereas some of the sheep could not so well be known by his description of them, others with them were brought before him, and he declared which were they, and which were not.

And accordingly he was cast by the jury and condemned, and after executed about the 8th of September, 1642. A very sad spectacle it was; for first the mare, and then the cow, and the rest of the lesser cattle were killed before his face, according to the law, Leviticus 20:15, and then he himself was executed. The cattle were all cast into a great and large pit that was digged of purpose for them, and no use made of any part of them.

Upon the examination of this person, and also of a former that had made some sodomitical attempts upon another, it being demanded of them how they came first to the knowledge and practice of such wickedness, the one confessed he had long used it in old England; and this youth last spoken of said he was taught it by another that had heard of such things from some in England when he was there, and they kept cattle together. By which it appears how one wicked person may infect many; and what care all ought to have what servants they bring into their families.

But it may be demanded how came it to pass that so many wicked persons and profane people should so quickly come over into this land, and mix themselves amongst them, seeing it was religious men that began the work, and they came for religion's sake. I confess this may be marveled at, at least in time to come, when the reasons thereof should not be known; and the more because here was so many hardships and wants met withal. I shall therefore endeavor to give some answer hereunto.

1. And first, according to that in the gospel, it is ever to be remembered that where the Lord begins to sow good seed, there the envious man will endeavor to sow tares.

2. Men being to come over into a wilderness, in which much labor and service was to be done about building and planting, etc., such as wanted help in that respect, when they could not have such as they would, were glad to take such as they could; and so many untoward servants, sundry of them proved, that were thus brought over, both men and womenkind; who, when their times were expired, became families of themselves, which gave increase hereunto.

3. Another and a main reason hereof was that men, finding so many godly disposed persons willing to come

into these parts, some began to make a trade of it, to transport passengers and their goods, and hired ships for that end; and then, to make up their freight and advance their profit, cared not who the persons were, so they had money to pay them. And by this means the country became pestered with many unworthy persons, who, being come over, crept into one place or other.

4. Again, the Lord's blessing usually following his people, as well in outward as spiritual things (though afflictions be mixed withal), do make many to adhere to the people of God, as many followed Christ, for the loaves' sake, John 6:26. and a mixed multitude came into the wilderness with the people of God out of Egypt of old, Exodus 12:38.

5. So also many were sent by their friends, some under hope that they would be made better; others that they might be eased of such burdens, and they kept from shame at home that would necessarily follow their dissolute courses. And thus, by one means or other, in twenty years' time, it is a question whether the greater part be not grown the worser. . . .

ANNO DOMINI 1643

I am to begin this year with that which was a matter of great sadness and mourning unto them all. About the 18th of April died their Reverend Elder, and my dear and loving friend, Mr. William Brewster; a man that had done and suffered much for the Lord Jesus and the gospel's sake, and had borne his part in well and woe with this poor persecuted church above thirty-six years in England, Holland, and in this wilderness, and done the Lord and them faithful service in his place and calling. And notwithstanding the many troubles and sorrows he passed through, the Lord upheld him to a great age. He was near fourscore years of age (if not all out) when he died. He had this blessing added by the Lord to all the rest, to die in his bed, in peace, amongst the midst of his friends, who mourned and wept over him, and ministered what help and comfort they could unto him, and he again recomforted them whilst he could.

His sickness was not long, and till the last day thereof he did not wholly keep his bed. His speech continued till somewhat more than half a day, and then failed him; and about nine or ten o'clock that evening he died, without any pangs at all. A few hours before, he drew his breath short, and some few minutes before his last, he drew his breath long, as a man fallen into a sound sleep, without any pangs or gaspings, and so sweetly departed this life unto a better. . . .

I cannot but here take occasion, not only to mention, but greatly to admire the marvelous providence of God, that notwithstanding the many changes and hardships that these people went through, and the many enemies they had and difficulties they met withal, that so many of them should live to very old age! It was not only this reverend man's condition (for one swallow makes no summer, as they say), but many more of them did the like, some dying about and before this time, and many still living, who attained to sixty years of age, and to sixty-five, divers to seventy and above, and some near eighty as he did. It must needs be more than ordinary, and above natural reason, that so it should be; for it is found in experience that change of air, famine, or unwholesome food, much drinking of water, sorrows and troubles, etc., all of them are enemies to health, causes of many diseases, consumers of natural vigor and the bodies of men, and shorteners of life.

And yet of all these things they had a large part, and suffered deeply in the same. They went from England to Holland, where they found both worse air and diet than that they came from; from thence (enduring a long imprisonment, as it were, in the ships at sea) into New England; and how it hath been with them here hath already been shown; and what crosses, troubles, fears, wants, and sorrows they had been liable unto, is easy to conjecture; so as in some sort they may say with the Apostle, 2 Corinthians 11:26–27, they were *in journeyings often, in perils of waters, in perils of robbers, in perils of their own nation, in perils among the heathen, in perils in the wilderness, in perils in*

the sea, in perils among false brethren; in weariness and painful-
ness, in watching often, in hunger and thirst, in fasting often, in
cold and nakedness. What was it then that upheld them? It was
God's visitation that preserved their spirits. . . .

By reason of the plottings of the Narragansetts (ever since the
Pequots' war), the Indians were drawn into a general conspiracy against the English in all parts, as was in part discovered the
year before; and now made more plain and evident by many
discoveries and free-confessions of sundry Indians (upon several occasions) from divers places concurring in one; with such
other concurring circumstances as gave them sufficiently to understand the truth thereof, and to think of means how to prevent the same, and secure themselves. Which made them enter
into [a] more near union and confederation.[1] . . .

And in . . . their first meeting held at Boston [on 7 Septem-
ber], amongst other things they had this matter of great consequence to consider on: the Narragansetts, after the subduing of
the Pequots, thought to have ruled over all the Indians about
them; but the English, especially those of Connecticut holding
correspondency and friendship with Uncas, sachem of the Mohegan Indians which lived near them (as the Massachusetts had
done with the Narragansetts), and he had been faithful to them
in the Pequot war, they were engaged to support him in his just
liberties, and were contented that such of the surviving Pequots
as had submitted to him should remain with him and quietly
under his protection. This did much increase his power and
augment his greatness, which the Narragansetts could not endure to see.

But Miantonomi, their chief sachem (an ambitious and politic
man), sought privately and by treachery (according to the Indian manner) to make him away, by hiring some to kill him.
Sometime they assayed to poison him; that not taking, then in
the night time to knock him on the head in his house, or secretly to shoot him, and such like attempts. But none of these
taking effect, he made open war upon him (though it was
against the covenants both between the English and them, as also
between themselves, and a plain breach of the same). He came
suddenly upon him with 900 or 1,000 men (never denouncing[2]

any war before). The other's power at that present was not above half so many; but it pleased God to give Uncas the victory, and he slew many of his men, and wounded many more; but the chief of all was, he took Miantonomi prisoner.

And seeing he was a great man, and the Narragansetts a potent people and would seek revenge, he would do nothing in the case without the advice of the English; so he (by the help and direction of those of Connecticut) kept him prisoner till this meeting of the commissioners. The commissioners weighed the cause and passages, as they were clearly represented and sufficiently evidenced betwixt Uncas and Miantonomi; and the things being duly considered, the commissioners apparently saw that Uncas could not be safe whilst Miantonomi lived, but, either by secret treachery or open force, his life would still be in danger.

Wherefore they thought he might justly put such a false and blood-thirsty enemy to death; but in his own jurisdiction, not in the English plantations. And they advised, in the manner of his death all mercy and moderation should be showed, contrary to the practice of the Indians, who exercise torture and cruelty. And, Uncas having hitherto showed himself a friend to the English, and in this craving their advice, if the Narragansett Indians or others shall unjustly assault Uncas for this execution, upon notice and request, the English promise to assist and protect him as far as they may against such violence. . . .

And Uncas followed this advice, and accordingly executed him, in a very fair manner, according as they advised, with due respect to his honor and greatness. But what followed on the Narragansetts' part will appear hereafter.

ANNO DOMINI 1644

Mr. Edward Winslow was chosen Governor this year.

Many having left this place (as is before noted) by reason of the straitness and barrenness of the same, and their finding of better accommodations elsewhere more suitable to their ends and minds; and sundry others still upon every occasion desiring their dismissions, the church began seriously to think whether it were not better jointly to remove to some other place, than to be thus weakened and, as it were, insensibly dissolved. Many meetings and much consultation was held hereabout, and divers were men's minds and opinions. Some were still for staying together in this place, alleging men might here live, if they would be content with their condition; and that it was not for want or necessity so much that they removed, as for the enriching of themselves. Others were resolute upon removal, and so signified that here they could not stay; but if the church did not remove, they must. Insomuch as many were swayed rather than there should be a dissolution, to condescend to a removal, if a fit place could be found that might more conveniently and comfortably receive the whole, with such accession of others as might come to them, for their better strength and subsistence; and some such like cautions and limitations. So as, with the aforesaid provisos, the greater part consented to a removal to a place called Nauset, which had been superficially viewed and the good will of the purchasers (to whom it belonged) obtained, with some addition thereto from the Court.

But now they began to see their error, that they had given away already the best and most commodious places to others, and now wanted themselves; for this place was about fifty miles from hence, and at an outside of the country, remote from all society. Also, that it would prove so strait, as it would not be competent to receive the whole body, much less be capable of any addition or increase; so as (at least in a short time) they should be worse there than they are now here. The which, with sundry other like considerations and inconveniences, made them change their resolutions; but such as were before resolved upon removal took advantage of this agreement and went on notwithstanding; neither could the rest hinder them, they having made some beginning.

And thus was this poor church left, like an ancient mother grown old and forsaken of her children (though not in their affections), yet in regard of their bodily presence and personal helpfulness. Her ancient members being most of them worn away by death; and these of later time being like children translated into other families, and she like a widow left only to trust in God. Thus she that had made many rich became herself poor.

Some things handled, and pacified by the commissioners this year.

Whereas, by a wise providence of God, two of the jurisdictions in the western parts, viz. Connecticut and New Haven, have been lately exercised by sundry insolencies and outrages from the Indians; as, first, an Englishman, running from his master out of the Massachusetts, was murdered in the woods in or near the limits of Connecticut jurisdiction; and about six weeks after, upon discovery by an Indian, the Indian sagamore in these parts promised to deliver the murderer to the English, bound. And having accordingly brought him within the sight of Uncaway,[1] by their joint consent, as it is informed, he was there unbound, and left to shift for himself. Whereupon ten Englishmen forthwith coming to the place, being sent by Mr. Ludlow at the Indians' desire to receive the murderer, who seeing him escaped, laid hold of eight of the Indians there present, amongst whom there was a sagamore or two and kept them in hold two days, till four sagamores engaged themselves within one month to deliver the prisoner. And about a week after this agreement, an Indian came presumptuously and with guile, in the day time, and murderously assaulted an English woman in her house at Stamford, and by three wounds, supposed mortal, left her for dead, after he had robbed the house.

By which passages the English were provoked, and called to a due consideration of their own safety; and the Indians generally in those parts arose in an hostile manner, refused to come to the English to carry on treaties of peace, departed from their wigwams, left their corn unweeded, and showed themselves tumultuously about some of the English plantations, and shot off pieces within hearing of the town; and some Indians came to the English and told them the Indians would fall upon them. So that most of the English thought it unsafe to travel in those parts by land, and some of the plantations were put upon strong watch and ward, night and day, and could not attend their private occasions, and yet distrusted their own strength for their defense. Whereupon Hartford and New Haven were sent unto for aid, and saw cause both to send into the weaker parts of their own jurisdiction thus in danger, and New Haven, for convenience of situation, sent aide to Uncaway, though belonging to Connecticut.

Of all which passages they presently acquainted the commissioners in the Bay, and had the allowance and approbation from the General Court there, with directions neither to hasten war nor to bear such insolencies too long. Which courses, though chargeable to themselves, yet through God's blessing they hope fruit is, and will be, sweet and wholesome to all the colonies; the murderers are since delivered to justice, the public peace preserved for the present, and probability it may be better secured for the future.

Thus this mischief was prevented, and the fear of a war hereby diverted. But now another broil was begun by the Narragansetts; though they unjustly had made war upon Uncas (as is before declared), and had, the winter before this, earnestly pressed the Governor of the Massachusetts that they might still make war upon them to revenge the death of their sagamore, which, being taken prisoner, was by them put to death (as before was noted), pretending that they had first received and accepted his ransom, and then put him to death. But the Governor refused their presents, and told them that it was themselves had done the wrong, and broken the conditions of peace; and he nor the English neither could nor would allow them to make any further war upon him, but if they did, must assist him, and oppose them; but if it did appear, upon good proof, that he had received a ransom for his life, before he put him to death, when the commissioners met, they should have a fair hearing, and they would cause Uncas to return the same.

But notwithstanding, at the spring of the year they gathered a great power, and fell upon Uncas, and slew sundry of his men, and wounded more, and also had some loss themselves. Uncas called for aid from the English; they told him what the Narragansetts objected, he denied the same; they told him it must come to trial, and if he was innocent, if the Narragansetts would not desist, they would aid and assist him. So at this meeting they sent both to Uncas and the Narragansetts, and required their sagamores to come or send to the commissioners now met at Hartford, and they should have a fair and impartial hearing in all their grievances, and would endeavor that all wrongs should be rectified where they should be found; and they promised that they should safely come and return without any danger or molestation; and sundry the like things, as appears more at large in the messenger's instructions.

Upon which the Narragansetts sent one sagamore and some other deputies, with full power to do in the case as should be meet. Uncas came in person, accompanied with some chief about him. After the agitation of the business, the issue was this. The commissioners declared to the Narragansett deputies as followeth:

1. That they did not find any proof of any ransom agreed on.
2. It appeared not that any wampum had been paid as a ransom, or any part of a ransom, for Miantonomi's life.
3. That if they had in any measure proved their charge against Uncas, the commissioners would have required him to have made answerable satisfaction.
4. That if hereafter they can make satisfying proof, the English will consider the same, and proceed accordingly.
5. The commissioners did require that neither themselves nor the Niantics[2] make any war or injurious assault upon Uncas or any of his company until they make proof of the ransom charged, and that due satisfaction be denied, unless he first assault them.
6. That if they assault Uncas, the English are engaged to assist him.

Hereupon the Narragansett sachem, advising with the other deputies, engaged himself in the behalf of the Narragansetts and Niantics that no hostile acts should be committed upon Uncas, or any of his, until after the next planting of corn; and that after that, before they begin any war, they will give thirty days' warning to the Governor of the Massachusetts or Connecticut. The commissioners approving of this offer, and taking their engagement under their hands, required Uncas, as he expected the continuance of the favor of the English, to observe the same terms of peace with the Narragansetts and theirs. . . .

ANNO DOMINI 1645

. . . Besides some underhand assaults made on both sides, the Narragansetts gathered a great power, and fell upon Uncas, and slew many of his men, and wounded more, by reason that they far exceeded him in number, and had got store of pieces, with which they did him most hurt. And as they did this without the knowledge and consent of the English (contrary to former agreement), so they were resolved to prosecute the same, notwithstanding anything the English said or should do against them. So, being encouraged by their late victory, and promise of assistance from the Mohawks (being a strong, warlike, and desperate people), they had already devoured Uncas and his in their hopes; and surely they had done it in deed, if the English had not timely set in for his aid. For those of Connecticut sent him forty men, who were a garrison to him, till the commissioners could meet and take further order.

Being thus met, they forthwith sent three messengers, viz. Sergeant John Davis, Benedict Arnold, and Francis Smith, with full and ample instructions, both to the Narragansetts and Uncas; to require them that they should either come in person or send sufficient men fully instructed to deal in the business; and if they refused or delayed, to let them know (according to former agreements) that the English are engaged to assist against these hostile invasions, and that they have sent their men to defend Uncas, and to know of the Narragansetts whether they will stand to the former peace, or they will assault the English also, that they may provide accordingly.

But the messengers returned not only with a slighting, but a threatening answer from the Narragansetts (as will more appear hereafter). Also they brought a letter from Mr. Roger Williams, wherein he assures them that the war would presently break forth, and the whole country would be all of aflame. And that the sachems of the Narragansetts had concluded a neutrality with the English of Providence and those of Aquidneck Island. Whereupon the commissioners, considering the great danger and provocations offered, and the necessity we should be put unto of making war with the Narragansetts, and being also careful in a matter of so great weight and general concernment to see the way cleared, and to give satisfaction to all the colonies, did think fit to advise with such of the magistrates and elders of the Massachusetts as were then at hand, and also with some of the chief military commanders there; who being assembled, it was then agreed,—

First, that our engagement bound us to aid and defend Uncas. Second, that this aid could not be intended only to defend him and his fort, or habitation, but (according to the common acceptation of such covenants, or engagements, considered with the grounds or occasion thereof) so to aid him as he might be preserved in his liberty and estate. Thirdly, that this aid must be speedy, lest he might be swallowed up in the meantime, and so come too late. Fourthly, the justice of this war being cleared to ourselves and the rest then present, it was thought meet that the case should be stated, and the reasons and grounds of the war declared and published. Fifthly, that a day of humiliation should be appointed, which was the fifth day of the week following. Sixthly, it was then also agreed by the commissioners that the whole number of men to be raised in all the colonies should be 300. Whereof from the Massachusetts 190, Plymouth 40, Connecticut 40, New Haven 30.

And considering that Uncas was in present danger, forty men of this number were forthwith sent from the Massachusetts for his succor; and it was but need, for the other forty from Connecticut had order to stay but a month, and their time being out, they returned; and the Narragansetts, hearing thereof, took the advantage, and came suddenly upon him, and gave him another blow, to his further loss, and were ready to do the like again; but these forty men being arrived, they returned, and did nothing.

The declaration which they set forth I shall not transcribe, it being very large, and put forth in print, to which I refer those that would see the same, in which all passages are laid open from the first. I shall only note their proud carriage, and answers to the three messengers sent from the commissioners. They received them with scorn and contempt, and told them they resolved to have no peace without Uncas's head. Also they gave them this further answer: that it mattered not who began the war, they were resolved to follow it, and that the English should withdraw their garrison from Uncas, or they would procure the Mohawks against them; and withal gave them this threatening answer: that they would lay the English cattle on heaps, as high as their houses, and that no Englishman should stir out of his door to piss, but he should be killed.

And whereas they required guides to pass through their country to deliver their message to Uncas from the commissioners, they denied them, but at length (in way of scorn) offered them an old Pequot woman. Besides also they conceived themselves in danger, for whilst the interpreter was speaking with them about the answer he should return, three men came and stood behind him with their hatchets, according to their murderous manner; but one of his fellows gave him notice of it, so they broke off and came away; with sundry such like affronts, which made those Indians they carried with them to run away for fear and leave them to go home as they could.

Thus whilst the commissioners in care of the public peace sought to quench the fire kindled amongst the Indians, these children of strife breathe out threatenings, provocations, and war against the English themselves. So that, unless they should dishonor and provoke God by violating a just engagement, and expose the colonies to contempt and danger from the barbarians, they cannot but exercise force, when no other means will prevail to reduce the Narragansetts and their confederates to a more just and sober temper.

So as hereupon they went on to hasten the preparations, according to the former agreement, and sent to Plymouth to send forth their forty men with all speed to lie at Seekonk,[1] lest any danger should befall it before the rest were ready, it lying next the enemy, and there to stay till the Massachusetts should join with them. Also Connecticut and New Haven forces were to join together, and march with all speed, and the Indian confederates of those parts with them. All which was done accordingly; and the soldiers of this place were at Seekonk, the place of their rendezvous, eight or ten days before the rest were ready; they were well armed all with snaphance pieces,[2] and went under the command of Captain Standish. Those from other places were led likewise by able commander[s], as Captain Mason for Connecticut, etc.; and Major Gibbons was made general over the whole, with such commissions and instructions as was meet. . . .

Pessacus, Mixanno, and Witowash, three principal sachems of the Narragansett Indians, and Aumsequen, deputy for the Niantics, with a large train of men, within a few days after came to Boston [and accepted a treaty by which they made reparation to the English and to Uncas]. . . . And thus was the war at this time stayed and prevented. . . .

From William Bradford and Edward Winslow, *Mourt's Relation*

Mourt's Relation *is the name that has come to be applied for the sake of convenience to a work that was originally published in London in 1622 under a title that began* A Relation, or Journal, of the Beginning and Proceedings of the English Plantation settled at Plymouth in New England. *The mysterious Mourt, to whom authorship of the book was later assigned, figures in the first edition only as the signer of a brief foreword, "G. Mourt." The signature seems to be a misreading of the name of George Morton, a member of the Leyden congregation who apparently was the recipient of the manuscript and the one who delivered it to the press.*

Although the identity of all those who contributed to the work is in doubt, it is evidently for the most part derived from journals kept by William Bradford and his chief lieutenant, Edward Winslow. Though lacking the eloquence and gravity of Bradford's Of Plymouth Plantation, *it is unexcelled in the immediacy and vividness of its account of the first year of the Pilgrims' encounter with the New World.*

[DISCOVERY]

Wednesday, the sixth of September [1620], the wind coming East-Northeast, a fine small gale, we loosed from Plymouth [England], having been kindly entertained and courteously used by divers friends there dwelling. And, after many difficulties in boisterous storms, at length by God's Providence upon the 9th of November following by break of the day we espied land, which we deemed to be Cape Cod, and so afterward it proved. And the appearance of it much comforted us, especially seeing so goodly a land, and wooded to the brink of the sea. It caused us to rejoice together and praise God that had given us once again to see land.

And thus we made our course south-southwest, purposing to go to a river ten leagues to the south of the Cape, but at night the wind being contrary, we put round again for the Bay of Cape Cod.[1] And upon the 11th of November, we came to an anchor in the Bay, which is a good harbor and pleasant Bay, circled round except in the entrance, which is about four miles over from land to land; compassed about to the very sea with oaks, pines, juniper, sassafras, and other sweet wood. It is a harbor wherein a thousand Sail of ships may safely ride. There we relieved ourselves with wood and water and refreshed our people; while our shallop[2] was fitted to coast the Bay to search for a habitation.

There was the greatest store of fowl that ever we saw. And every day we saw whales playing hard by us. Of which in that place, if we had instruments and means to take them, we might have made a very rich return, which to our great grief we wanted. Our Master[3] and his Mate and others experienced in fishing professed we might have made £3,000 or £4,000 worth of oil. They preferred it before Greenland whale-fishing; and purpose the next winter to fish for whale here.

For cod, we assayed; but found none. There is good store, no doubt, in their season. Neither got we any fish all the time we lay there, but some few little ones on the shore. We found great mussels and very fat and full of sea pearl, but we could not eat them; for they made us all sick that did eat, as well sailors as passengers. They caused to cast and scour,[4] but they were soon well again.

The Bay is so round and circling that before we could come to anchor, we went round all the points of the compass. We could not come near the shore by three-quarters of an English mile because of shallow water, which was a great prejudice to us. For our people, going on shore, were forced to wade a bow-shot or two in going a-land; which caused many to get colds and coughs, for it was many times freezing cold weather. . . .

So soon as we could, we set ashore fifteen or sixteen men well armed; with some to fetch wood, for we had none left, as also to see what the land was and what inhabitants they could meet with. They found it to be a small neck of land. On this side where we lay is the Bay; and the further side, the sea. The ground or earth sandhills, much like the dunes of Holland, but much better. The crust of the earth, a spit's depth[5] excellent black earth, all wooded with oaks, pines, sassafras, juniper, birch, holly, vines, some ash, walnut. The wood for the most part open and without underwood, fit either to go or ride in.

At night, our people returned; but found not any person nor habitation, and laded their boat with juniper, which smelled very sweet and strong; and of which we burnt the most part of the time we lay there. Monday, the 13th of November, we unshipped our shallop and drew her on land to mend and repair her, having been forced to cut her down in bestowing her betwixt the decks; and she was much opened[6] with the people's lying in her. Which kept us long there, for it was sixteen or seventeen days before the Carpenter had finished her. Our people went on shore to refresh themselves; and our women to wash, as they had great need.

But whilst we lay thus still, hoping our shallop would be ready in five or six days at the furthest, but our Carpenter made slow work of it. So that some of our people, impatient of delay, desired for our better furtherance to travel by land into the country (which was not without appearance of danger, not having the shallop with them, nor means to carry provision but on their backs), to see whether it might be fit for us to seat in or no. And the rather because as we sailed into the harbor, there seemed to be a river[7] opening itself into the mainland. The willingness of the persons was liked, but the thing itself, in regard of the danger, was rather permitted than approved.

And so with cautions, directions, and instructions, sixteen men were set out, with every man his musket, sword, and corselet, under the conduct of Captain Miles Standish, unto whom were adjoined for council and advice William Bradford, Stephen

Hopkins, and Edward Tilley.[8] Wednesday, the 15th of November, they were set ashore; and when they had ordered themselves in the order of a Single File and marched about the space of a mile, by the sea they espied five or six people with a dog coming towards them, who were savages, who, when they saw them, ran into the wood and whistled the dog after them, etc. First, they supposed them to be Master Jones, the Master, and some of his men; for they were ashore and knew of their coming, but after they knew them to be Indians, they marched after them into the woods lest other of the Indians should lie in ambush.

But when the Indians saw our men following them, they ran away with might and main, and our men turned out of the wood after them, for it was the way they intended to go; but they could not come near them. They followed them that night about ten miles by the trace of their footings; and saw how they had come the same way they went, and, at a turning, perceived how they run up a hill to see whether they followed them. At length, night came upon them; and they were constrained to take up their lodging. So they set forth three sentinels; and the rest, some kindled a fire, and others fetched wood, and there held our rendezvous that night.

In the morning, so soon as we could see the trace, we proceeded on our journey and had the track until we had compassed the head of a long creek, and there they took into another wood and we after them; supposing to find some of their dwellings. But we marched through boughs and bushes and under hills and valleys, which tore our very armor in pieces, and yet could meet with none of them, nor their houses, nor find any fresh water, which we greatly desired and stood in need of. For we brought neither beer nor water with us; and our victuals were only biscuit and Holland cheese, and a little bottle of *aquavitae,* so as we were sore athirst.

About ten a clock, we came into a deep valley, full of brush, wood-gale,[9] and long grass; through which we found little paths or trac[k]s. And there we saw a deer and found springs of fresh water, of which we were heartily glad and sat us down and drank our first New England water with as much delight as ever we drank drink in all our lives.

When we had refreshed ourselves, we directed our course full south, that we might come to the shore, which, within a short while after, we did; and there made a fire that they in the ship might see where we were, as we had direction; and so marched on towards this supposed river. And as we went into another valley, we found a fine clear pond of fresh water being about a musket-shot broad and twice as long. There grew also many small vines, and fowl and deer haunted there. There grew much sassafras. From thence, we went on, and found much plain ground, about fifty acres, fit for the plow; and some signs where the Indians had formerly planted their corn. After this, some thought it best for nearness of the river to go down and travel on the sea-sands, by which means some of our men were tired, and lagged behind.

So we stayed, and gathered them up; and struck into the land again, where we found a little path to certain heaps of sands, one whereof was covered with old mats and had a wooden thing, like a mortar, whelmed[10] on the top of it, and an earthen pot laid in a little hole at the end thereof. We, musing what it might be, digged and found a bow, and, as we thought, arrows, but they were rotten. We supposed that there were many other things, but because we deemed them graves, we put in the bow again and made it up as it was, and left the rest untouched, because we thought it would be odious unto them to ransack their sepulchers.

We went on further and found new stubble of which they had gotten corn this year; and many walnut trees, full of nuts; and great store of strawberries, and some vines.

Passing thus a field or two, which were not great, we came to another, which had also been newly gotten, and there we found where a house had been, and four or five old planks laid together. Also we found a great kettle, which had been some ship's kettle and brought out of Europe. There was also a heap of sand, made like the former, but it was newly done. We might see how they had paddled it with their hands. Which we digged up, and in it we found a little old basket full of fair Indian corn. And digged further and found a fine great new basket full of very fair corn of this year; with some thirty-six goodly ears of corn, some yellow, and some red, and others mixed with blue; which was a very goodly sight. The basket was round and narrow at the top. It held about three or four bushels; which was as much as two of us could lift up from the ground and was very hand-somely and cunningly made. But whilst we were busy about these things, we set our men sentinel in a round ring; all but two or three, which digged up the corn.

We were in suspense what to do with it, and the kettle, and, at length, after much consultation, we concluded to take the kettle and as much of the corn as we could carry away with us. And when our shallop came, if we could find any of the people, and come to parley with them; we would give them the kettle again, and satisfy them for their corn. So we took all the ears, and put a good deal of the loose corn in the kettle, for two men to bring away on a staff. Besides, they that could put any into their pockets, filled the same. The rest, we buried again, for we were so laden with armor, that we could carry no more.

Not far from this place, we found the remainder of an old fort or palisade, which, as we conceived, had been made by some Christians. This was also hard by that place which we thought had been a river; unto which we went and found it so to be; di-viding itself into two arms by a high bank standing-right by the cut, or mouth, which came from the sea. That which was next unto us was the less; the other arm was more than twice as big and not unlikely to be a harbor for ships. But whether it be a fresh river or only an indraught of the sea, we had no time to discover, for we had commandment to be out but two days. Here also we saw two canoes, the one on the one side, and the other on the other side. We could not believe it was a canoe till we came near it.

So we returned, leaving the further discovery hereof to our shallop, and came that night back to the Fresh Water Pond. And there we made our rendezvous that night, making a great fire and a barricade to windward of us; and kept good watch with three sentinels all night, every one standing when his turn came; while five or six inches of Match[11] were burning. It proved a very rainy night. In the morning, we took our kettle and sunk it in the Pond, and trimmed our muskets, for few of them would go off because of the wet, and so coasted the wood again to come home, in which we were shrewdly puzzled and lost our way.

As we wandered, we came to a tree where a young sprit[12] was bowed down over a bow, and some acorns strewed underneath. Stephen Hopkins said it had been to catch some deer. So as we were looking at it, William Bradford being in the rear, when he came, looked also upon it; and as he went about, it gave a sudden jerk up, and he was immediately caught by the leg. It was a very pretty device, made with a rope of their own making; and having a noose as artificially made as any roper in England can make, and as like ours as can be, which we brought away with us.

In the end, we got out of the wood and were fallen about a mile too high above the creek. Where we saw three bucks, but we had rather have had one of them. We also did spring three couple of partridges, and, as we came along by the creek, we saw great flocks of wild geese and ducks; but they were very fearful of us. So we marched some while in the woods, some while on the sands, and other while in the water up to the knees, till at length we came near the ship; and then we shot off our pieces, and the long boat came to fetch us. Master Jones and Master Carver,[13] being on the shore with many of our people, came to meet us.

And thus we came, both weary and welcome, home, and delivered in our corn into the store to be kept for seed. For we knew not how to come by any, and therefore were very glad, purposing so soon as we could meet with any of the inhabitants of that place to make them large satisfaction. This was our first discovery, whilst our shallop was in repairing.

Our people did make things as fitting as they could and time would in seeking out wood, and helving[14] of tools, and sawing of timber to build a new shallop, but the discommodiousness of the harbor did much hinder us. For we could neither go to nor come from the shore but at high water; which was much to our hindrance and hurt. For oftentimes they waded to the middle of the thigh and oft to the knees to go and come from land. Some did it necessarily, and some for their own pleasure, but it brought to the most, if not to all, coughs and colds (the weather proving suddenly cold and stormy), which afterward turned to the scurvy, whereof many died.

When our shallop was fit (indeed before she was fully fitted; for there was two days' work after bestowed on her), there was appointed some twenty-four men of our own and armed, then to go and make a more full discovery of the rivers before mentioned. Master Jones was desirous to go with us and took such of his sailors as he thought useful for us, so as we were in all about thirty-four men. We made Master Jones our leader, for we thought it best herein to gratify his kindness and forwardness.

When we were set forth, it proved rough weather and cross winds; so as we were constrained, some in the shallop, and others in the long boat, to row to the nearest shore the wind would suffer them to go unto and then to wade out above the knees. The wind was so strong as the shallop could not keep the water but was forced to harbor there that night. But we marched six or seven miles further and appointed the shallop to come to us as soon as they could. It blowed and did snow all that day and night and froze withal. Some of our people that are dead took the original of their death here.

The next day, about eleven o'clock, our shallop came to us, and we shipped ourselves; and the wind being good, we sailed to the river we formerly discovered, which we named Cold Harbor, to which when we came, we found it not navigable for ships; yet we thought it might be a good harbor for boats, for it flows there twelve feet at high water. We landed our men between the two creeks and marched some four or five miles by the greater of them, and the shallop followed us.

At length, night grew on; and our men were tired with marching up and down the steep hills and deep valleys, which lay half a foot thick with snow. Master Jones, wearied with marching, was desirous we should take up our lodging; though some of us would have marched further. So we made there our rendezvous for that night under a few pine trees; and, as it fell out, we got three fat geese and six ducks to our supper; which we ate with soldiers' stomachs, for we had eaten little all that day. Our resolution was next morning to go up to the head of this river, for we supposed it would prove fresh water.

But in the morning, our resolution held not; because many liked not the hilliness of the soil and badness of the harbor. So we turned towards the other creek that we might go over and look for the rest of the corn that we left behind when we were here before. When we came to the creek, we saw the canoe lie on the dry ground, and a flock of geese in the river, at which one made a shot and killed a couple of them. And we launched the canoe and fetched them, and when we had done, she carried us over by seven or eight at once.

This done, we marched to the place where we had the corn formerly, which place we called Cornhill, and digged and found the rest; of which we were very glad. We also digged in a place a little further off and found a bottle of oil. We went to another place which we had seen before and digged, and found more corn, viz. two or three baskets' full of Indian wheat[15] and a bag of beans, with a good many of fair wheat ears. Whilst some of us were digging up this, some others found another heap of corn, which they digged up also. So as we had in all about ten bushels; which will serve us sufficiently for seed.

And sure it was God's good Providence that we found this corn; for else we know not how we should have done. For we knew not how we should find or meet with any of the Indians, except it be to do us a mischief. Also we had never in all likelihood seen a grain of it if we had not made our first journey, for the ground was now covered with snow and so hard frozen that we were fain with our cutlasses and short swords to hew and carve the ground a foot deep, and then wrest it up with levers, for we had forgot to bring other tools.

Whilst we were in this employment, foul weather being towards,[16] Master Jones was earnest to go aboard [the *Mayflower*], but sundry of us desired to make further discovery and to find out the Indians' habitations. So we sent home with him our weakest people and some that were sick and all the corn; and eighteen of us stayed still and lodged there that night, and desired that the shallop might return to us next day and bring us some mattocks and spades with them. The next morning we followed certain beaten paths and tracks of the Indians into the woods, supposing they would have led us into some town or houses. After we had gone a while, we lighted upon a very broad beaten path, well nigh two feet broad. Then we lighted all our Matches and prepared ourselves; concluding we were near their dwellings, but, in the end, we found it to be only a path made to drive deer in when the Indians hunt, as we supposed.

When we had marched five or six miles into the woods and could find no signs of any people; we returned again another way. And as we came into the plain ground, we found a place like a grave, but it was much bigger and longer than any we had yet seen. It was also covered with boards; so as we mused what it should be and resolved to dig it up.

Where we found first a mat, and under that a fair bow, and there, another mat, and under that, a board about three-quarters [of a yard] long, finely carved and painted, with three tines or broaches[17] on the top like a crown. Also between the mats, we found bowls, trays, dishes, and such like trinkets. At length, we came to a fair new mat, and under that, two bundles; the one bigger, the other less. We opened the greater and found in it a great quantity of fine and perfect red powder, and in it the bones and skull of a man. The skull had fine yellow hair still on it and some of the flesh unconsumed. There were bound up with it a knife, a pack-needle,[18] and two or three old iron things. It was bound up in a sailor's canvas cassock, and a pair of cloth breeches. The red powder was a kind of embalment and yielded a strong but no offensive smell. It was as fine as any flour.

We opened the less bundle likewise and found of the same powder in it and the bones and head of a little child. About the legs and other parts of it were bound strings and bracelets of fine white beads. There was also by it a little bow about three-quarters [of a yard] long and some other odd knacks. We brought sundry of the prettiest things away with us and covered up the corpse again. After this, we digged in sundry like places but found no more corn, nor any things else but graves.

There was variety of opinions amongst us about the embalmed person. Some thought it was an Indian lord and king. Others said the Indians have all black hair, and never any was seen with brown or yellow hair. Some thought it was a Christian of special note, which had died amongst them, and they thus buried him to honor him. Others thought they had killed him and did it in triumph over him.

Whilst we were thus ranging and searching, two of the sailors, which were newly come on the shore, by chance espied two houses which had been lately dwelt in; but the people were gone. They, having their pieces and hearing nobody, entered the houses and took out some things, and durst not stay but came again and told us. So some seven or eight of us went with them and found how we had gone within a flight shot[19] of them before. The houses were made with long young sapling trees, bent and both ends stuck in the ground. They were made round like an arbor and covered down to the ground with thick and well wrought mats; and the door was not over a yard high, made of a mat to open. The chimney was a wide open hole in the top, for which they had a mat to cover it close when they pleased. One might stand and go upright in them. In the midst of them were four little trunches[20] knocked into the ground and small sticks laid over, on which they hung their pots and what they had to seethe.[21] Round about the fire, they lay on mats, which are their beds. The houses were double matted, for as they were matted without, so were they within with newer and fairer mats.

In the houses, we found wooden bowls, trays, and dishes; earthen pots; hand baskets made of crab shells wrought together, also an English pail or bucket; it wanted a bail, but it had two iron ears. There were also baskets of sundry sorts, bigger and some lesser, finer and some coarser. Some were curiously wrought with black and white in pretty works, and sundry other of their household stuff. We found also two or three deer's heads, one whereof had been newly killed, for it was still fresh. There was also a company of deer's feet stuck up in the houses. Harts' horns and eagles' claws and sundry like things there were. Also two or three baskets full of parched acorns, pieces of fish, and a piece of a broiled herring. We found also a little silk grass and a little tobacco seed, with some other seeds which we

knew not. Without, were sundry bundles of flags and sedge bul-
rushes and other stuff to make mats. There was thrust into a
hollow tree, two or three pieces of venison, but we thought it fitter for the dogs than for us. Some of the best things we took
away with us, and left the houses standing still as they were.

So, it growing towards night and the tide almost spent, we
hasted with our things down to the shallop, and got aboard that
night, intending to have brought some beads and other things
to have left in the houses in sign of peace, and that we meant to
truck[22] with them. But it was not done by means of our hasty
coming away from Cape Cod, but, so soon as we can meet conveniently with them, we will give them full satisfaction. Thus
much of our Second Discovery.

Having thus discovered this place, it was controversial
amongst us what to do touching our abode and settling there.
Some thought it best, for many reasons, to abide there. As first,
that there was a convenient harbor for boats though not for
ships. Secondly, good corn-ground ready to our hands, as we
saw by experience in the goodly corn it yielded, which would
again agree with the ground and be natural seed for the same.
Thirdly, Cape Cod was like to be a place of good fishing, for we
saw daily great whales of the best kind for oil and bone come
close aboard our ship; and in fair weather swim and play about
us. There was once one, when the sun shone warm, came and
lay above water, as if she had been dead, for a good while together, within half a musket shot of the ship. At which, two
were prepared to shoot to see whether she would stir or no. He
that gave fire first, his musket flew in pieces, both stock and
barrel, yet, thanks be to God, neither he nor any man else was
hurt with it, though many were there about. But when the whale
saw her time, she gave a snuff, and away. Fourthly, the place
was likely to be healthful, secure, and defensible.

But the last and especial reason was that now the heart of
winter and unseasonable weather was come upon us so that we
could not go upon coasting and discovery without danger of
losing men and boat; upon which would follow the overthrow
of all, especially considering what variable winds and sudden
storms do there arise. Also cold and wet lodging had so tainted

our people (for scarce any of us was free from vehement coughs) as if they should continue long in that estate, it would endanger the lives of many and breed diseases and infection amongst us. Again, we had yet some beer, butter, flesh, and other such victuals, which would quickly be all gone, and then we should have nothing to comfort us in the great labor and toil we were like to undergo at the first. It was also conceived, whilst we had competent victuals, that the ship would stay with us, but when that grew low, they would be gone and let us shift as we could.

Others again urged greatly the going to Agawam,[23] a place twenty leagues off to the northwards; which they had heard to be an excellent harbor for ships, better ground and better fishing. Secondly, for anything we knew, there might be hard by us a far better seat, and it should be a great hindrance to seat where we should remove again. Thirdly, the water was but in ponds; and it was thought there would be none in summer, or very little. Fourthly, the water there must be fetched up a steep hill.

But to omit many reasons and replies used hereabouts, it was in the end concluded to make some discovery within the Bay, but in no case so far as Agawam. Besides, Robert Coppin, our Pilot, made relation of a great navigable river and good harbor in the other headland of the Bay almost right over against Cape Cod, being a right line, not much above eight leagues distant, in which he had been once. And because that one of the wild men with whom they had some trucking stole a harping iron[24] from them, they called it Thievish Harbor.[25] And beyond that place, they were enjoined not to go. Whereupon a Company was chosen to go out upon a third discovery. Whilst some were employed in this discovery, it pleased God that Mistress White was brought to bed of a son; which was called Peregrine.

The 5th day [of December], we, through God's mercy, escaped a great danger by the foolishness of a boy; one of [John] Billington's sons who, in his father's absence, had got gunpowder and had shot off a piece or two, and made squibs. And there being a fowling piece charged in his father's cabin, shot her off in the cabin; there being a little barrel of powder half full scattered in and about the cabin; the fire being within four feet of the bed between the decks; and many flints and iron things about the cabin; and many people about the fire, and yet, by God's mercy, no harm done.

Wednesday, the 6th of December, it was resolved our discoverers should set forth, for the day before was too foul weather. And so they did, though it was well over the day ere all things could be ready. So [eight] of our men were appointed, who were of themselves willing to undertake it, . . . and three of London, . . . and two of our seamen. . . . Of the ship's company, there went two of the Master's Mates, . . . the Master Gunner, and three sailors. The Narration of which Discovery follows, penned by one of the company.

Wednesday, the 6th of December we set out, being very cold and hard weather. We were a long while after we launched from the ship before we could get clear of a sandy point which lay within less than a furlong of the same. In which time, two were very sick, and Edward Tilley had like to have swooned with cold. The Gunner was also sick unto death, but hope of trucking made him go, and so remained all that day and the next night. At length, we got clear of the sandy point and got up our sails; and within an hour or two we got under the weather shore and then had smoother water and better sailing, but it was very cold; for the water froze on our clothes and made them many times like coats of iron.

We sailed six or seven leagues by the shore; but saw neither river nor creek. At length we met with a tongue of land, being flat, off from the shore, with a sandy point. We bore up to gain the point and found there a fair income or road of a Bay,[26] being a league over at the narrowest, and some two or three in length. But we made right over to the land before us and left the discovery of this income till the next day. As we drew near to the shore, we espied some ten or twelve Indians very busy about a black thing, what it was we could not tell, till afterwards they saw us and ran to and fro, as if they had been carrying something away.

We landed a league or two from them and had much ado to put ashore anywhere, it lay so full of flat sands. When we came to shore, we made us a barricade and got firewood and set out our sentinels and betook us to our lodging, such as it was. We saw the smoke of the fire which the savages made that night about four or five miles from us.

In the morning, we divided our company. Some eight in the shallop and the rest on the shore went to discover this place, but we found it only to be a bay without either river or creek coming into it. Yet we deemed it to be as good a harbor as Cape Cod. For they that sounded it found a ship might ride in five fathom water. We, on the land, found it to be a level soil but none of the fruitfullest. We saw two becks[27] of fresh water, which were the first running streams that we saw in the country, but one might stride over them. We found also a great fish called a grampus[28] dead on the sands. They in the shallop found two of them also in the bottom of the bay, dead in like sort. They were cast up at high water and could not get off for the frost and ice. They were some five or six paces long, and about two inches thick of fat, and fleshed like a swine. They would have yielded a great deal of oil, if there had been time and means to have taken it. So we finding nothing for our turn, both we and the shallop returned.

We then directed our course along the sea sands to the place where we first saw the Indians. When we were there, we saw it was also a grampus which they were cutting up. They cut it into long rands or pieces about an ell[29] long and two handful broad. We found here and there a piece scattered by the way, as it seemed, for haste. This place the most were minded we should call the Grampus Bay, because we found so many of them there. We followed the track of the Indians' bare feet a good way on the sands. At length, we saw where they struck into the woods by the side of a pond. As we went to view the place, one said he thought he saw an Indian house among the trees. So went up to see; and here we and the shallop lost sight of one another till night, it being now about nine or ten o'clock.

So we lighted on a path, but saw no house and followed a great way into the woods. At length, we found where corn had been set,[30] but not that year. Anon we found a great burying place, one part whereof was encompassed with a large palisade like a churchyard, with young spires[31] of four or five yards long set as close one by another as they could, two or three feet in the ground. Within it was full of graves, some bigger and some less. Some were also paled about, and others had like an Indian house made over them, but not matted. Those graves were more sumptuous than those at Cornhill. Yet we digged none of them up, but only viewed them and went our way. Without the palisade were graves also, but not so costly.

From this place we went, and found more corn ground, but not of this year. As we ranged, we lighted on four or five Indian houses which had been lately dwelt in, but they were uncovered and had no mats about them; else they were like those we found at Cornhill, but had not been so lately dwelt in. There was nothing left but two or three pieces of old mats, a little sedge. Also a little further we found two baskets full of parched acorns hid in the ground, which we supposed had been corn, when we began to dig the same. We cast earth thereon again and went our way.

All this while, we saw no people. We went ranging up and down till the sun began to draw low, and then we hastened out of the woods that we might come to our shallop; which, when we were out of the woods, we espied a great way off and called them to come unto us; the which they did as soon as they could, for it was not yet high water. They were exceeding glad to see us, for they feared, because they had not seen us in so long a time, thinking we would have kept by the shore side. So, being both weary and faint, for we had eaten nothing all that day, we fell to make our rendezvous and get firewood, which always cost us a great deal of labor. By that time we had done, and our shallop come to us, it was within night, and we fed upon such victuals as we had and betook us to our rest, after we had set our watch.

About midnight, we heard a great and hideous cry; and our sentinels called, "Arm! Arm!" So we bestirred ourselves, and shot off a couple of muskets; and noise ceased. We concluded that it was a company of wolves or foxes. For one told us he had heard such a noise in Newfoundland.

About five o'clock in the morning, we began to be stirring,

and two or three which doubted whether their pieces would go off or no, made trial of them and shot them off, but thought nothing at all. After prayer, we prepared ourselves for breakfast and for a journey, and it being now the twilight in the morning, it was thought meet to carry the things down to the shallop. Some said it was not best to carry the armor down. Others said they would be readier. Two or three said they would not carry theirs till they went themselves, but mistrusting nothing at all. As it fell out, the water not being high enough, they laid the things down on the shore and came up to breakfast.

Anon, all upon a sudden, we heard a great and strange cry, which we knew to be the same voices, though they varied their notes. One of our company, being abroad, came running in and cried, "They are men! Indians! Indians!" and withal their arrows came flying amongst us. Our men ran out with all speed to recover their arms, as, by the good Providence of God, they did. In the mean time, Captain Miles Standish, having a snaphance[32] ready, made a shot, and after him another. After they two had shot, other two of us were ready, but he wished us not to shoot till we could take aim, for we knew not what need we should have. And there were four only of us which had their arms there ready and stood before the open side of our barricade, which was first assaulted. They thought it best to defend it; lest the enemy should take it and our stuff, and so have the more vantage against us.

Our care was no less for the shallop, but we hoped all the rest would defend it. We called unto them to know how it was with them. And they answered, "Well! Well!" every one; and "Be of good courage!" We heard three of their pieces go off, and the rest called for a firebrand to light their Matches. One took a log out of the fire on his shoulder, and went and carried it unto them, which was thought did not a little discourage our enemies. The cry of our enemies was dreadful, especially when our men ran out to recover their arms. Their note was after this manner, "Woath! Woach! Ha! Ha! Hach! Woach!"

Our men were no sooner come to their arms; but the enemy were ready to assault them. There was a lusty man, and no whit less valiant, who was thought to be their Captain, stood behind a tree within half a musket shot of us, and there let his arrows fly at us. He was seen to shoot three arrows, which were all avoided. For he at whom the first arrow was aimed, saw it and stooped down, and it flew over him. The rest were avoided also. He stood three shots of a musket. At length, one took, as he said, full aim at him, after which he give an extraordinary cry, and away they went all. We followed them about a quarter of a mile, but we left six to keep our shallop; for we were careful of our business. Then we shouted all together two several times, and shot off a couple of muskets, and so returned. This we did that they might see we were not afraid of them; nor discouraged. Thus it pleased God to vanquish our enemies and give us deliverance.

By their noise, we could not guess that they were less than thirty or forty; though some thought that they were many more. Yet in the dark of the morning we could not so well discern them among the trees, as they could see us by our fireside. We took up eighteen of their arrows; which we have sent to England by Master Jones, some whereof were headed with brass, others with hart's horn; and others with eagles' claws. Many more, no doubt, were shot, for these we found were almost covered with leaves. Yet, by the especial Providence of God, none of them either hit or hurt us, though many came close by us, and on every side of us and some coats which hung up in our barricade were shot through and through. So, after we had given God thanks for our deliverance, we took our shallop and went on our journey, and called this place "The First Encounter."[33]

From hence, we intended to have sailed to the aforesaid Thievish Harbor if we found no convenient harbor by the way. Having the wind good, we sailed all that day along the coast about fifteen leagues, but saw neither river, nor creek, to put into. After we had sailed an hour or two, it began to snow and rain, and to be bad weather. About the midst of the afternoon, the wind increased, and the seas began to be very rough, and the hinges of the rudder broke, so that we could steer no longer with it, but two men with much ado were fain to serve with a couple of oars. The seas were grown so great that we were much troubled and in great danger, and night grew on.

Anon, Master Coppin bade us be of good cheer, he saw the harbor. As we drew near, the gale being stiff, and we, bearing great sail to get in, split our mast in three pieces; and was like to have cast away our shallop; yet, by God's mercy, recovering ourselves, we had the flood with us and struck into the harbor. Now he that thought that had been the place was deceived, it being a place where not any of us had been before, and coming into the harbor, he that was our Pilot did bear up northward; which if we had continued, we had been cast away.

Yet still the Lord kept us, and we bore up for an island before us, and recovering that island, being compassed about with many rocks and dark night growing upon us, it pleased the divine Providence that we fell upon a place of sandy ground, where our shallop did ride safe and secure all that night; and coming upon [the] strange island, kept our watch all night in the rain upon that island, and in the morning we marched about it, and found no inhabitants at all. And here we made our rendezvous all that day, being Saturday, 10th of December. On the Sabbath Day, we rested, and on Monday we sounded the harbor,[34] and found it a very good harbor for our shipping. We marched also into the land and found divers cornfields and little running brooks, a place very good for situation. So we returned to our ship again with good news to the rest of our people, which did much comfort their hearts.

[SETTLEMENT]

On the 10th day [of December 1620, the *Mayflower*] weighed anchor, to go to the place we had discovered; and coming within two leagues of the land, we could not fetch the harbor, but were fain to put room again towards Cape Cod, our course lying West, and the wind was at northwest. But it pleased God that the next day, being Saturday the 16th, the wind came fair; and we put to sea again and came safely into a safe harbor. And within half an hour, the wind changed, so as if we had been let-ted[1] but a little, we had gone back to Cape Cod.

This harbor is a bay greater than Cape Cod, compassed with

a goodly land, and in the bay, two fine islands uninhabited wherein is nothing but wood: oaks, pines, walnut, beech, sassafras, vines, and other trees which we know not. This bay is a most hopeful place, innumerable store of fowl and excellent good, and cannot but be of fish in their seasons. Skate, cod, turbot, and herring we have tasted of; abundance of mussels, the greatest and best that we ever saw; crabs and lobsters in their time, infinite. It is in fashion like a sickle or fishhook.

Monday, the 13th day, we went a-land, manned with the Master of the ship and three or four of the sailors. We marched along the coast in the woods some seven or eight miles; but saw not an Indian nor an Indian house; only we found where formerly had been some inhabitants; and where they had planted their corn. We found not any navigable river but four or five small running brooks of very sweet fresh water that all ran into the sea. The land for the crust of the earth is a spit's depth excellent black mould and fat in some places. Two or three great oaks, but not very thick; pines, walnut, beech, ash, birch, hazel, holly, aspen, sassafras in abundance, and vines everywhere; cherry-trees, plum-trees, and many others which we knew not. Many kinds of herbs we found here in winter, as strawberry leaves innumerable, sorrel, yarrow, chervil, brooklime, liverwort, watercresses, great store of leeks and onions, and an excellent strong kind of flax and hemp. Here are sand, gravel, and excellent clay, no better in the world, excellent for pots and will wash like soap; and great store of stone, though somewhat soft; and the best water that ever we drank; and the brooks now begin to be full of fish.

That night, many being weary with marching, we went aboard again. The next morning, being Tuesday, the 19th of December, we went again to discover further. Some went on land, and some in the shallop. The land we found as the former day we did. And we found a creek and went up three English miles. A very pleasant river. At full sea, a bark of thirty tons may go up, but at low water, scarce our shallop could pass. This place[2] we had a great liking to plant in, but that it was so far from our fishing, our principal profit; and so encompassed with woods that we should be in much danger of the savages; and our number being so little, and so much ground to clear. So as we thought good to quit and clear that place till we were of more strength.

Some of us having a good mind for safety to plant in the greater isle,[3] we crossed the bay, which there is five or six miles over, and found the isle about a mile and a half or two miles about, all wooded, and no fresh water but two or three pits that we doubted of fresh water in summer, and so full of wood as we could hardly clear so much as to serve us for corn. Besides, we judged it cold for our corn and some part very rocky. Yet divers thought of it as a place defensible and of great security. That night we returned again a-shipboard with resolution the next morning to settle on some of those places.

So, in the morning, after we had called on God for direction, we came to this resolution: to go presently ashore again and to take a better view of two places which we thought most fitting for us. For we could not now take time for further search or consideration, our victuals being much spent, especially our beer, and it being now the 20th of December.

After our landing and viewing of the places so well as we could; we came to a conclusion by most voices to set on the mainland on the first place, on a high ground where there is a great deal of land cleared and hath been planted with corn three or four years ago; and there is a very sweet brook runs under the hillside, and many delicate springs of as good water as can be drunk; and where we may harbor our shallops and boats exceeding well; and in this brook, much good fish in their seasons; on the further side of the river also, much corn ground cleared. In one field is a great hill on which we point[4] to make a Platform and to plant our ordnance, which will command all round about. From thence we may see into the Bay and far into the sea, and we may see thence Cape Cod. Our greatest labor will be the fetching of our wood, which is half a quarter of an English mile; but there is enough so far off. What people inhabit here, we know not, for as yet we have seen none. So there we made our rendezvous and a place for some of our people, about twenty resolving in the morning to come all ashore and to build houses.

But the next morning, being Thursday the 21st of December, it was stormy and wet that we could not go ashore. And those that remained there all night could do nothing but were wet, not having daylight enough to make them a sufficient court of guard[5] to keep them dry. All that night it blew and rained extremely. It was so tempestuous that the shallop could not go on land so soon as was meet, for they had no victuals on land. About eleven a clock, the shallop went off with much ado with provisions, but could not return, it blew so strong. And was such foul weather that we were forced to let fall our anchor and ride with three anchors ahead.

Friday, the 22nd, the storm still continued that we could not get a-land, nor they come to us aboard. This morning, good wife Allerton was delivered of a son, but dead born. Saturday, the 23rd, so many of us as could went ashore, felled and carried timber to provide ourselves stuff for building. Sunday, the 24th, our people on shore heard a cry of some savages, as they thought, which caused an alarm and to stand on their guard expecting an assault, but all was quiet.

Monday, the 25th day, we went on shore, some to fell timber, some to saw, some to rive,[6] and some to carry, so no man rested all that day. But towards night, some, as they were at work, heard a noise of some Indians; which caused us all to go to our muskets. But we heard no further, so we came aboard again, and left some twenty to keep the court of guard. That night we had a sore storm of wind and rain.

Monday, the 25th, being Christmas Day, we began to drink water aboard. But at night the Master caused us to have some beer. And so on board, we had divers times, now and then, some beer, but on shore none at all. Tuesday, the 26th, it was foul weather, that we could not go ashore. Wednesday, the 27th, we went to work again.

Thursday, the 28th of December so many as could went to work on the hill, where we purposed to build our Platform for our ordnance, and which doth command all the plain and the bay, and from whence we may see far into the sea and might be easier impaled, having two rows of houses and a fair street. So in the afternoon, we went to measure out the grounds. And first, we took notice how many families there were, willing all single men that had no wives to join some family as they thought fit, that so we might build fewer houses. Which was done, and we reduced them to nineteen families. To greater families, we allotted larger plots: to every person, half a Pole[7] in breadth and three in length. And so lots were cast where every man should lie. Which was done and staked out. We thought this proportion was large enough at the first for houses and gardens to impale them around, considering the weakness of our people, many of them growing ill with colds, for our former Discoveries in frost and storms and the wading at Cape Cod had brought much weakness amongst us, which increased so every day, more and more; and after was the cause of many of their deaths.

Friday and Saturday we fitted ourselves for our labor, but our people on shore were much troubled and discouraged with rain and wet those days, being very stormy and cold. We saw great smokes of fire made by the Indians about six or seven miles from us, as we conjectured. Monday, the 1st of January [1621], we went betimes to work. We were much hindered in lying so far off from the land and fain to go as the tide served, that we lost much time. For our ship drew so much water that she lay a mile and almost a half off, though a ship of seventy or eighty tons at high water may come to the shore.

Wednesday, the 3rd of January, some of our people being abroad to get and gather thatch, they saw great fires of the Indians, and were at their cornfields, yet saw none of the savages nor had seen any of them since we came to this bay. Thursday, the 4th of January, Captain Miles Standish with four or five more went to see if they could meet with any of the savages in that place where the fires were made. They went to some of their houses but not lately inhabited, yet they could not meet with any. As they came home, they shot at an eagle and killed her, which was excellent meat. It was hardly to be discerned from mutton.

Friday, the 5th of January. One of the sailors found alive upon the shore a herring; which the Master had to his supper, which put us in hope of fish; but as yet we had got but one cod.

We wanted small hooks. . . . Monday, the 8th day of January, was a very fair day; and we went betimes to work. Master Jones sent the shallop, as he had formerly done, to see where fish could be got. They had a great storm at sea and were in some danger. At night, they returned with three great seals and an excellent good cod, which did assure us that we should have plenty of fish shortly.

This day, Francis Billington (having, the week before, seen from the top of a tree on a high hill, a great sea, as he thought) went with one of the Master's Mates to see it. They went three miles and then came to a great water divided into two great lakes, the bigger of them five or six miles in circuit, and in it an isle of a cable's length[8] square; the other, three miles in compass. In their estimation, they are fine fresh water; full of fish and fowl. A brook issues from it. It will be an excellent help for us in time. They found seven or eight Indian houses, but not lately inhabited. When they saw the houses, they were in some fear, for they were but two persons and one piece.

Tuesday, the 9th January, was a reasonable fair day, and we went to labor that day in the building of our town in two rows of houses for more safety. We divided by lot the plot of ground whereon to build our town. After the proportion formerly allotted, we agreed that every man should build his own house, thinking by that course men would make more haste than working in common. The common house, in which for the first we made our rendezvous, being nearly finished, wanted only covering, it being about twenty feet square. Some would make mortar, and some gather thatch, so that in four days half of it was thatched. Frost and foul weather hindered us much. This time of the year seldom could we work half the week.

Thursday the 11th, William Bradford being at work, for it was a fair day, was vehemently taken with a grief and pain, and so shot to his huckle-bone[9] it was doubted that he would have instantly died. He got cold in the former discoveries, especially the last, and felt some pain in his ankles by times. But he grew a little better towards night, and in time, through God's mercy in the use of means, recovered.

Friday, the 12th, . . . two of our people put us in great sorrow and care. There were four sent to gather and cut thatch in the morning; and two of them, John Goodman and Peter Browne, having cut thatch all the forenoon, went to a further place and willed the other two to bind up that which was cut and to follow them. So they did, being about a mile and a half from our Plantation. But when the two came after, they could not find them nor hear anything of them at all, though they hallooed and shouted as loud as they could. So they returned to the Company, and told them of it. Whereupon Master Carver and three or four more went to seek them but could hear nothing of them. So they returning, sent more, but that night they could hear nothing at all of them. The next day they armed ten or twelve men out, verily thinking the Indians had surprised them, but could neither see nor hear anything at all. So they returned with much discomfort to us all.

These two that were missed at dinner time took their meat in their hands, and would go walk and refresh themselves. So going a little off, they found a lake of water and, having a great mastiff bitch with them and a spaniel, by the waterside they found a great deer. The dogs chased him, and they followed so far as they lost themselves and could not find the way back. They wandered all that afternoon, being wet, and at night it did freeze and snow. They were slenderly appareled and had no weapons, but each one his sickle, nor any victuals. They ranged up and down and could find none of the savages' habitations.

When it drew to night, they were much perplexed, for they could find neither harbor nor meat, but in frost and snow were forced to make the earth their bed, and the element their covering. And another thing did very much terrify them. They heard, as they thought, two lions roaring exceedingly for a long time together and a third that they thought was very near them. So, not knowing what to do, they resolved to climb up into a tree as their safest refuge; though that would prove an intolerable cold lodging. So they stood at the tree's root, that, when the lions came, they might take their opportunity of climbing up. The bitch they were fain to hold by the neck; for she would have been gone to the lion. But it pleased God so to dispose that the wild beasts came not. So they walked up and down under the tree all night. It was an extremely cold night.

So soon as it was light, they traveled again, passing by many lakes and brooks and woods, and in one place where the savages had burnt the space of five miles in length, which is a fine champaign country and even. In the afternoon, it pleased God from a high hill they discovered the two isles in the bay and so that night got to the Plantation; being ready to faint with travail and want of victuals and almost famished with cold. John Goodman was fain to have his shoes cut off his feet, they were so swelled with cold, and it was a long while after ere he was able to go.

Those on the shore were much comforted at their return, but they on shipboard were grieved, as deeming them lost; but the next day, being the 14th of January, in the morning about six of the clock, the wind being very great; they on shipboard spied their great new rendezvous on fire, which was to them a new discomfort, fearing, because of the supposed loss of the men, that the savages had fired them. Neither could they presently go to them for want of water, but after three-quarters of an hour they went, as they had purposed the day before to keep the Sabbath on shore, because now there was the greater number of people. At their landing, they heard good tidings of the return of the two men and that the house was fired occasionally[10] by a spark that flew into the thatch, which instantly burnt it all up, but the roof stood and little hurt.

The most loss was Master Carver's and William Bradford's, who then lay sick in bed; and if they had not risen with good speed, had been blown up with powder, but, through God's mercy, they had no harm. The house was as full of beds as they could lie one by another, and their muskets were charged, but, blessed be God, there was no harm done. . . .

The 19th day [of January], we resolved to make a Shed to put our common provision in; of which some were already set on shore, but at noon it rained that we could not work. This day, in the evening, John Goodman went abroad to use his lame feet that were pitifully ill with the cold he had got, having a little spaniel with him. A little way from the Plantation, two great wolves ran after the dog. The dog ran to him and betwixt his legs for succor. He had nothing in his hand, but took up a stick and threw at one of them and hit him, and they presently ran both away, but came again. He got a pale board in his hand, and they sat both on their tails grinning at him a good while, and went their way and left him. . . .

Tuesday and Wednesday, 30th and 31st of January, cold frosty weather and sleet, that we could not work. In the morning, the Master and others saw two savages that had been on the island near our ship. What they came for, we could not tell. They were going so far back again before they were descried, that we could not speak with them.

Sunday, the 4th of February, was very wet and rainy with the greatest gusts of wind that ever we had since we came forth, that though we rode in a very good harbor, yet we were in danger because our ship was light, the goods taken out and she unballasted. And it caused much daubing of our houses to fall down.

Friday the 9th, still the cold weather continued that we could do little work. That afternoon, our little house for our sick people was set on fire by a spark that kindled in the roof, but no great harm was done. That evening, the Master, going ashore, killed five geese, which he friendly distributed among the sick people. He found also a good deer killed. The savages had cut off the horns; and a wolf was eating of him. How he came there we could not conceive.

Friday, the 16th day, was a fair day, but the northerly wind continued, which continued the frost. This day, after noon, one of our people being a-fowling and having taken a stand by the creek side in the reeds about a mile and a half from our Plantation, there came by him twelve Indians, marching towards our Plantation, and in the woods he heard the noise of many more. He lay close till they were passed, and then, with what speed he could, he went home and gave the alarm. So the people abroad in the woods returned and armed themselves, but saw none of them. Only toward the evening, they made a great fire about the place where they were first discovered.

Captain Miles Standish and Francis Cook being at work in

the woods, coming home, left their tools behind them, but before they returned, their tools were taken away by the savages. This coming of the savages gave us occasion to keep more strict watch and to make our pieces and furniture[11] ready, which by the moisture and rain were out of temper. Saturday, the 17th day, in the morning, we called a meeting for the establishing of military Orders amongst ourselves, and we chose Miles Standish our Captain, and gave him authority of command in affairs.

And as we were in consultation hereabouts, two savages presented themselves upon the top of a hill over against our Plantation about a quarter of a mile and less, and made signs unto us to come unto them. We likewise made signs unto them to come to us. Whereupon we armed ourselves and stood ready, and sent two over the brook towards them, to wit, Captain Standish and Stephen Hopkins, who went towards them. Only one of them had a musket, which they laid down on the ground in their sight in sign of peace and to parley with them, but the savages would not tarry their coming. A noise of a great many more was heard behind the hill, but no more came in sight. This caused us to plant our great ordnance in places most convenient.

Wednesday, the 21st of February, the Master came on shore with many of his sailors and brought with him one of the great pieces called a Minion[12] and helped us to draw it up the hill, with another piece that lay on shore, and mounted them and a Saker[13] and two Bases.[14] He brought with him a very fat goose to eat with us; and we had a fat crane and a mallard and a dried neat's tongue,[15] and so we were kindly and friendly together.

Saturday, the 3rd of March, the wind was south; the morning, misty; but towards noon, warm and fair weather. The birds sang in the woods most pleasantly. At one of the clock, it thundered, which was the first we heard in that country. It was strong and great claps, but short. But after an hour it rained very sadly till midnight.

Wednesday, the 7th of March, the wind was full east; cold, but fair. That day Master Carver with five others went to the great ponds, which seem to be excellent fishing places. All the way they went they found it exceedingly beaten and haunted with deer, but they saw none. Amongst other fowl, they saw a milk-white fowl with a very black head. This day, some garden seeds were sown.

Friday, the 16th. . . . This morning, we determined to conclude of the military Orders which we had begun to consider of before, but were interrupted by the savages; as we mentioned formerly. And whilst we were busied hereabout, we were interrupted again, for there presented himself a savage,[16] which caused an alarm. He very boldly came all alone and along the houses straight to the rendezvous, where we intercepted him, not suffering him to go in, as undoubtedly he would out of his boldness.

He saluted us in English and bade us "Welcome!" for he had learned some broken English amongst the Englishmen that came to fish at Monhegan,[17] and knew by name the most of the Captains, Commanders, and Masters that usually come. He was a man free in speech, so far as he could express his mind and of a seemly carriage. We questioned him of many things. He was the first savage we could meet withal. He said he was not of these parts but of Morattigon, and one of the Sagamores or Lords thereof; and had been eight months in these parts, it lying hence a day's sail with a great wind and five days by land. He discoursed of the whole country and of every province and of their Sagamores, and their number of men and strength.

The wind beginning to rise a little, we cast a horseman's coat about him, for he was stark naked, only a leather about his waist, with a fringe about a span[18] long or little more. He had a bow and two arrows; the one headed and the other unheaded. He was a tall straight man, the hair of his head black; long behind, only short before; none on his face at all. He asked some beer, but we gave him strong water and biscuit and butter and cheese and pudding and a piece of a mallard, all which he liked well and had been acquainted with such amongst the English. He told us the place where we now live is called Patuxet, and that about four years ago all the inhabitants died of an extraordinary plague; and there is neither man, woman, nor child remaining, as indeed we have found none, so as there is none to hinder our possession or to lay claim unto it.

All the afternoon, we spent in communication with him. We would gladly have been rid of him at night, but he was not willing to go this night. Then we thought to carry him on shipboard, wherewith he was well content and went into the shallop, but the wind was high and the water scant, that it could not return back. We lodged him that night at Stephen Hopkins's house, and watched him. The next day he went away back to the Massasoits,[19] from whence he said he came, who are our next bordering neighbors. They are sixty strong, as he saith.

The Nausets are as near southeast of them and are a hundred strong; and those were they of whom our people were encountered, as we before related. They are much incensed and provoked against the English, and about eight months ago slew three Englishmen, and two more hardly escaped by flight to Monhegan. They were Sir Fernando Gorges's men,[20] as this savage told us. As he did likewise of the *huggerie*, that is, fight, that our discoverers had with the Nausets, and of our tools that were taken out of the woods, which we willed him should be brought again, otherwise we would right ourselves. These people are ill affected towards the English by reason of one Hunt, a Master of a ship, who deceived the people and got them, under color of trucking with them, twenty out of this very place where we inhabit and seven from the Nausets and carried them away, and sold them for slaves for £20 a man; like a wretched man that cares not what mischief he doth for his profit.

Saturday, in the morning, we dismissed the savage and gave him a knife, a bracelet, and a ring. He promised within a night or two to come again and to bring with him some of the Massasoits, our neighbors, with such beavers' skins as they had to truck with us. . . .

On [Sunday] came again the savage, and brought with him five other tall proper men. They had every man a deer's skin on him; and the principal of them had a wild cat's skin, or such like, on the one arm. They had, most of them, long hose up to their groins, close made, and above their groins to their waist, another leather. They were altogether like the Irish trousers. They are of complexion like our English Gypsies, no hair, or very little, on their faces. On their heads, long hair to their shoulders, only cut before; some trussed up before with a feather, broadwise like a fan; another [with a] fox's tail hanging out. These left, according to our charge given him before, their bows and arrows a quarter of a mile from our town.

We gave them entertainment as we thought was fitting them. They did eat liberally of our English victuals. They made semblance unto us of friendship and amity. They sang and danced after their manner like antics.[21] They brought with them in a thing like a bow-case, which the principal of them had about his waist, a little of their corn pounded to powder, which put to a little water, they eat. He had a little tobacco in a bag, but none of them drank[22] but when he listed.[23] Some of them had their faces painted black from the forehead to the chin, four or five fingers broad; others after other fashions as they liked.

They brought three or four skins, but we would not truck at all that day; but wished them to bring more, and we would truck for all, which they promised within a night or two and would leave these behind them, though we were not willing they should. And they brought us all our tools again, which were taken in the woods in our men's absence.

So, because of the day, we dismissed them so soon as we could. But Samoset, our first acquaintance, either was sick or feigned himself so and would not go with them, and stayed with us till Wednesday morning. Then we sent him to them to know the reason they came not according to their words; and we gave him a hat, a pair of stockings and shoes, a shirt, and a piece of cloth to be about his waist.

The Sabbath Day, when we sent them from us, we gave every one of them some trifles, especially the principal of them. We carried[24] them along with our arms to the place where they left their bows and arrows, whereat they were amazed; and two of them began to slink away, but the others called them. When they took their arrows, we bade them farewell; and they were glad. And so, with many thanks given us, they departed, with promise they would come again. . . .

Thursday, the 22nd of March [1621], was a very fair warm day. About noon, we met again about our public business, but we had scarce been an hour together but Samoset came again, and Squanto, the only native of Patuxet, where we now inhabit, who was one of the twenty captives that by Hunt were carried away and had been in England and dwelt in Cornhill [London] with Master John Slany, a Merchant, and could speak a little English, with three others; and they brought with them some few skins to truck and some red herrings newly taken and dried but not salted.

And signified unto us that their great Sagamore Massasoit was hard by with Quadequina his brother and all their men. They could not well express in English what they would, but, after an hour, the King came to the top of a hill over against us and had in his train sixty men, that we could well behold them and they us. We were not willing to send our Governor to them, and they unwilling to come to us. So Squanto went again unto him; who brought word that we should send one to parley with him, which we did, which was Edward Winslow, to know his mind and to signify the mind and will of our Governor, which was to have trading and peace with him. We sent to the King a pair of knives and a copper chain with a jewel to it. To Quadequina we sent likewise a knife and a jewel to hang in his ear. And withal a pot of strong water, a good quantity of biscuit, and some butter, which were all willingly accepted.

Our messenger made a speech unto him that King James saluted him with words of love and peace and did accept of him as his friend and ally; and that our Governor desired to see him, and to truck with him, and to confirm a peace with him as his next neighbor. He liked well of the speech and heard it attentively, though the interpreters did not well express it. After he had eaten and drunk himself and given the rest to his company, he looked upon our messenger's sword and armor which he had on with intimation of his desire to buy it, but, on the other side, our messenger showed his unwillingness to part with it. In the end, he left him in the custody of Quadequina his brother and came over the brook and some twenty men following him, leaving all their bows and arrows behind them. We kept six or seven as hostages for our messenger.

Captain Standish and Master Williamson met the King at the

brook, with half a dozen musketeers. They saluted him, and he them. So on going over, the one on the one side, and the other on the other, conducted him to a house then in building, where we placed a green rug and three or four cushions. Then instantly came our Governor with drum and trumpet after him, and some few musketeers. After salutations, our Governor kissing his hand, the King kissed him, and so they sat down. The Governor called for some strong water and drank to him, and he drank a great draught that made him sweat all the while after. He called for a little fresh meat, which the King did eat willingly and did give his followers.

They then treated of peace, which was:

1. That neither he, nor any of his, should injure, or do hurt, to any of our people.
2. And if any of his did hurt to any of ours, he should send the offender, that we might punish him.
3. That if any of our tools were taken away, when our people were at work, he should cause them to be restored; and if ours did any harm to any of his, we would do the like to them.
4. If any did unjustly war against him, we would aid him. If any did war against us, he should aid us.
5. He should send to his neighboring confederates to certify them of this, that they might not wrong us; but might be likewise comprised in the conditions of Peace.
6. That when their men came to us, they should leave their bows and arrows behind them, as we should do our pieces when we came to them.
7. Lastly, that doing thus, King JAMES would esteem of him as his friend and ally.

All which the King seemed to like well, and it was applauded of his followers. All the while he sat by the Governor, he trembled for fear. In his person, he is a very lusty man in his best years, an able body, grave of countenance, and spare of speech. In his attire, little or nothing differing from the rest of his followers, only in a great chain of white bone beads about his neck; and at it, behind his neck, hangs a little bag of tobacco, which he drank and gave us to drink. His face was painted with a sad[25] red like murrey,[26] and oiled both head and face that he looked greasily. All his followers likewise were in their faces in part or in whole painted; some black, some red, some yellow, and some white; some with crosses and other antic works. Some had skins on them, and some naked; all strong, tall, all men in appearance.

So, after all was done, the Governor conducted him to the brook, and there they embraced each other, and he departed, we diligently keeping our hostages. We expected our messenger's coming, but anon word was brought us that Quadequina was coming, and our messenger was stayed till his return. Who presently came and a troop with him. So likewise we entertained him and conveyed him to the place prepared. He was very fearful of our pieces and made signs of dislike that they should be carried away, whereupon commandment was given that they should be laid away. He was a very proper tall young man of a very modest and seemly countenance, and he did kindly like of our entertainment. So we conveyed him likewise, as we did the King, but divers of their people stayed still. When he was returned, then they dismissed our messenger. Two of his people would have stayed all night, but we would not suffer it.

One thing I forgot. The King had in his bosom, hanging at a string, a great long knife. He marveled much at our trumpet, and some of his men would sound it as well as they could.

Samoset and Squanto, they stayed all night with us; and the King and all his men lay all night in the woods, not above half an English mile from us; and all their wives and women with them. They said that within eight or nine days they would come and set corn on the other side of the brook and dwell there all summer; which is hard by us. That night we kept good watch, but there was no appearance of danger.

The next morning divers of their people came over to us hoping to get some victuals, as we imagined. Some of them told us the King would have some of us come see him. Captain Standish and Isaac Allerton[27] went venturously, who were welcomed of him after their manner. He gave them three or four groundnuts and some tobacco.

We cannot yet conceive but that he is willing to have peace with us. For they have seen our people sometimes alone, two or three, in the woods at work and fowling, when as they offered them no harm, as they might easily have done. And especially because he hath a potent adversary, the Narragansetts,[28] that are at war with him, against whom he thinks we may be some strength to him, for our pieces are terrible unto them. This morning they stayed till ten or eleven of the clock; and our Governor bade them send the King's kettle and filled it full of peas, which pleased them well. And so they went their way.

Friday [the 23rd March,] was a very fair day. Samoset and Squanto still remained with us. Squanto went at noon to fish for eels. At night he came home with as many as he could well lift in one hand; which our people were glad of. They were fat and sweet. He trod them out with his feet; and so caught them with his hands without any other instrument.

This day, we proceeded on with our common business, from which we had been so often hindered by the savages' coming, and concluded both of Military orders and of some Laws and Orders as we thought behoveful for our present estate and condition. And did likewise choose our Governor for this year; which was Master John Carver, a man well approved amongst us.

[THE FIRST THANKSGIVING]

[Since our arrival a year ago] we have built seven dwelling houses, and four for the use of the Plantation, and have made preparation for divers others. We set, last Spring, some twenty acres of Indian corn and sowed some six acres of barley and peas; and, according to the manner of the Indians, we manured our ground with herrings, or rather shads, which we have in great abundance and take with great ease at our doors.

Our corn did prove well, and, God be praised! we had a good increase of Indian corn; and our barley indifferent good; but our peas not worth the gathering; for we feared they were too late sown. They came up very well and blossomed, but the sun parched them in the blossom.

Our harvest being gotten in, our Governor sent four men on fowling, that so we might, after a more special manner, rejoice together after we had gathered the fruit of our labors. They four in one day killed as much fowl as, with a little help besides, served the Company almost a week. At which time, amongst other recreations, we exercised our Arms, many of the Indians coming amongst us.

And, amongst the rest, their greatest King, Massasoit, with some ninety men, whom for three days we entertained and feasted. And they went out and killed five deer, which they brought to the Plantation and bestowed on our Governor, and upon the Captain[1] and others. . . .

We have found the Indians very faithful in their Covenant of Peace with us; very loving and ready to pleasure us. We often go to them; and they come to us. Some of us have been fifty miles by land in the country with them. . . . There is now great peace amongst the Indians themselves, which was not formerly; neither would have been but for us; and we, for our parts, walk as peaceably and safely in the wood as in the highways in England. We entertain them familiarly in our houses; and they, as friendly, bestowing their venison on us. They are a people without any religion,[2] or knowledge of any God, yet very trusty,[3] quick of apprehension, ripe witted, just. . . .

From Edward Winslow,
Good News from New England
(1625)

Edward Winslow (1595–1655), perhaps the most talented of the leaders of the settlement at Plymouth, published this early account of the colony in England, where he had been sent as its agent. At home both in the New World wilderness and in the political and commercial spheres of the Old World, he was a skillful emissary to the Native Americans of New England and a shrewd negotiator with the London speculators who held the debt of the colony. Here he shows us the Pilgrim spirit at its courageous and generous best and at its brutal and self-righteous worst.

[AN ERRAND OF MERCY]

... [In March of 1623] news came to Plymouth that Massa-soit[1] was like to die; and that, at the same time, there was a Dutch ship driven so high on the shore by stress of weather right before his dwelling[2] that, till the tides increased, she could not be got off.

Now it being a commendable manner of the Indians when any, especially of note, are dangerously sick, for all that profess friendship to them to visit them in their extremity; either in their persons, or else to send some acceptable persons to them. Therefore it was thought meet, being a good and warrantable action, that as we had ever professed friendship, so we should now maintain the same by observing this their laudable custom; and the rather because we desired to have some conference with the

Dutch; not knowing when we should have so fit an opportunity.

To that end, myself having formerly been there[3] and understanding in some measure the Dutch tongue; the Governor again laid this service upon myself; and fitted me with some cordials to administer to him, having one, Master John Hampden (a Gentleman of London who then wintered with us and desired much to see the country) for my consort; and Hobbamock[4] for our guide.

So we set forward and lodged the first night at Namasket,[5] where we had friendly entertainment. The next day, about one of the clock, we came to a ferry in Corbitant's country,[6] where, on discharge of my piece, divers Indians came to us from a house not far off. There they told us that Massasoit was dead and that day buried; and that the Dutch would be gone before we could get thither, having hove off their ship already. This news struck us blank, but especially Hobbamock, who desired we might return with all speed.

I told him I would first think of it. Considering now that he being dead Corbitant was the most like to succeed him, and that we were not above three miles from Mattapoisett,[7] his dwelling place, although he were but a hollow-hearted friend towards us, I thought no time so fit as this to enter into more friendly terms with him and the rest of the Sachems round about; hoping, through the blessing of God, it would be a means in that unsettled state to settle their affections towards us.

And though it were somewhat dangerous in respect of our personal safety, because myself and Hobbamock had been employed upon a service against him[8] which he might now fitly revenge, yet esteeming it the best means, leaving the event to God in his mercy, I resolved to put it in practice, if Master Hampden and Hobbamock durst attempt it with me. Whom I found willing to that, or any other course [that] might tend to the general good.

So we went towards Mattapoisett. In the way, Hobbamock, manifesting a troubled spirit, broke forth into these speeches, *Neen womasu Sagimus! Neen womasu Sagimus!* etc., "My loving Sachem! My loving Sachem! Many have I known; but never any like thee!"

And turning him to me, said, whilst I lived, I should never see

his like amongst the Indians; saying [Massasoit] was no liar. He
was not bloody and cruel like other Indians. In anger and passion, he was soon reclaimed; easy to be reconciled towards such
as had offended him; ruled by reason in such measure as he
would not scorn the advice of mean men; and that he governed
his men better with few strokes than others did with many;
truly loving where he loved. Yea, he feared we had not a faithful friend left among the Indians, showing how he ofttimes restrained their malice, etc., continuing a long speech, with such
signs of lamentation and unfeigned sorrow as it would have
made the hardest heart relent.

At length, we came to Mattapoisett and went to the *Sachimo
Comaco*; for so they call the Sachem's place; though they call
an ordinary house *Witeo*. But Corbitant the Sachem was not at
home, but at Pokanoket,[9] which was some five or six miles off.
The Squa[w] Sachem, for so they call the Sachem's wife, gave
us friendly entertainment.

Here we inquired again concerning Massasoit. They thought
him dead but knew no certainty. Whereupon I hired one to go
with all expedition to Pokanoket that we might know the certainty thereof, and withal to acquaint Corbitant with our there
being. About half an hour before sunsetting, the messenger returned and told us that he was not yet dead, though there was no
hope we should find him living. Upon this, we were much revived
and set forward with all speed, though it was late within night ere
we got thither. About two of the clock that afternoon, the Dutchmen departed, so that in that respect our journey was frustrate.

When we came thither, we found the house so full of men as
we could scarce get in, though they used their best diligence to
make way for us. There were they, in the midst of their charms
for him, making such a hellish noise as it distempered us that
were well; and therefore unlike to ease him that was sick.
About him were six or eight women, who chafed his arms, legs,
and thighs to keep heat in him.

When they had made an end of their charming, one told him
that his friends the English were come to see him. Having understanding left, but his sight was wholly gone; he asked, "Who
was come?"

They told him, "Winsnow." For they cannot pronounce the letter *l*, but ordinarily *n* in the place thereof.

He desired to speak with me. When I came to him and they told him of it; he put forth his hand to me, which I took. Then he said twice, though very inwardly, *Keen Winsnow?* which is to say, "Art thou Winslow?" I answered, *Ahhe*; that is, "Yes." Then he doubled[10] these words, *Malta neen wonckanet namen Winsnow!* that is to say, "Oh Winslow, I shall never see thee again."

Then I called Hobbamock and desired him to tell Massasoit that the Governor, hearing of his sickness, was sorry for the same; and though by reason of many businesses he could not come himself; yet he sent me with such things for him as he thought most likely to do him good in this his extremity. And whereof, if he pleased to take, I would presently give him.

Which he desired. And having a confection of many comfortable conserves,[11] etc., on the point of my knife, I gave him some; which I could scarce get through his teeth. When it was dissolved in his mouth, he swallowed the juice of it, whereat those that were about him much rejoiced; saying he had not swallowed anything in two days before.

Then I desired to see his mouth, which was exceedingly furred; and his tongue swelled in such a manner as it was not possible for him to eat such meat as they had, his passage being stopped up. Then I washed his mouth and scraped his tongue; and got abundance of corruption out of the same. After which I gave him more of the confection, which he swallowed with more readiness. Then he desiring to drink, I dissolved some of it in water and gave him thereof. Within half an hour, this wrought a great alteration in him in the eyes of all that beheld him. Presently after, his sight began to come to him, which gave him and us good encouragement.

In the meantime, I inquired how he slept; and when he went to the stool? They said he slept not in two days before and had not had a stool in five. Then I gave him more and told him of a mishap we had, by the way, in breaking a bottle of drink which the Governor also sent him, saying if he would send any of his men to Patuxet,[12] I would send for more of the same; also for chickens to make him broth and for other things which I knew were good for him, and would stay[13] the return of the messenger, if he desired.

This he took marvelous kindly and appointed some, who were ready to go by two of the clock in the morning, against which time I made ready a letter, declaring therein our good success, the state of his body, etc., desiring to send me such things as I sent for, and such physic as the Surgeon durst administer to him.

He requested me that the day following I would take my piece and kill some fowl, and make him some English pottage[14] such as he had eaten at Plymouth, which I promised. After his stomach coming to him,[15] I must needs make him some without fowl, before I went abroad. Which somewhat troubled me, being unaccustomed and unacquainted in such businesses; especially having nothing to make it comfortable, my consort being as ignorant as myself. But being we must do somewhat, I caused a woman to bruise some corn and take the flour from it; and we set the groats, or broken corn, in a pipkin, for they have earthen pots of all sizes.

When the day broke, we went out, it being now March, to seek herbs, but could not find any but strawberry leaves, of which I gathered a handful and put in the same. And because I had nothing to relish it, I went forth again and pulled up a sassafras root, and sliced a piece thereof, and boiled it till it had a good relish, and then took it out again. The broth being boiled, I strained it through my handkerchief and gave him at least a pint, which he drank and liked it very well. After this, his sight mended more and more. Also he had three moderate stools and took some rest. Insomuch as we with admiration blessed God for giving his blessing to such raw and ignorant means, making no doubt of his recovery; himself and all of them acknowledging us the Instruments of his preservation.

The morning he caused me to spend in going from one to another amongst those that were sick in the town, requesting me to wash their mouths also, and give to each of them some of the same I gave him, saying they were good folk. This pains I took with willingness; though it were much offensive to me, not being accustomed with such poisonous savors.

After dinner, he desired me to get him a goose or duck and make him some pottage therewith with as much speed as I could. So I took a man with me and made a shot at a couple of ducks some six score paces off, and killed one, at which he wondered. So we returned forthwith and dressed it, making more broth therewith, which he much desired. Never did I see a man so low brought recover in that measure in so short a time.

The fowl being extraordinary fat, I told Hobbamock I must take off the top thereof,[16] saying it would make him very sick again, if he did eat it. This he acquainted Massasoit therewith, who would not be persuaded to it, though I pressed it very much, showing the strength thereof and the weakness of his stomach, which could not possibly bear it. Notwithstanding he made a gross meal of it and ate as much as would well have satisfied a man in health. About an hour after, he began to be very sick, and straining very much, cast up the broth again; and in overstraining himself, began to bleed at the nose and so continued the space of four hours. Then they all wished he had been ruled, concluding now he would die, which we much feared also. They asked me what I thought of him? I answered [that] his case was desperate, yet it might be it would save his life. For if it ceased in time, he would forthwith sleep and take rest, which was the principal thing he wanted. Not long after, his blood stayed,[17] and he slept at least six or eight hours.

When he awaked, I washed his face and bathed and suppled his beard and nose with a linen cloth. But on a sudden he chopped[18] his nose in the water and drew up some therein and sent it forth with such violence as he began to bleed afresh. Then they thought there was no hope, but we perceived it was but the tenderness of his nostril, and therefore told them I thought it would stay presently, as indeed it did.

The messengers were now returned. But finding his stomach come to him, he would not have the chickens killed, but kept them for breed. Neither durst we give him any physic which was then sent; because his body was so much altered since our instructions. Neither saw we any need, not doubting now of his recovery, if he were careful.

Many whilst we were there came to see him, some, by their

report, from a place not less than a hundred miles. To all that came, one of his chief men related the manner of his sickness; how near he was spent; how, amongst others, his friends the English came to see him; and how suddenly they recovered him to this strength they saw, he being now able to sit upright of himself.

The day before our coming another Sachem, being there, told him that now he might see how hollow-hearted the English were, saying if we had been such friends in deed as we were in show, we would have visited him in this his sickness. Using many arguments to withdraw his affections and to persuade him to give way to some things against us which were motioned[19] to him not long before.

But upon this his recovery, he broke forth into these speeches: "Now I see the English are my friends and love me; and whilst I live, I will never forget this kindness they have showed me."

Whilst we were there, our entertainment exceeded all other strangers'.

Divers other things were worth the noting, but I fear I have been too tedious.

[A PILGRIM ATROCITY]

At our coming away [from Massasoit], he called Hobbamock to him, and privately (none hearing save two or three of his *Pnieses*,[1] who are of his Council) revealed the plot of the Massachusetts[2] . . . against Master Weston's Colony,[3] and so against us, . . . saying that [a number of nearby Native peoples] were joined with them. Himself also in his sickness was earnestly solicited, but he would neither join therein, nor give way to any of his. Therefore (as we respected the lives of our countrymen and our own after-safety) he advised us to kill the men of Massachusetts, who were the authors of this intended mischief.

And whereas we were wont to say we would not strike a stroke till they first began, if, said he, upon this intelligence they [at Plymouth] make this answer, tell them when their countrymen at Wessagussett are killed, they being not able to defend themselves, that then it will be too late to recover their lives. Nay, through the multitude of adversaries, they shall with great difficulty preserve their own. And therefore he counseled without delay to take away the principals, and then the plot would cease. With this, he charged [Hobbamock] thoroughly to acquaint me by the way, that I might inform the Governor thereof at my first coming home. . . .

[Miles Standish was sent to defeat the plot, and] being now come to the Massachusetts went first to the ship[4] but found neither man, nor so much as a dog therein. Upon the discharge of a musket; the Master [of the *Swan*] and some others of the Plantation showed themselves, who were on shore gathering groundnuts and getting other food. After salutation, Captain Standish asked them how they durst so leave the ship and live in such security.

Who answered like men senseless of their own misery [that] they feared not the Indians, but lived and suffered them to lodge with them; not having sword or gun, or needing the same. To which the Captain answered, if there were no cause, he was the gladder. But upon further inquiry understanding that those in whom John Sanders[5] had received most special confidence and left in his stead to govern the rest were at the Plantation, thither he went.

And, to be brief, made known the Indians' purpose and the end of his own coming, as also . . . that if afterward they durst not there stay, it was the intendment of the Governors and People of Plymouth there to receive them till they could be better provided; but if they conceived of any other course that might be more likely for their good, that himself should further them therein to the uttermost of his power.

These men, comparing other circumstances with that they now heard, answered they could expect no better, and it was God's mercy that they were not killed before his coming; desiring therefore that he would neglect no opportunity to proceed.

Hereupon he advised them to secrecy, yet withal to send special command to [the] one third of their Company that were farthest off to come home, and there enjoined them, on pain of death, to keep the town, himself allowing them a pint of Indian corn to a man for a day, though that store he had was spared out of our seed.

The weather proving very wet and stormy, it was the longer before he could do anything. In the meantime an Indian came to him and brought some furs, but rather to gather what he could from the Captain's [proceedings] than coming then for trade. And though the Captain carried things as smoothly as he possibly could, yet at his return he reported he saw by his eyes that he was angry in his heart, and therefore [they] began to suspect themselves discovered. This caused one Pecksuot, who was a *Pniese*, being a man of a notable spirit, to come to Hobbamock, who was then with them, and told him he understood that the Captain was come to kill himself and the rest of the savages there. "Tell him," said he, "we know it, but fear him not, neither will we shun him. But let him begin when he dare; he shall not take us at unawares."

Many times after, divers of them severally or a few together came to the Plantation to him, where they would whet and sharpen the points of their knives before his face and use many other insulting gestures and speeches. Amongst the rest, Wituwamat bragged of the excellency of his knife; on the end of the handle there was pictured a woman's face. "But," said he, "I have another at home wherewith I have killed both French and English, and that hath a man's face on it; and by and by these two must marry." Further, he said of that knife he there had, *Hinnaim namen, hinnaim michen, matta cuts,* that is to say, "By and by it should see; and by and by it should eat, but not speak."

Also Pecksuot, being a man of greater stature than the Captain, told him [that] though he were a great Captain, yet he was but a little man. And, said he, "Though I be no Sachem; yet I am a man of great strength and courage." These things the Captain observed, yet bore with patience for the present.

On the next day, seeing he could not get many of them together at once; and this Pecksuot and Wituwamat [being] both together with another man and a youth of some eighteen years of age, which was brother to Wituwamat and villain-like trod in his steps, daily putting many tricks upon the weaker sort of

[English]men; and having about as many of his own Company in a room with them [Standish] gave the word to his men.

And the door being fast shut, [he] began himself with Pecksuot; and snatching [Pecksuot's] own knife from his neck, though with much struggling, killed him therewith; the point whereof he had made as sharp as a needle, and ground the back also to an edge. Wituwamat and the other man, the rest killed and took the youth, whom the Captain caused to be hanged. But it is incredible how many wounds these two *Pnieses* received before they died, not making any fearful noise, but catching at their weapons and striving to the last.

Hobbamock stood by all this time as a spectator and meddled not, observing how our men demeaned themselves in this action. All being here ended, smiling he broke forth into these speeches to the Captain: "Yesterday Pecksuot, bragging of his own strength and stature, said [that] though you were a great Captain; yet you were but a little man. But today, I see you are big enough to lay him on the ground."

But to proceed. There being some women [there] at the same time, Captain Standish left them in the custody of Master Weston's people at the town [of Wessagussett] and sent word to another Company that had intelligence of things to kill those Indian men that were amongst them. These killed two more.

Himself also with some of his own men went to another place, where they killed another; and, through the negligence of one man, an Indian escaped, who discovered and crossed[6] their proceedings. . . .

Captain Standish took the one half of his men and one or two of Master Weston's and Hobbamock, still seeking to make spoil of them and theirs. At length, they espied a file of Indians, which made towards them amain. And there being a small advantage in the ground by reason of a hill near them; both companies strove for it. Captain Standish got it. Whereupon they retreated and took each man his tree, letting fly their arrows amain, especially at himself and Hobbamock. Whereupon Hobbamock cast off his coat; and being a known *Pniese*, theirs being now killed, chased them so fast as our people were not able to hold way with him. Insomuch as our men could have but one certain mark, and then but the arm and half face of a notable villain as he drew at Captain Standish. Who, together with another, both discharged [their muskets] at once at him, and broke his arm. Whereupon [the Indians] fled into a swamp.

When they were in the thicket, they parleyed, but to small purpose, getting nothing but foul language. So our Captain dared the Sachem to come out and fight like a man, showing how base and womanlike he was in tonguing it as he did. But he refused and fled.

So the Captain returned to the Plantation [at Wessagussett], where he released the women, and would not take their beaver coats from them, nor suffer the least discourtesy to be offered them. Now were Master Weston's men resolved to leave their Plantation, and go for Monhegan, hoping to get passage and return [to England] with the fishing ships.

The Captain told them that for his own part he durst there live with fewer men than they were; yet since they were otherwise minded, according to his order from the Governors and People of Plymouth he would help them with corn competent for their provision by the way. Which he did, scarce leaving himself more than brought them home. Some of them disliked the choice of the body to go to Monhegan; and therefore desiring to go with him to Plymouth, he took them into the shallop.

And seeing them set sail [for Monhegan], and clear of the Massachusetts Bay, he took leave and returned to Plymouth, whither he came in safety, blessed be God! and brought the head of Wituwamat with him.

From Thomas Morton,
New English Canaan,
The Third Book (1632)

Thomas Morton (1576?–1647?) is chiefly known to students of American history and literature as the antithesis of the Pilgrims of Plymouth and the Puritans of Massachusetts Bay. To their piety, discipline, and sobriety, he opposed a pagan delight in revelry and self-indulgence. They expressed themselves in the "plain style," a simple and direct form of writing whose only embroidery is its steady reference to the events and phrasing of the Bible; Morton customarily writes in a fantastic style, charged with word-play and classical allusion in a mannered display of wit and learning. They are instruments of the Reformation; he is a child of the Renaissance. But the argument can be made that Morton was more significantly the first Englishman to view the American wilderness as the locus of freedom and joy rather than as a wasteland to be redeemed through hardship and toil. Three times he came to New England, where, in old age still an avid hunter, he died. Here in four brief chapters from his only book, the New English Canaan, *he gives his version of the massacre at Wessagussett in 1623 together with a mock-heroic account of his own encounter with the Pilgrim Fathers in 1628.*

CHAPTER 5

Of a Massacre made upon the Savages
at Wessagussett.[1]

. . . Some of the plantation [at Wessagussett], about three persons, went to live with [Obtakiest][2] and his company, and had very good quarter. . . . There they purposed to stay until Master Weston's arrival, but the Plymouth men intending no good to him (as appeared by the consequence) came in the mean time to Wessagussett, and there pretended to feast the Savages of those parts, bringing with them Pork and things for the purpose, which they set before the Savages. They ate thereof without suspicion of any mischief, who were taken upon a watchword given, and with their own knives (hanging about their necks) were by the Plymouth planters stabbed and slain, one of which were hanged up there, after the slaughter.

In the meantime the Sachem had knowledge of this accident by one that ran to his Countrymen at the Massachusetts,[3] and gave them intelligence of the news; after which time the Savages there consulting of the matter, in the night (when the other English, fearless of danger, were asleep) knocked them all in the head in revenge of the death of their Countrymen. But if the Plymouth Planters had really intended good to Master Weston, or those men, why had they not kept the Savages alive in Custody, until they had secured the other English? Who by means of this evil managing of the business lost their lives and the whole plantation was dissolved thereupon, as was likely for fear of a revenge to follow, as a relation to[4] this cruel antecedent. And when Master Weston came over, he found things at an evil exigent[5] by means thereof, but could not tell how it was brought about.

The Savages of the Massachusetts that could not imagine from whence these men should come or to what end, seeing them perform such unexpected actions, neither could tell by what name properly to distinguish them, did from that time afterwards call the English Planters *Wotawquenange*, which in their language signifieth "stabbers" or "Cutthroats," and this name was received by those that came thereafter for good, being then unacquainted with the signification of it, for many years following, until from a Southerly Indian that understood English well, I was by demonstration made to conceive the interpretation of it and rebuked these other, that it was not forborne. The other calling us by the name of *Wotoquansawge*, what that doth signify he said he was not able by any demonstration to express, and my neighbors durst no more in my hearing call us by the name formerly used, for fear of my displeasure.

CHAPTER 14

Of the Revels of New Canaan

The Inhabitants of Passonagessit[1] (having translated the name of their habitation from that ancient Savage name to Ma-re Mount;[2] and being resolved to have the new name confirmed for a memorial to after ages) did devise amongst themselves to have it performed in a solemn manner with Revels and merriment after the old English custom, prepared to set up a Maypole upon the festival day of Philip and [James];[3] and therefore brewed a barrel of excellent beer and provided a case of bottles to be spent, with other good cheer, for all comers of that day. And because they would have it in a complete form, they had prepared a song fitting to the time and present occasion.

And upon May Day they brought the Maypole to the place appointed, with drums, guns, pistols, and other fitting instruments, for that purpose; and there erected it with the help of Savages that came thither of purpose to see the manner of our Revels. A goodly pine tree of eighty foot long was reared up, with a pair of buck's horns nailed on somewhat near unto the top of it, where it stood as a fair sea mark for directions how to find out the way to mine Host of Ma-re Mount.[4] . . .

The setting up of his Maypole was a lamentable spectacle to the precise separatists[5] that lived at new Plymouth. They termed it an Idol; yea they called it the Calf of Horeb,[6] and stood at defiance with the place, naming it Mount Dagon;[7] threatening to make it a woeful mount and not a merry mount. . . .

There was likewise a merry song made, which (to make their Revels more fashionable) was sung with a Chorus, every man bearing his part; which they performed in a dance hand in hand about the Maypole, while one of the Company sung and filled out the good liquor like Ganymede[8] and Jupiter.

THE SONG

Drink and be merry, merry, merry boys
Let all your delight be in Hymen's joys,
Io to Hymen[9] now the day is come,
About the merry Maypole take a Room.
Make green garlands, bring bottles out;
And fill sweet Nectar, freely about,
Uncover thy head, and fear no harm,
For here's good liquor to keep it warm.
Then drink and be merry, etc.
Io to Hymen, etc.
Nectar is a thing assign'd,
By the Deities' own mind,
To cure the heart oppressed with grief,
And of good liquors is the chief
Then drink, etc.
Io to Hymen, etc.
Give to the Melancholy man,
A cup or two oft now and then;
This physic will soon revive his blood,
And make him be of a merrier mood.
Then drink, etc.
Io to Hymen, etc.
Give to the Nymph that's free from scorn,
No Irish stuff nor Scotch[10] overworn,
Lasses in beaver coats come away,
Ye shall be welcome to us night and day.
To drink and be merry, etc.
Io to Hymen, etc.

This harmless mirth made by young men (that lived in hope
to have wives brought over to them, that would save them a labor to make a voyage to fetch any over) was much distasted of
the precise Separatists that keep much ado about the tithe of
Mint and Cummin;[11] troubling their brains more than reason
would require about things that are indifferent; and from that
time sought occasion against my honest Host of Ma-re Mount

to overthrow his undertakings, and to destroy his plantation quite and clean. . . .

CHAPTER 15

*Of a great Monster supposed to be at Ma-re Mount
and the preparation made to destroy it.*

The Separatists envying the prosperity and hope of the Plantation at Ma-re Mount (which they perceived began to come forward, and to be in a good way for gain in the Beaver trade) conspired together against mine Host especially (who was the owner of that Plantation), and made up a party against him, and mustered up what aid they could, accounting of him as of a great Monster.

Many threatening speeches were given out both against his person and his Habitation, which they divulged should be consumed with fire. And taking advantage of the time when his company (which seemed little to regard their threats) were gone up into the Inlands to trade with the Savages for Beaver.

They set upon my honest host at a place called Wessagussett, where (by accident) they found him. The inhabitants there were in good hope of the subversion of the plantation at Ma-re Mount (which they principally aimed at), and the rather, because mine host was a man that endeavored to advance the dignity of the Church of England, which they (on the contrary part) would labor to vilify with uncivil terms, inveighing against the sacred book of common prayer, and mine host that used it in a laudable manner amongst his family, as a practice of piety.

There he would be a means to bring sacks to their mill (such is the thirst after Beaver) and help the conspirators too. [They] surprise[d] mine host (who was there all alone), and they charged him (because they would seem to have some reasonable cause against him, to set a gloss upon their malice) with criminal things which indeed had been done by such a person but was of their conspiracy. Mine host demanded of the conspirators who it was that was author of that information that seemed to be their ground for what they now intended. And because they answered they would not tell him, he as peremptorily replied, that he would not stay, whether he had, or he had not done as they had been informed.

The answer made no matter (as it seemed) whether it had been negatively or affirmatively made, for they had resolved what he should suffer, because (as they boasted) they were now become the greater number. They had shaken off their shackles of servitude, and were become Masters, and masterless people.

It appears they were like bears' whelps in former time, when mine host's plantation was of as much strength as theirs, but now (theirs being stronger) they (like overgrown bears) seemed monstrous. In brief, mine host must endure to be their prisoner, until they could contrive it so that they might send him for England (as they said), there to suffer according to the merit of the fact, which they intended to father upon him, supposing (belike) it would prove a heinous crime.

Much rejoicing was made that they had gotten their capital enemy (as they concluded him), whom they purposed to hamper in such sort that he should not be able to uphold his plantation at Ma-re Mount. The Conspirators sported themselves at my honest host that meant them no hurt; and were so jocund that they feasted their bodies, and fell to tippling, as if they had obtained a great prize; like the Trojans when they had the custody of Hippeus's pine-tree horse.[1]

Mine host feigned grief, and could not be persuaded either to eat or drink, because he knew emptiness would be a means to make him as watchful as the Geese kept in the Roman Capital,[2] whereon the contrary part, the conspirators would be so drowsy that he might have an opportunity to give them a slip, instead of a tester.[3] Six persons of the conspiracy were set to watch him at Wessagussett. But he kept waking; and in the dead of night (one lying on the bed for further surety), up gets mine Host and got to the second door that he was to pass, which (notwithstanding the lock) he got open and shut it after him with such violence that it affrighted some of the conspirators.

The word, which was given with an alarm, was, "Oh, he's gone, he's gone, what shall we do, he's gone?" The rest (half

asleep) start up in a maze and, like rams, ran their heads one
at another full butt in the dark. Their grand leader Captain
Shrimp[4] took on furiously, and tore his clothes for anger to see
the empty nest, and their bird gone. The rest were eager to have
torn their hair from their heads, but it was so short[5] that it
would give them no hold. Now Captain Shrimp thought in the
loss of this prize (which he accounted his Masterpiece) all his
honor would be lost forever.

In the meantime mine Host was got home to Ma-re Mount
through the woods, eight miles, round about the head of the
river Monatoquit[6] that parted the two Plantations, finding his
way by the help of the lightning (for it thundered as he went
terribly) and there he prepared powder three pounds dried for
his present employment, and four good guns for him and the
two assistants left at his house, with bullets of several sizes
three hundred, or thereabouts, to be used if the conspirators
should pursue him thither. And these two persons promised
their aids in the quarrel and confirmed that promise with a
health in good rosa solis.[7]

Now Captain Shrimp, the first Captain in the Land (as he
supposed), must do some new act to repair this loss, and to vin-
dicate his reputation, who had sustained blemish by this over-
sight. Begins now to study how to repair or survive his honor in
this manner; calling of Council, they conclude.[8]

He takes eight persons more to him, and (like the nine Worthies[9] of New Canaan) they embark with preparation against
Ma-re Mount, where this Monster of a man (as their phrase
was) had his den; the whole number (had the rest not been from
home, being but seven) would have given Captain Shrimp (a
quondam Drummer) such a welcome, as would have made him
wish for a Drum as big as Diogenes's tub,[10] that he might have
crept into it out of sight.

Now the nine Worthies are approached; and mine Host prepared, having intelligence by a Savage, that hastened in love from
Wessagussett to give him notice of their intent. One of mine Host's
men proved a craven; the other had proved his wits to purchase a
little valor, before mine Host had observed his posture. The nine
worthies coming before the Den of this supposed Monster (this

seven headed hydra,[11] as they termed him) and began like Don
Quixote against the Windmill to beat a par[le]y,[12] and to offer
quarter (if mine Host would yield) for they resolved to send him
for England, and bade him lay by his arms.

But he (who was the Son of a Soldier) having taken up arms
in his just defense, replied that he would not lay by those arms,
because they were so needful at Sea, if he should be sent over.
Yet to save the effusion of so much worthy blood as would have
issued out of the veins of these nine worthies of New Canaan, if
mine Host should have played upon them out at his portholes
(for they came within danger like a flock of wild geese, as if
they had been tailed one to another, as colts to be sold at a fair)
mine Host was content to yield upon quarter; and did capitu-
late with them in what manner it should be for more certainty,
because he knew what Captain Shrimp was.

He expressed that no violence should be offered to his person, none to his goods, nor any of his Household, but that he
should have his arms, and what else was requisite for the voyage, which, their Herald returns, it was agreed upon and should
be performed.

But mine Host no sooner had set open the door and issued
out, but instantly Captain Shrimp, and the rest of the worthies
stepped to him, laid hold of his arms; and had him down, and
so eagerly was every man bent against him (not regarding any
agreement made with such a carnal man) that they fell upon
him, as if they would have eaten him. Some of them were so violent that they would have a slice with scabbard and all for
haste, until an old Soldier (of the Queen's as the Proverb is) that
was there by accident clapped his gun under the weapons, and
sharply rebuked these worthies for their unworthy practices. So
the matter was taken into more deliberate consideration.

Captain Shrimp and the rest of the nine worthies made themselves (by this outrageous riot) Masters of mine Host of Ma-re
Mount, and disposed of what he had at his plantation. This
they knew (in the eye of the Savages) would add to their glory;
and diminish the reputation of mine honest Host, whom they
practiced to be rid of upon any terms, as willingly as if he had
been the very Hydra of the time.

CHAPTER 16

*How the nine worthies put mine Host of Ma-re Mount
into the enchanted Castle at Plymouth, and terrified
him with the Monster Briareus.[1]*

The nine Worthies of New Canaan having now the Law in
their own hands, there being no general Governor in the Land,
nor none of the Separation that regarded the duty they owe
their Sovereign, whose natural born Subjects they were; though
translated out of Holland from whence they had learned to
work all to their own ends and make a great show of Religion
but no humanity, for they were now to sit in Council on the
cause.

And much it stood mine honest Host upon to be very cir-
cumspect, and to take Aeacus[2] to task, for that his voice was
more allowed of than both the other; and had not mine Host
confounded all the arguments that Aeacus could make in their
defense and confuted him that swayed the rest, they would have
made him unable to drink in such manner of merriment any
more. So that following this private counsel given him by one
that knew who ruled the roost, the Hurricane ceased that else
would split his pinnace.[3]

A conclusion was made, and sentence given, that mine Host
should be sent to England a prisoner. But when he was brought
to the ships for that purpose, no man durst be so foolhardy as
to undertake [to] carry him. So these Worthies set mine Host
upon an Island without gun, powder, or shot, or dog, or so much
as a knife, to get thing to feed upon or any other clothes to shelter him with at winter than a thin suit which he had on at that
time. Home he could not get to Ma-re Mount upon this Island.
He stayed a month at least, and was relieved by the Savages that
took notice that mine Host was a Sachem of Passonagessit, and
would bring bottles of strong liquor to him, and unite themselves into a league of brotherhood with mine Host; so full of
humanity are these infidels before these Christians.

From this place for England, sailed mine Host in a Plymouth
ship[4] (that came into the Land to fish upon the Coast) that

landed him safe in England at Plymouth, and he stayed in England until the ordinary time for shipping to set forth for these parts; and then returned, no man being able to tax[5] him of anything.

But the Worthies (in the meantime) hoped they had been rid of him.

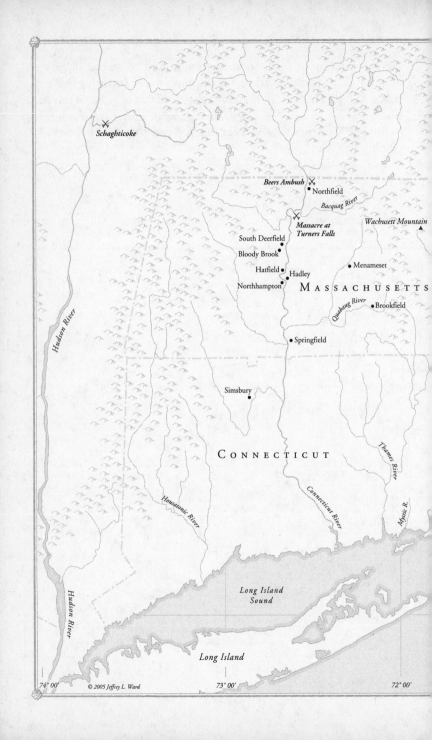

Schaghticoke

Beers Ambush
Northfield
Bacquag River

Massacre at
Turners Falls
Wachusett Mountain ▲

South Deerfield

Bloody Brook

Hatfield • • Hadley
Northhampton •
M A S S A C H U S E T T S

Menameset •

Quabaug River • Brookfield

• Springfield

Hudson River

Simsbury •

C O N N E C T I C U T

Thames River

Housatonic River

Connecticut River

Mystic R.

*Long Island
Sound*

Hudson River

Long Island

74° 00'   © 2005 Jeffrey L. Ward   73° 00'   72° 00'

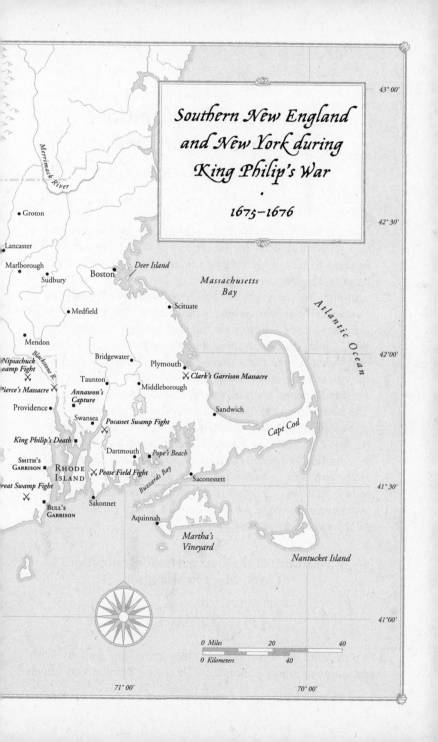

Southern New England
and New York during
King Philip's War

·

1675–1676

43° 00'

42° 30'

42° 00'

41° 30'

41° 00'

Merrimack River

· Groton

Lancaster ·

Marlborough ·

· Sudbury

Boston ·

Deer Island

*Massachusetts
Bay*

· Medfield

· Scituate

Atlantic Ocean

· Mendon

Bridgewater ·

Plymouth ·

✕ *Clark's Garrison Massacre*

*Nipsachuck
Swamp Fight* ✕

Taunton ·

Middleborough ·

Pierce's Massacre ✕

*Annawon's
Capture* ■

Blackstone R.

Providence ·

Swansea ·

✕ *Pocasset Swamp Fight*

Sandwich ·

Cape Cod

King Philip's Death ■

Dartmouth ·

Pope's Beach ■

SMITH'S
GARRISON ■

RHODE
ISLAND

✕ *Pease Field Fight*

Buzzards Bay

Saconessett ·

Great Swamp Fight
✕

■ BULL'S
GARRISON

Sakonnet ·

Aquinnah ·

*Martha's
Vineyard*

Nantucket Island

0 Miles   20   40

0 Kilometers   40

71° 00'

70° 00'

From Mary Rowlandson, *The Sovereignty and Goodness of God*, 1682

Mary White Rowlandson (c.1637–1711), born in England two generations after the passengers of the Mayflower, *was brought to New England as an infant. In 1653 she and her parents joined the new settlement of Lancaster on the Massachusetts frontier, where, three years later, she married Lancaster's minister, Joseph Rowlandson. On the 10th of February, 1676, during the final throes of King Philip's War, Lancaster was attacked by a powerful force of Natives that overwhelmed the settlement's defenses, killed most of its inhabitants, and carried off twenty-four survivors, including Rowlandson and her three children, as captives.*

The Sovereignty and Goodness of God is her account of that ordeal. Framed in the Calvinist idiom of her culture, the little book presents an intimate and powerful depiction of personal experience in the darkest days of New England. It is the first and in many ways the most compelling of the many captivity narratives that for the next two hundred years were to shape white America's image of the Native peoples it was dispossessing.

A Narrative of the Captivity and Restoration of Mrs. Mary Rowlandson

[THE ATTACK]

On the tenth of February, 167[6], came the Indians with great numbers upon Lancaster.[1] Their first coming was about

Sun-rising. Hearing the noise of some Guns, we looked out; several Houses were burning and the Smoke ascending to Heaven. There were five persons taken in one house. The Father and the Mother and a sucking Child they knocked on the head; the other two they took and carried away alive. There were two others who, being out of their Garrison[2] upon some occasion, were set upon; one was knocked on the head, the other escaped. Another there was who running along was shot and wounded and fell down. He begged of them his life, promising them Money (as they told me), but they would not hearken to him but knocked him in head, and stripped him naked, and split open his Bowels. Another, seeing many of the Indians about his Barn, ventured and went out but was quickly shot down. There were three others belonging to the same Garrison who were killed. The Indians, getting up upon the roof of the Barn, had advantage to shoot down upon them over their Fortification. Thus these murderous wretches went on burning and destroying before them.

At length they came and beset our own house, and quickly it was the dolefullest day that ever mine eyes saw. The House stood upon the edge of a hill; some of the Indians got behind the hill, others into the Barn, and others behind anything that could shelter them; from all which places they shot against the House, so that the Bullets seemed to fly like hail; and quickly they wounded one man among us, then another, and then a third. About two hours (according to my observation in that amazing time) they had been about the house before they prevailed to fire it, which they did with Flax and Hemp which they brought out of the Barn, and there being no defense about the House, only two Flankers[3] at two opposite corners and one of them not finished. They fired it once and one ventured out and quenched it, but they quickly fired it again, and that took.

Now is the dreadful hour come that I have often heard of (in time of War, as it was the case of others) but now mine eyes see it. Some in our house were fighting for their lives, others wallowing in their blood, the House on fire over our heads, and the bloody Heathen ready to knock us on the head if we stirred out. Now might we hear Mothers and Children crying out for themselves and one another, "Lord, what shall we do?" Then I took my Children (and one of my sisters, hers) to go forth and leave the house, but as soon as we came to the door and appeared, the Indians shot so thick that the bullets rattled against the House, as if one had taken an handful of stones and threw them, so that we were fain to give back. We had six stout Dogs belonging to our Garrison, but none of them would stir, though another time, if any Indian had come to the door, they were ready to fly upon him and tear him down. The Lord hereby would make us the more to acknowledge his hand, and to see that our help is always in him.

But out we must go, the fire increasing and coming along behind us roaring, and the Indians gaping before us with their Guns, Spears, and Hatchets to devour us. No sooner were we out of the House, but my Brother-in-Law (being before wounded in defending the house in or near the throat) fell down dead, whereat the Indians scornfully shouted and hallooed, and were presently upon him, stripping off his clothes. The bullets flying thick, one went through my side, and the same (as would seem) through the bowels and hand of my dear Child in my arms. One of my elder Sister's Children named William had then his Leg broken, which the Indians perceiving, they knocked him on head.

Thus were we butchered by those merciless Heathen, standing amazed with the blood running down to our heels. My eldest Sister, being yet in the House and seeing those woeful sights, the Infidels hauling Mothers one way and Children another, and some wallowing in their blood, and her elder Son telling her that her Son William was dead and myself was wounded, she said, "And, Lord, let me die with them," which was no sooner said but she was struck with a Bullet and fell down dead over the threshold. . . . The Indians laid hold of us, pulling me one way, and the Children another, and said, "Come, go along with us." I told them they would kill me; they answered [that] if I were willing to go along with them, they would not hurt me.

Oh, the doleful sight that now was to behold at this House! . . . Of thirty seven persons who were in this one House, none escaped either present death or a bitter captivity, save only one, who might say as he (Job 1:15), "And I only am escaped alone to tell the News." There were twelve killed, some shot, some stabbed with their Spears, some knocked down with their Hatchets. When we are in prosperity, Oh, the little that we think of such dreadful sights, and to see our dear Friends, and Relations lie bleeding out their heart-blood upon the ground. There was one who was chopped into the head with a Hatchet and stripped naked, and yet was crawling up and down. It is a solemn sight to see so many Christians lying in their blood, some here, and some there, like a company of Sheep torn by Wolves, all of them stripped naked by a company of hell-hounds, roaring, singing, ranting, and insulting, as if they would have torn our very hearts out; yet the Lord by his Almighty power preserved a number of us from death, for there were twenty-four of us taken alive and carried Captive.

I had often before this said that if the Indians should come, I should choose rather to be killed by them than taken alive, but when it came to the trial, my mind changed. Their glittering weapons so daunted my spirit, that I chose rather to go along with those (as I may say) ravenous Beasts, than that moment to end my days. And that I may the better declare what happened to me during that grievous Captivity, I shall particularly speak of the several Removes[4] we had up and down the Wilderness.

THE FIRST REMOVE

Now away we must go with those Barbarous Creatures, with our bodies wounded and bleeding, and our hearts no less than our bodies. About a mile we went that night, up upon a hill within sight of the Town, where they intended to lodge. There was hard by a vacant house (deserted by the English before, for fear of the Indians). I asked them whether I might not lodge in the house that night to which they answered, "What, will you love Englishmen still?" This was the dolefullest night that ever my eyes saw. Oh, the roaring and singing and dancing and yelling of those black creatures in the night, which made the place a lively resemblance of hell. And as miserable was the waste that was there made of Horses, Cattle, Sheep, Swine, Calves, Lambs, Roasting Pigs, and Fowl (which they had plundered in the Town), some roasting, some lying and burning, and some boiling to feed our merciless Enemies; who were joyful enough though we were disconsolate.

To add to the dolefulness of the former day and the dismalness of the present night, my thoughts ran upon my losses and sad bereaved condition. All was gone, my Husband gone (at least separated from me, he being in the Bay;[1] and to add to my grief, the Indians told me they would kill him as he came homeward), my Children gone, my Relations and Friends gone, our House and home and all our comforts within door and without, all was gone except my life, and I knew not but the next moment that might go too. There remained nothing to me but one poor wounded Babe, and it seemed at present worse than death that it was in such a pitiful condition bespeaking Compassion, and I had no refreshing for it, nor suitable things to revive it. Little do many think what is the savageness and brutishness of this barbarous Enemy, ay, even those that seem to profess[2] more than others among them, when the English have fallen into their hands.

Those seven that were killed at Lancaster the summer before upon a Sabbath day and the one that was afterward killed upon a weekday were slain and mangled in a barbarous manner by One-eyed John and Marlboro's Praying-Indians, which Captain Moseley brought to Boston,[3] as the Indians told me.

THE SECOND REMOVE

But now, the next morning, I must turn my back upon the Town, and travel with them into the vast and desolate Wilderness, I knew not whither. It is not my tongue or pen can express the sorrows of my heart and bitterness of my spirit that I had at this departure, but God was with me in a wonderful manner, carrying me along, and bearing up my spirit that it did not quite fail. One of the Indians carried my poor wounded Babe upon a horse; it went moaning all along, "I shall die, I shall die." I went on foot after it with sorrow that cannot be expressed. At length I took it off the horse and carried it in my arms till my strength failed, and I fell down with it. Then they set me upon a horse with my wounded Child in my lap, and there being no furniture[1] upon the horse back, as we were going down a steep hill, we both fell over the horse's head, at which they like inhumane creatures laughed and rejoiced to see it, though I thought we should there have ended our days, as overcome with so many difficulties. But the Lord renewed my strength still and carried me along, that I might see more of his Power; yea, so much that I could never have thought of, had I not experienced it.

After this it quickly began to snow, and when night came on, they stopped,[2] and now down I must sit in the snow by a little fire, and a few boughs behind me, with my sick Child in my lap and calling much for water, being now (through the wound) fallen into a violent Fever. My own wound also growing so stiff that I could scarce sit down or rise up; yet so it must be that I must sit all this cold winter night upon the cold snowy ground, with my sick Child in my arms, looking that every hour would be the last of its life; and having no Christian friend near me, either to comfort or help me. Oh, I may see the wonderful power of God, that my Spirit did not utterly sink under my affliction. Still the Lord upheld me with his gracious and merciful Spirit, and we were both alive to see the light of the next morning.

THE THIRD REMOVE

The morning being come, they prepared to go on their way. One of the Indians got up upon a horse, and they set me up behind him, with my poor sick Babe in my lap. A very wearisome and tedious day I had of it; what with my own wound, and my Child's being so exceeding sick and in a lamentable condition with her wound. It may be easily judged what a poor feeble condition we were in, there being not the least crumb of refreshing that came within either of our mouths from Wednesday night to Saturday night, except only a little cold water.

This day in the afternoon, about an hour by Sun, we came to the place where they intended, *viz.* an Indian Town called Wenimesset, northward of Quabaug.[1] When we were come, Oh, the number of Pagans (now merciless enemies) that there came about me, that I may say as David, Psalm 27:13, "I had fainted, unless I had believed," etc. The next day was the Sabbath. . . . This day there came to me one Robert Pepper (a man belonging to Roxbury) who was taken in Captain Beers's Fight,[2] and had been now a considerable time with the Indians; and up with them almost as far as Albany to see King Philip,[3] as he told me, and was now very lately come into these parts. Hearing, I say, that I was in this Indian Town, he obtained leave to come and see me. He told me he himself was wounded in the leg at Captain Beers's Fight; and was not able some time to go but as they carried him, and as he took Oaken leaves and laid to his wound, and through the blessing of God he was able to travel again. Then I took Oaken leaves and laid to my side, and with the blessing of God it cured me also; yet before the cure was wrought, I may say, as it is in Psalm 38:5–6, "My wounds stink and are corrupt, I am troubled, I am bowed down greatly, I go mourning all the day long." I sat much alone with a poor wounded Child in my lap, which moaned night and day, having nothing to revive the body or cheer the spirits of her, but instead of that, sometimes one Indian would come and tell me one hour that "your Master will knock your Child in the head," and then a second, and then a third, "your Master will quickly knock your Child in the head."

This was the comfort I had from them, miserable comforters are ye all, as he said.[4] Thus nine days I sat upon my knees with my Babe in my lap, till my flesh was raw again. My Child being even ready to depart this sorrowful world, they bade me carry it out to another Wigwam (I suppose because they would not be troubled with such spectacles), whither I went with a very heavy heart, and down I sat with the picture of death in my lap. About two hours in the night, my sweet Babe like a Lamb departed this life, on February 18, 167[6], it being about six years and five months old. It was nine days from the first wounding in this miserable condition, without any refreshing of one nature or other except a little cold water. I cannot but take notice how at another time I could not bear to be in the room where any dead person was, but now the case is changed; I must and could lie down by my dead Babe, side by side all the night after. I have thought since of the wonderful goodness of God to me in preserving me in the use of my reason and senses in that distressed time, that I did not use wicked and violent means to end my own miserable life.

In the morning, when they understood that my child was dead, they sent for me home to my Master's Wigwam (by my Master in this writing must be understood Quinnapin,[5] who was a Sagamore and married King Philip's wife's Sister; not that he first took me, but I was sold to him by another Narragansett Indian, who took me when first I came out of the Garrison). I went to take up my dead child in my arms to carry it with me, but they bid me let it alone. There was no resisting, but go I must and leave it. When I had been at my master's wigwam, I took the first opportunity I could get to go look after my dead child. When I came, I asked them what they had done with it? Then they told me it was upon the hill; then they went and showed me where it was, where I saw the ground was newly digged, and there they told me they had buried it. There I left that Child in the Wilderness, and must commit it and myself also in this Wilderness-condition to him who is above all.

God having taken away this dear Child, I went to see my daughter Mary, who was at this same Indian Town at a Wigwam not very far off, though we had little liberty or opportunity to see one another. She was about ten years old, and taken from the door at first by a Praying-Indian and afterward sold for a gun. When I came in sight, she would fall a weeping; at which they were provoked and would not let me come near her, but bade me be gone; which was a heart-cutting word to me. I had one Child dead, another in the Wilderness, I knew not where, the third they would not let me come near to. . . . I could not sit still in this condition, but kept walking from one place to another. And as I was going along, my heart was even overwhelmed with the thoughts of my condition, and that I should have Children, and a Nation which I knew not ruled over them.

Whereupon I earnestly entreated the Lord that he would consider my low estate, and show me a token for good, and if it were his blessed will, some sign and hope of some relief.

And indeed quickly the Lord answered in some measure my poor prayers, for as I was going up and down mourning and lamenting my condition, my Son came to me and asked me how I did. I had not seen him before since the destruction of the Town, and I knew not where he was till I was informed by himself that he was amongst a smaller parcel of Indians whose place was about six miles off. With tears in his eyes, he asked me whether his Sister Sarah was dead and told me he had seen his Sister Mary; and prayed me that I would not be troubled in reference to himself. The occasion of his coming to see me at this time was this. There was, as I said, about six miles from us, a small Plantation of Indians, where it seems he had been during his Captivity. And at this time, there were some Forces of the Indians gathered out of our company and some also from them (among whom was my Son's master) to go to assault and burn Medfield.[6] In this time of the absence of his master, his dame brought him to see me. I took this to be some gracious answer to my earnest and unfeigned desire.

The next day, *viz.* to this, the Indians returned from Medfield, all the company, for those that belonged to the other small company came through the Town that now we were at. But before they came to us, Oh! the outrageous roaring and whooping that there was. They began their din about a mile before they came to us. By their noise and whooping they signified how many they had destroyed (which was at that time twenty-three). Those that were with us at home were gathered together as soon as they heard the whooping, and every time that the other went over their number, these at home gave a shout that the very Earth rung again. And thus they continued till those that had been upon the expedition were come up to the Sagamore's Wigwam, and then, Oh, the hideous insulting and triumphing that there was over some Englishmen's scalps that they had taken (as their manner is) and brought with them.

I cannot but take notice of the wonderful mercy of God to

me in those afflictions in sending me a Bible. One of the Indians that came from Medfield fight had brought some plunder, came to me, and asked me if I would have a Bible, he had got one in his Basket. I was glad of it and asked him whether he thought the Indians would let me read? He answered, "Yes." So I took the Bible, and in that melancholy time, it came into my mind to read first the 28th Chapter of Deuteronomy, which I did, and when I had read it, my dark heart wrought on this manner: That there was no mercy for me, that the blessings were gone, and the curses come in their room, and that I had lost my opportunity. But the Lord helped me still to go on reading till I came to Chapter 30, the seven first verses, where I found there was mercy promised again if we would return to him by repentance; and though we were scattered from one end of the Earth to the other, yet the Lord would gather us together, and turn all those curses upon our Enemies. I do not desire to live to forget this Scripture, and what comfort it was to me.

Now the Indians began to talk of removing from this place, some one way, and some another. There were now besides myself nine English Captives in this place (all of them Children, except one Woman). I got an opportunity to go and take my leave of them, they being to go one way, and I another. I asked them whether they were earnest with God for deliverance; they told me they did as they were able, and it was some comfort to me that the Lord stirred up Children to look to him. The Woman, *viz.* Goodwife Joslin, told me she should never see me again, and that she could find in her heart to run away. I wished her not to run away by any means, for we were near thirty miles from any English Town, and she very big with Child, and had but one week to reckon; and another Child in her Arms, two years old, and bad Rivers there were to go over, and we were feeble with our poor and coarse entertainment. I had my Bible with me, I pulled it out, and asked her whether she would read; we opened the Bible and lighted on Psalm 27, in which Psalm we especially took notice of that [last verse], "Wait on the Lord, Be of good courage, and he shall strengthen thine Heart, wait I say on the Lord."

THE FOURTH REMOVE

And now I must part with that little Company I had. Here I parted from my Daughter Mary (whom I never saw again till I saw her in Dorchester, returned from Captivity), and from four little Cousins and Neighbors, some of which I never saw afterward; the Lord only knows the end of them. Amongst them also was that poor Woman before mentioned, who came to a sad end, as some of the company told me in my travel. She having much grief upon her Spirit about her miserable condition, being so near her time, she would be often asking the Indians to let her go home. They not being willing to that and yet vexed with her importunity, gathered a great company together about her and stripped her naked, and set her in the midst of them; and when they had sung and danced about her (in their hellish manner) as long as they pleased, they knocked her on head, and the child in her arms with her. When they had done that, they made a fire and put them both into it, and told the other Children that were with them, that if they attempted to go home, they would serve them in like manner. The Children said she did not shed one tear, but prayed all the while.

But to return to my own Journey; we traveled about half a day or little more and came to a desolate place in the Wilderness,[1] where there were no Wigwams or Inhabitants before. We came about the middle of the afternoon to this place, cold and wet, and snowy, and hungry, and weary, and no refreshing for man, but the cold ground to sit on, and our poor Indian cheer.

Heart-aching thoughts here I had about my poor Children, who were scattered up and down among the wild beasts of the forest. My head was light and dizzy (either through hunger or hard lodging, or trouble or altogether), my knees feeble, my body raw by sitting double night and day, that I cannot express to man the affliction that lay upon my Spirit, but the Lord helped me at that time to express it to himself. I opened my Bible to read, and the Lord brought that precious Scripture to me, Jeremiah 31:16, "Thus saith the Lord, refrain thy voice from weeping, and thine eyes from tears, for thy work shall be rewarded, and they shall come again from the land of the Enemy." This was a sweet Cordial to me; when I was ready to faint, many and many a time have I sat down, and wept sweetly over this Scripture. At this place we continued about four days.

THE FIFTH REMOVE

The occasion (as I thought) of their moving at this time was the English Army, it being near and following them. For they went as if they had gone for their lives for some considerable way, and then they made a stop, and chose some of their stoutest men, and sent them back to hold the English Army in play whilst the rest escaped. And then, like Jehu,[1] they marched on furiously, with their old and with their young. Some carried their old decrepit mothers, some carried one, and some another. Four of them carried a great Indian upon a Bier, but going through a thick Wood with him, they were hindered, and could make no haste; whereupon they took him upon their backs, and carried him, one at a time, till they came to Bacquag River.[2]

Upon a Friday a little after noon we came to this River. When all the company was come up and were gathered together, I thought to count the number of them, but they were so many, and being somewhat in motion, it was beyond my skill. In this travel, because of my wound, I was somewhat favored in my load. I carried only my knitting work and two quarts of parched meal. Being very faint, I asked my mistress[3] to give me one spoonful of the meal, but she would not give me a taste. They quickly fell to cutting dry trees to make Rafts to carry them over the river, and soon my turn came to go over. By the advantage of some brush which they had laid upon the Raft to sit upon, I did not wet my foot (which many of themselves at the other end were mid-leg deep), which cannot but be acknowledged as a favor of God to my weakened body, it being a very cold time. I was not before acquainted with such kind of doings or dangers. . . . A certain number of us got over the River that night, but it was the night after the Sabbath before all the company was got over. On the Saturday they boiled an old Horse's leg which they had got, and so we drank of the broth as soon as they thought it was ready, and when it was almost all gone, they filled it up again.

The first week of my being among them, I hardly ate anything; the second week, I found my stomach grow very faint for want of something; and yet it was very hard to get down their filthy trash. But the third week, though I could think how formerly my stomach would turn against this or that, and I could starve and die before I could eat such things, yet they were sweet and savory to my taste. I was at this time knitting a pair of white cotton stockings for my mistress, and had not yet wrought upon a Sabbath day. When the Sabbath came they bade me go to work. I told them it was the Sabbath-day and desired them to let me rest, and told them I would do as much more tomorrow; to which they answered me they would break my face.

And here I cannot but take notice of the strange providence of God in preserving the heathen. They were many hundreds, old and young, some sick, and some lame, many had Papooses at their backs. The greatest number at this time with us were Squaws, and they traveled with all they had, bag and baggage, and yet they got over this River aforesaid. And on Monday they set their Wigwams on fire, and away they went. On that very day came the English Army after them to this River and saw the smoke of their Wigwams, and yet this River put a stop to them. God did not give them courage or activity to go over after us. We were not ready for so great a mercy as victory and deliverance; if we had been, God would have found out a way for the English to have passed this River, as well as for the Indians with their Squaws and Children, and all their Luggage. . . .

THE SIXTH REMOVE

On Monday (as I said) they set their Wigwams on fire and went away. It was a cold morning, and before us there was a great Brook with ice on it. Some waded through it up to the knees and higher, but others went till they came to a Beaver dam, and

I amongst them, where through the good providence of God, I did not wet my foot. I went along that day mourning and lamenting, leaving farther my own Country, and traveling into the vast and howling Wilderness, and I understood something of Lot's Wife's Temptation, when she looked back.[1] We came that day to a great Swamp,[2] by the side of which we took up our lodging that night. When I came to the brow of the hill that looked toward the Swamp, I thought we had been come to a great Indian Town (though there were none but our own Company). The Indians were as thick as the trees. It seemed as if there had been a thousand Hatchets going at once. If one looked before one, there was nothing but Indians, and behind one, nothing but Indians, and so on either hand, I myself in the midst, and no Christian soul near me, and yet how hath the Lord preserved me in safety? Oh, the experience that I have had of the goodness of God, to me and mine!

THE SEVENTH REMOVE

After a restless and hungry night there, we had a wearisome time of it the next day. The Swamp by which we lay was, as it were, a deep Dungeon, and an exceeding high and steep hill before it. Before I got to the top of the hill, I thought my heart and legs and all would have broken and failed me. What through faintness and soreness of body, it was a grievous day of travel to me. As we went along, I saw a place where English Cattle had been; that was comfort to me, such as it was. Quickly after that we came to an English Path, which so took with me that I thought I could have freely lain down and died. That day, a little after noon, we came to Squakeag,[1] where the Indians quickly spread themselves over the deserted English Fields, gleaning what they could find. Some picked up ears of Wheat that were crickled[2] down, some found ears of Indian Corn, some found Ground-nuts,[3] and others sheaves of Wheat that were frozen together in the shock and went to threshing of them out.

Myself got two ears of Indian Corn, and whilst I did but turn my back, one of them was stolen from me, which much troubled me. There came an Indian to them at that time with a basket of Horse-liver. I asked him to give me a piece. "What," says he, "can you eat Horse-liver?" I told him I would try if he would give a piece, which he did, and I laid it on the coals to roast; but before it was half ready they got half of it away from me, so that I was fain to take the rest and eat it as it was with the blood about my mouth, and yet a savory bit it was to me, for "to the hungry Soul every bitter thing is sweet."[4] A solemn sight methought it was to see Fields of wheat and Indian Corn forsaken and spoiled, and the remainders of them to be food for our merciless Enemies. That night we had a mess of wheat for our Supper.

THE EIGHTH REMOVE

On the morrow morning we must go over the River, *i.e.,* Connecticut, to meet with King Philip. Two Canoesfull they had carried over. The next Turn I myself was to go; but as my foot was upon the Canoe to step in, there was a sudden outcry among them, and I must step back; and instead of going over the River, I must go four or five miles up the River farther Northward. Some of the Indians ran one way, and some another. The cause of this rout was, as I thought, their espying some English Scouts who were thereabout.

In this travel up the River, about noon the Company made a stop and sat down; some to eat, and others to rest them. As I sat amongst them musing of things past, my Son Joseph unexpectedly came to me. We asked of each other's welfare, bemoaning our doleful condition, and the change that had come upon us. We had Husband and Father, and Children, and Sisters, and Friends, and Relations, and House, and Home, and many Comforts of this Life, but now we may say, as Job, "Naked came I out of my Mother's Womb, and naked shall I return. The Lord gave, and the Lord hath taken away, Blessed be the Name of the Lord."[1] I asked him whether he would read; he told me he earnestly desired it. I gave him my Bible, and he lighted upon that comfortable Scripture, Psalm 118:17–18, "I shall not die but live, and declare the works of the Lord. The Lord hath chastened me sore, yet he hath not given me over to death." "Look here, Mother," says he, "did you read this?" . . .

We traveled on till night, and in the morning we must go over the River to Philip's Crew. When I was in the Canoe, I could not but be amazed at the numerous crew of Pagans that were on the Bank on the other side. When I came ashore,[2] they gathered all about me, I sitting alone in the midst. I observed they asked one another questions, and laughed and rejoiced over their Gains and Victories. Then my heart began to fail, and I fell a-weeping, which was the first time to my remembrance that I wept before them. Although I had met with so much Affliction, and my heart was many times ready to break, yet could I not shed one tear in their sight, but rather had been all this while in amaze and like one astonished. But now I may say as, Psalm 137:1, "By the Rivers of Babylon, there we sat down; yea, we wept when we remembered Zion." There one of them asked me why I wept, I could hardly tell what to say. Yet I answered, they would kill me. "No," said he, "none will hurt you." Then came one of them and gave me two spoonfuls of Meal to comfort me, and another gave me half a pint of Peas, which was more worth than many Bushels at another time.

Then I went to see King Philip. He bade me come in and sit down, and asked me whether I would smoke it (a usual Compliment nowadays amongst Saints and Sinners), but this no way suited me. For though I had formerly used Tobacco, yet I had left it ever since I was first taken. It seems to be a Bait the Devil lays to make men lose their precious time. I remember with shame how formerly, when I had taken two or three pipes, I was presently ready for another, such a bewitching thing it is. But I thank God he has now given me power over it. Surely there are many who may be better employed than to lie sucking a stinking Tobacco-pipe.

Now the Indians gather their Forces to go against Northampton. Overnight one went about yelling and hooting to give notice of the design. Whereupon they fell to boiling of Ground-nuts and parching of Corn (as many as had it) for their

Provision, and in the morning away they went. During my abode in this place, Philip spoke to me to make a shirt for his boy, which I did, for which he gave me a shilling. I offered the money to my master, but he bade me keep it, and with it I bought a piece of Horse flesh. Afterwards he asked me to make a Cap for his boy, for which he invited me to Dinner. I went, and he gave me a Pancake about as big as two fingers; it was made of parched wheat, beaten, and fried in Bear's grease, but I thought I never tasted pleasanter meat in my life. There was a Squaw who spoke to me to make a shirt for her *Sannup*[3] for which she gave me a piece of Bear. Another asked me to knit a pair of Stockings, for which she gave me a quart of Peas. I boiled my Peas and Bear together and invited my master and mistress to dinner, but the proud Gossip,[4] because I served them both in one Dish, would eat nothing except one bit that he gave her upon the point of his knife.

Hearing that my son was come to this place, I went to see him and found him lying flat upon the ground. I asked him how he could sleep so? He answered me that he was not asleep, but at Prayer; and lay so, that they might not observe what he was doing. I pray God he may remember these things now he is re-turned in safety.

At this Place (the Sun now getting higher) what with the beams and heat of the Sun, and the smoke of the Wigwams, I thought I should have been blind. I could scarce discern one Wigwam from another. There was here one Mary Thurston of Medfield, who, seeing how it was with me, lent me a Hat to wear, but as soon as I was gone, the Squaw (who owned that Mary Thurston) came running after me and got it away again. Here was the Squaw that gave me one spoonful of Meal. I put it in my Pocket to keep it safe, yet notwithstand-ing somebody stole it, but put five Indian Corns in the room of it, which Corns were the greatest Provisions I had in my travel for one day.

The Indians returning from Northampton brought with them some Horses and Sheep and other things which they had taken. I desired them that they would carry me to Albany upon one of those Horses and sell me for Powder, for so they had sometimes discoursed. I was utterly hopeless of getting home on foot, the way that I came. I could hardly bear to think of the many weary steps[5] I had taken to come to this place.

THE NINTH REMOVE

But instead of going either to Albany or homeward, we must go five miles up the River, and then go over it. Here we abode a while.[1] Here lived a sorry Indian, who spoke to me to make him a shirt. When I had done it, he would pay me nothing. But he living by the River side, where I often went to fetch water, I would often be putting of him in mind and calling for my pay. At last he told me if I would make another shirt for a Papoose not yet born, he would give me a knife, which he did when I had done it. I carried the knife in, and my master asked me to give it him, and I was not a little glad that I had anything that they would accept of and be pleased with. When we were at this place, my Master's maid came home. She had been gone three weeks into the Narragansett Country to fetch Corn, where they had stored up some in the ground; she brought home about a peck and half of Corn. This was about the time that their great Captain, Naananto,[2] was killed in the Narragansett Country.

My Son being now about a mile from me, I asked liberty to go and see him. They bade me go, and away I went, but quickly lost myself traveling over Hills and through Swamps, and could not find the way to him. And I cannot but admire at the wonderful power and goodness of God to me, in that, though I was gone from home and met with all sorts of Indians, and those I had no knowledge of, and there being no Christian soul near me, yet not one of them offered the least imaginable miscarriage to me. I turned homeward again and met with my master. He showed me the way to my Son. When I came to him, I found him not well, and withal he had a boil on his side, which much troubled him. We bemoaned one another awhile, as the Lord helped us, and then I returned again.

When I was returned, I found my self as unsatisfied as I was

before. I went up and down mourning and lamenting; and my
spirit was ready to sink with the thoughts of my poor Children.
My Son was ill, and I could not but think of his mournful
looks, and no Christian Friend was near him to do any office of
love for him, either for Soul or Body. And my poor Girl, I knew
not where she was, nor whether she was sick or well, or alive or
dead. I repaired under these thoughts to my Bible (my great
comfort in that time) and that Scripture came to my hand, *Cast
thy burden upon the Lord, and He shall sustain thee*, Psalm
55:22.

But I was fain to go and look after something to satisfy my
hunger, and going among the Wigwams, I went into one and
there found a Squaw who showed herself very kind to me, and
gave me a piece of Bear. I put it into my pocket and came
home, but could not find an opportunity to broil it, for fear
they would get it from me, and there it lay all that day and
night in my stinking pocket. In the morning I went to the same
Squaw, who had a Kettle of Ground-nuts boiling. I asked her
to let me boil my piece of Bear in her Kettle, which she did,
and gave me some Ground-nuts to eat with it; and I cannot but
think how pleasant it was to me. I have sometime seen Bear
baked very handsomely among the English, and some like it,
but the thoughts that it was Bear made me tremble; but now
that was savory to me that one would think was enough to
turn the stomach of a brute Creature.

One bitter cold day, I could find no room to sit down before
the fire. I went out and could not tell what to do, but I went into
another Wigwam, where they were also sitting round the fire, but
the Squaw laid a skin for me and bid me sit down, and gave me
some Ground-nuts, and bade me come again, and told me they
would buy me, if they were able, and yet these were strangers to
me that I never saw before.

THE TENTH REMOVE

That day a small part of the Company removed about three-
quarters of a mile, intending further the next day. When they

came to the place where they intended to lodge and had pitched their wigwams, being hungry I went again back to the place we were before at to get something to eat, being encouraged by the Squaw's kindness, who bade me come again. When I was there, there came an Indian to look after me, who when he had found me, kicked me all along. I went home and found Venison roasting that night, but they would not give me one bit of it. Sometimes I met with favor, and sometimes with nothing but frowns.

THE ELEVENTH REMOVE

The next day in the morning they took their Travel, intending a day's journey up the River.[1] I took my load at my back, and quickly we came to wade over the River and passed over tiresome and wearisome hills.[2] One hill was so steep that I was fain to creep up upon my knees, and to hold by the twigs and bushes to keep myself from falling backward. My head also was so light that I usually reeled as I went; but I hope all these wearisome steps that I have taken are but a forewarning to me of the heavenly rest[3]. . . .

THE TWELFTH REMOVE

It was upon a Sabbath-day-morning that they prepared for their Travel. This morning I asked my master whether he would sell me to my Husband; he answered me *Nux*,[1] which did much rejoice my spirit. My mistress, before we went, was gone to the burial of a Papoose, and returning, she found me sitting and reading in my Bible. She snatched it hastily out of my hand and threw it out of doors. I ran out and caught it up, and put it into my pocket, and never let her see it afterward. Then they packed up their things to be gone and gave me my load. I complained it was too heavy, whereupon she gave me a slap in the face and bade me go. I lifted up my heart to God, hoping the Redemption was not far off, and the rather because their insolency grew worse and worse.

But the thoughts of my going homeward (for so we bent our course) much cheered my Spirit, and made my burden seem light, and almost nothing at all. But (to my amazement and great perplexity) the scale was soon turned, for when we had gone a little way, on a sudden my mistress gives out she would go no further, but turn back again, and said I must go back again with her, and she called her *Sannup*, and would have had him gone back also. But he would not, but said he would go on and come to us again in three days.

My Spirit was upon this, I confess, very impatient, and almost outrageous. I thought I could as well have died as went back. I cannot declare the trouble that I was in about it, but yet back again I must go. As soon as I had an opportunity, I took my Bible to read, and that quieting Scripture came to my hand, Psalm 46:10, "Be still, and know that I am God," which stilled my spirit for the present. But a sore time of trial, I concluded, I had to go through, my master being gone, who seemed to me the best friend that I had of an Indian, both in cold and hunger, and quickly so it proved. Down I sat, with my heart as full as it could hold, and yet so hungry that I could not sit neither, but going out to see what I could find, and walking among the Trees, I found six Acorns and two Chestnuts, which were some refreshment to me.

Towards Night I gathered me some sticks for my own comfort, that I might not lie a-cold, but when we came to lie down, they bade me go out and lie somewhere else, for they had company (they said) come in more than their own. I told them I could not tell where to go; they bade me go look. I told them if I went to another Wigwam they would be angry and send me home again. Then one of the Company drew his sword and told me he would run me thorough if I did not go presently. Then was I fain to stoop to this rude fellow and to go out in the night, I knew not whither. Mine eyes have seen that fellow afterwards walking up and down Boston under the appearance of a Friend-Indian, and several others of the like Cut.[2]

I went to one Wigwam, and they told me they had no room. Then I went to another, and they said the same. At last an old Indian bade me come to him, and his Squaw gave me some

Ground-nuts. She gave me also something to lay under my head, and a good fire we had; and through the good providence of God, I had a comfortable lodging that night. In the morning, another Indian bade me come at night, and he would give me six Ground-nuts, which I did. We were at this place and time about two miles from Connecticut River. We went in the morning to gather Ground-nuts to the River, and went back again that night. I went with a good load at my back (for they when they went though but a little way would carry all their trumpery with them). I told them the skin was off my back, but I had no other comforting answer from them than this, that it would be no matter if my head were off too.

THE THIRTEENTH REMOVE

Instead of going toward the Bay, which was that I desired, I must go with them five or six miles down the River into a mighty Thicket of Brush,[1] where we abode almost a fortnight. Here one asked me to make a shirt for her Papoose, for which she gave me a mess of Broth, which was thickened with meal made of the Bark of a Tree, and to make it the better, she had put into it about a handful of Peas and a few roasted Ground-nuts. I had not seen my son a pretty while, and here was an Indian of whom I made inquiry after him, and asked him when he saw him. He answered me that such a time his master roasted him, and that himself did eat a piece of him, as big as his two fingers, and that he was very good meat. But the Lord upheld my Spirit under this discouragement; and I considered their horrible addictedness to lying, and that there is not one of them that makes the least conscience of speaking of truth.

In this place on a cold night as I lay by the fire, I removed a stick that kept the heat from me. A Squaw moved it down again, at which I looked up, and she threw a handful of ashes in mine eyes; I thought I should have been quite blinded and have never seen more, but lying down, the water run out of my eyes and carried the dirt with it, that by the morning I recovered my sight again. Yet upon this, and the like occasions, I hope it is not too much to say with Job, "Have pity upon me, have pity upon me, Oh ye my Friends, for the Hand of the Lord has touched me."[2] And here I cannot but remember how many times sitting in their Wigwams and musing on things past, I should suddenly leap up and run out, as if I had been at home, forgetting where I was, and what my condition was. But when I was without, and saw nothing but Wilderness and Woods and a company of barbarous heathens, my mind quickly returned to me, which made me think of that spoken concerning Sampson, who said, " 'I will go out and shake myself as at other times,' but he wist not that the Lord was departed from him."[3]

About this time I began to think that all my hopes of Restoration would come to nothing. I thought of the English Army, and hoped for their coming and being taken by them, but that failed. I hoped to be carried to Albany, as the Indians had discoursed before, but that failed also. I thought of being sold to my Husband, as my master spoke, but instead of that, my master himself was gone, and I left behind, so that my Spirit was now quite ready to sink. I asked them to let me go out and pick up some sticks, that I might get alone and pour out my heart unto the Lord. Then also I took my Bible to read, but I found no comfort here neither, which many times I was wont to find. So easy a thing it is with God to dry up the Streams of Scripture-comfort from us. Yet I can say that in all my sorrows and afflictions, God did not leave me to have my impatience work towards himself, as if his waves were unrighteous. But I knew that he laid upon me less then I deserved. . . .

About this time they came yelping from Hadley,[4] where they had killed three Englishmen, and brought one Captive with them, *viz.* Thomas Read. They all gathered about the poor Man, asking him many Questions. I desired also to go and see him; and when I came, he was crying bitterly, supposing they would quickly kill him. Whereupon I asked one of them whether they intended to kill him. He answered me they would not. He being a little cheered with that, I asked him about the welfare of my Husband. He told me he saw him such a time in the Bay, and he was well, but very melancholy. By which I certainly understood (though I suspected it before) that whatsoever the

Indians told me respecting him was vanity and lies. Some of them told me he was dead, and they had killed him. Some said he was Married again, and that the Governor wished him to Marry, and told him he should have his choice, and that all [were] persuaded I was dead. So like were these barbarous creatures to him who was a liar from the beginning.[5]

As I was sitting once in the Wigwam here, Philip's Maid came in with the Child in her arms, and asked me to give her a piece of my Apron to make a flap for it; I told her I would not. Then my Mistress bade me give it, but still I said no. The maid told me if I would not give her a piece, she would tear a piece off it. I told her I would tear her Coat then. With that my Mistress rises up and takes up a stick big enough to have killed me and struck at me with it, but I stepped out, and she struck the stick into the Mat of the Wigwam. But while she was pulling of it out, I ran to the Maid and gave her all my Apron, and so that storm went over.

Hearing that my Son was come to this place, I went to see him and told him his Father was well, but very melancholy. He told me he was as much grieved for his Father as for himself. I wondered at his speech, for I thought I had enough upon my spirit in reference to myself to make me mindless of my Husband and everyone else, they being safe among their Friends. He told me also that a while before, his Master (together with other Indians) were going to the French for Powder; but by the way the Mohawks[6] met with them and killed four of their Company, which made the rest turn back again, for which I desire that myself and he may bless the Lord; for it might have been worse with him had he been sold to the French than it proved to be in his remaining with the Indians.

I went to see an English Youth in this place; one John Gilbert of Springfield. I found him lying without doors upon the ground. I asked him how he did; he told me he was very sick of a flux,[7] with eating so much blood. They had turned him out of the Wigwam and with him an Indian Papoose, almost dead (whose Parents had been killed), in a bitter cold day without fire or clothes. The young man himself had nothing on but his shirt and waistcoat. This sight was enough to melt a heart of flint. There they lay quivering in the Cold, the youth round like a dog, the Papoose stretched out with his eyes and nose and mouth full of dirt, and yet alive and groaning. I advised John to go and get to some fire. He told me he could not stand, but I persuaded him still lest he should lie there and die; and with much ado I got him to a fire, and went myself home.

As soon as I was got home, his Master's Daughter came after me to know what I had done with the Englishman. I told her I had got him to a fire in such a place. Now had I need to pray Paul's Prayer, 2 Thessalonians 3:2, "That we may be delivered from unreasonable and wicked men." For her satisfaction I went along with her and brought her to him. But before I got home again, it was noised about that I was running away and getting the English youth along with me. [So] that as soon as I came in, they began to rant and domineer, asking me where I had been, and what I had been doing, and saying they would knock him on the head. I told them I had been seeing the English Youth, and that I would not run away. They told me I lied, and taking up a Hatchet, they came to me and said they would knock me down if I stirred out again, and so confined me to the Wigwam.

Now may I say with David, 2 Samuel 24:14. "I am in a great strait." If I keep in, I must die with hunger, and if I go out, I must be knocked in head. This distressed condition held that day and half the next, and then the Lord remembered me, whose mercies are great. Then came an Indian to me with a pair of stockings that were too big for him, and he would have me ravel them out and knit them fit for him. I showed myself willing, and bid him ask my mistress if I might go along with him a little way. She said yes, I might, but I was not a little refreshed with that news that I had my liberty again. Then I went along with him, and he gave me some roasted Ground-nuts, which did again revive my feeble stomach. . . .

Then my Son came to see me, and I asked his master to let him stay awhile with me that I might comb his head and look over him, for he was almost overcome with lice. He told me, when I had done, that he was very hungry, but I had nothing to relieve him; but bid him go into the Wigwams as he went along, and see if he could get anything among them. Which he did, and it seems tarried a little too long; for his Master was angry with him and beat him, and then sold him. Then he came running to tell me he had a new Master, and that he had given him some Ground-nuts already. Then I went along with him to his new Master who told me he loved him, and he should not want. So his Master carried him away, and I never saw him afterward till I saw him at Piscataqua in Portsmouth.[8]

That night they bade me go out of the Wigwam again. My Mistress's Papoose was sick, and it died that night, and there was one benefit in it, that there was more room. I went to a Wigwam, and they bade me come in, and gave me a skin to lie upon and a mess of Venison and Ground-nuts, which was a choice Dish among them. On the morrow they buried the Papoose, and afterward, both morning and evening, there came a company to mourn and howl with her, though I confess I could not much condole with them. Many sorrowful days I had in this place, often getting alone. . . . I remembered how on the night before and after the Sabbath, when my Family was about me, and Relations and Neighbors with us, we could pray and sing, and then refresh our bodies with the good creatures of God, and then have a comfortable Bed to lie down on. But instead of all this, I had only a little Swill for the body, and then like a Swine, must lie down on the ground. I cannot express to man the sorrow that lay upon my Spirit; the Lord knows it. Yet that comfortable Scripture would often come to my mind, "For a small moment have I forsaken thee, but with great mercies will I gather thee."[9]

THE FOURTEENTH REMOVE

Now must we pack up and be gone from this Thicket, bending our course toward the Bay-towns, I having nothing to eat by the way this day but a few crumbs of Cake that an Indian gave my girl the same day we were taken. She gave it me, and I put it in my pocket. There it lay till it was so moldy (for want of good baking) that one could not tell what it was made of. It fell all to crumbs and grew so dry and hard that it was like little flints, and this refreshed me many times, when I was ready to faint. It was in my thoughts when I put it into my mouth that if ever I returned, I would tell the World what a blessing the Lord gave to such mean food.

As we went along, they killed a Deer with a young one in her. They gave me a piece of the Fawn, and it was so young and tender that one might eat the bones as well as the flesh, and yet I thought it very good. When night came on we sat down; it rained, but they quickly got up a Bark Wigwam, where I lay dry that night. I looked out in the morning, and many of them had lain in the rain all night, I saw by their Reeking.[1] Thus the Lord dealt mercifully with me many times, and I fared better than many of them. In the morning they took the blood of the Deer and put it into the Paunch, and so boiled it. I could eat nothing of that, though they ate it sweetly. And yet they were so nice[2] in other things, that when I had fetched water, and had put the Dish I dipped the water with into the Kettle of water which I brought, they would say they would knock me down, for they said it was a sluttish trick.

THE FIFTEENTH REMOVE

We went on our Travel. I having got one handful of Ground-nuts for my support that day, they gave me my load, and I went on cheerfully (with the thoughts of going homeward), having my burden more on my back than my spirit. We came to Bacquag River again that day, near which we abode a few days. Sometimes one of them would give me a Pipe, another a little Tobacco, another a little Salt, which I would change for a little Victuals. I cannot but think what a Wolfish appetite persons have in a starving condition, for many times when they gave me that which was hot, I was so greedy that I should burn my mouth, that it would trouble me hours after, and yet I should quickly do the same again. And after I was thoroughly hungry,

I was never again satisfied. For though sometimes it fell out, that I got enough, and did eat till I could eat no more, yet I was as unsatisfied as I was when I began. . . .

THE SIXTEENTH REMOVE

We began this Remove with wading over Bacquag River. The water was up to the knees and the stream very swift, and so cold that I thought it would have cut me in sunder. I was so weak and feeble that I reeled as I went along, and thought there I must end my days at last, after my bearing and getting through so many difficulties. The Indians stood laughing to see me staggering along, but in my distress the Lord gave me experience of the truth and goodness of that promise, Isaiah 43:2, "When thou passest thorough the Waters, I will be with thee, and through the Rivers, they shall not overflow thee." Then I sat down to put on my stockings and shoes with the tears running down mine eyes and many sorrowful thoughts in my heart, but I got up to go along with them.

Quickly there came up to us an Indian who informed them that I must go to Wachusett[1] to my master, for there was a Letter come from the Council[2] to the Sagamores about redeeming the Captives, and that there would be another in fourteen days, and that I must be there ready. My heart was so heavy before that I could scarce speak or go in the path, and yet now so light that I could run. My strength seemed to come again and recruit my feeble knees and aching heart. Yet it pleased them to go but one mile that night, and there we stayed two days.

In that time came a company of Indians to us, near thirty, all on horseback. My heart skipped within me, thinking they had been Englishmen at the first sight of them, for they were dressed in English Apparel, with Hats, white Neckcloths, and Sashes about their waists, and Ribbons upon their shoulders, but when they came near, there was a vast difference between the lovely faces of Christians and the foul looks of those Heathens, which much damped my spirit again.

THE SEVENTEENTH REMOVE

A comfortable Remove it was to me, because of my hopes. They gave me a pack, and along we went cheerfully, but quickly my will proved more than my strength. Having little or no refreshing, my strength failed me, and my spirit were almost quite gone. . . . At night we came to an Indian Town, and the Indians sat down by a Wigwam discoursing, but I was almost spent and could scarce speak. I laid down my load, and went into the Wigwam, and there sat an Indian boiling of Horses' feet (they being wont to eat the flesh first, and when the feet were old and dried and they had nothing else, they would cut off the feet and use them). I asked him to give me a little of his Broth, or Water they were boiling in. He took a dish and gave me one spoonful of Samp,[1] and bid me take as much of the Broth as I would. Then I put some of the hot water to the Samp and drank it up, and my spirit came again. He gave me also a piece of the Rough or Ridding[2] of the small Guts, and I broiled it on the coals. . . .

THE EIGHTEENTH REMOVE

We took up our packs and along we went, but a wearisome day I had of it. As we went along I saw an English-man stripped naked and lying dead upon the ground, but knew not who it was. Then we came to another Indian Town, where we stayed all night. In this Town there were four English Children, Captives; and one of them my own Sister's. I went to see how she did, and she was well, considering her Captive-condition. I would have tarried that night with her, but they that owned her would not suffer it. Then I went into another Wigwam, where they were boiling Corn and Beans, which was a lovely sight to see, but I could not get a taste thereof. Then I went to another Wigwam, where there were two of the English Children. The Squaw was boiling Horses' feet; then she cut me off a little piece and gave one of the English Children a piece also. Being very hungry I had quickly eat up mine, but the Child could not bite it, it was so tough and sinewy but lay sucking, gnawing, chewing and slabbering of it in the mouth and hand. Then I took it of the Child and ate it myself, and savory it was to my taste. Then I may say as Job 6:7, "The things that my soul refused to touch are as my sorrowful meat." Thus the Lord made that pleasant refreshing, which another time would have been an abomination. Then I went home to my mistress's Wigwam, and they told me I disgraced my master with begging, and if I did so any more, they would knock me in head. I told them they had as good knock me in head as starve me to death.

THE NINETEENTH REMOVE

They said, when we went out, that we must travel to Wachusett this day. But a bitter weary day I had of it, traveling now three days together, without resting any day between. At last, after many weary steps, I saw Wachusett hills, but many miles off. Then we came to a great Swamp, through which we traveled up to the knees in mud and water, which was heavy going to one tired before. Being almost spent, I thought I should have sunk down at last, and never got out; but I may say, as in Psalm 94:18, "When my foot slipped, thy mercy, O Lord, held me up."

Going along, having indeed my life but little spirit, Philip, who was in the Company, came up and took me by the hand, and said, "Two weeks more and you shall be Mistress again." I asked him if he spoke true. He answered, "Yes, and quickly you shall come to your master again," who had been gone from us three weeks. After many weary steps we came to Wachusett, where he was and glad I was to see him. He asked me when I washed me. I told him not this month. Then he fetched me some water himself and bid me wash, and gave me the Glass to see how I looked; and bid his Squaw give me something to eat. So she gave me a mess of Beans and meat and a little Ground-nut Cake. I was wonderfully revived with this favor showed me. . . .

My master had three Squaws, living sometimes with one, and sometimes with another one, this old Squaw at whose Wigwam I was, and with whom my Master had been those three weeks. Another was Weetamoo, with whom I had lived and served all this while. A severe and proud Dame she was, bestowing every day in dressing herself neat as much time as any of the Gentry of the land, powdering her hair and painting her face, going with Necklaces, with Jewels in her ears and Bracelets upon her hands. When she had dressed herself, her work was to make Girdles of Wampum and Beads. The third Squaw was a younger one, by whom he had two Papooses.

By that time I was refreshed by the old Squaw with whom my master was, Weetamoo's Maid came to call me home, at which I fell a weeping. Then the old Squaw told me, to encourage me, that if I wanted victuals, I should come to her, and that I should lie there in her Wigwam. Then I went with the maid and quickly came again and lodged there. The Squaw laid a Mat under me and a good Rug over me, the first time I had any such kindness showed me. I understood that Weetamoo thought that if she should let me go and serve with the old Squaw, she would be in danger to lose not only my service, but the redemption-pay also. And I was not a little glad to hear this; being by it raised in my hopes that in God's due time there would be an end of this sorrowful hour. Then came an Indian and asked me to knit him three pair of Stocking, for which I had a Hat and a silk Handkerchief. Then another asked me to make her a shift, for which she gave me an Apron.

Then came Tom and Peter,[1] with the second Letter from the Council about the Captives. Though they were Indians, I got them by the hand and burst out into tears; my heart was so full that I could not speak to them; but recovering myself, I asked them how my husband did, and all my friends and acquaintance. They said, "They are all very well but melancholy." They brought me two Biscuits and a pound of Tobacco. The Tobacco I quickly gave away. When it was all gone, one asked me to give him a pipe of Tobacco. I told him it was all gone; then [he] began he to rant and threaten. I told him when my Husband came I would give him some. "Hang him, Rogue (says he), I will knock out his brains, if he comes here." And then again, in the same breath they would say that if there should come an hundred without Guns, they would do them no hurt. So unstable and like madmen they were. So that fearing the worst, I durst not send to my Husband, though there were some thoughts of his coming to Redeem and fetch me, not knowing what might follow. For there was little more trust to them than to the master they served.[2]

When the Letter was come, the Sagamores met to consult about the Captives and called me to them to inquire how much my husband would give to redeem me. When I came I sat down among them, as I was wont to do, as their manner is. Then they bade me stand up and said they were the General Court.[3] They bid me speak what I thought he would give. Now knowing that all we had was destroyed by the Indians, I was in a great strait. I thought if I should speak of but a little, it would be slighted and hinder the matter; if of a great sum, I knew not where it would be procured. Yet at a venture, I said Twenty pounds, yet desired them to take less, but they would not hear of that, but sent that message to Boston, that for Twenty pounds I should be redeemed. It was a Praying-Indian that wrote their Letter for them.

There was another Praying-Indian, who told me that he had a brother that would not eat Horse, his conscience was so tender and scrupulous (though as large as hell, for the destruction of poor Christians). Then he said he read that Scripture to him, 2 Kings, 6:25, "There was a famine in Samaria, and behold they besieged it, until an Ass's head was sold for fourscore pieces of silver, and the fourth part of a Kab[4] of Dove's dung, for five pieces of silver." He expounded this place to his brother, and showed him that it was lawful to eat that in a Famine which is not at another time. And now, says he, he will eat Horse with any Indian of them all. There was another Praying-Indian, who when he had done all the mischief that he could, betrayed his own Father into the English hands, thereby to purchase his own life. Another Praying-Indian was at Sudbury-fight;[5] though, as he deserved, he was afterward hanged for it. There was another Praying-Indian, so wicked and cruel, as to wear a string about his neck strung with Christians' fingers. Another Praying-Indian, when they went to Sudbury-fight, went with them, and his Squaw also with him with her Papoose at her back.

Before they went to that fight, they got a company together to *Powwow*.[6] The manner was as followeth. There was one that kneeled upon a Deerskin, with the company round him in a ring who kneeled, and striking upon the ground with their hands and with sticks and muttering or humming with their mouths. Besides him who kneeled in the ring, there also stood one with a Gun in his hand. Then he on the Deerskin made a speech, and all manifested assent to it, and so they did many times together. Then they bade him with the Gun go out of the ring, which he did, but when he was out, they called him in again; but he seemed to make a stand; then they called the more earnestly, till he returned again. Then they all sang.

Then they gave him two Guns, in either hand one. And so he on the Deerskin began again; and at the end of every sentence in his speaking, they all assented, humming or muttering with their mouths and striking upon the ground with their hands. Then they bade him with the two Guns go out of the ring again; which he did, a little way. Then they called him in again, but he made a stand. So they called him with greater earnestness, but he stood reeling and wavering as if he knew not whether he should stand or fall, or which way to go. Then they called him with exceeding great vehemency, all of them, one and another. After a little while he turned in, staggering as he went, with his Arms stretched out, in either hand a Gun. As soon as he came in, they all sang and rejoiced exceedingly a while. And then he upon the Deerskin made another speech unto which they all assented in a rejoicing manner, and so they ended their business and forthwith went to Sudbury-fight.

To my thinking, they went without any scruple but that they should prosper and gain the victory. And they went out not so rejoicing, but they came home with as great a Victory. For they said they had killed two Captains and almost an hundred men. One Englishman they brought along with them, and he said it was too true, for they had made sad work at Sudbury, as indeed it proved. Yet they came home without that rejoicing and triumphing over their victory which they were wont to show at other times, but rather like Dogs (as they say) which have lost their ears. Yet I could not perceive that it was for their own loss of men. They said they had not lost above five or six, and I missed none except in one Wigwam. When they went, they acted as if the Devil had told them that they should gain the victory, and now they acted as if the Devil had told them they should have a fall. Whither it were so or no, I cannot tell, but so it proved, for quickly they began to fall, and so held on that Summer till they came to utter ruin. They came home on a Sabbath day, and the *Powwow* that kneeled upon the Deerskin came home (I may say without abuse) as black as the Devil.[7]

When my master came home, he came to me and bid me make a shirt for his Papoose of a Holland-laced Pillowbere.[8] About that time there came an Indian to me and bid me come to his Wigwam, at night, and he would give me some Pork and Ground-nuts. Which I did, and as I was eating, another Indian said to me, "he seems to be your good Friend, but he killed two Englishmen at Sudbury, and there lie their Clothes behind you." I looked behind me, and there I saw bloody Clothes with Bullet-holes in them; yet the Lord suffered not this wretch to do me any hurt. Yea, instead of that, he many times refreshed me. Five or six times did he and his Squaw refresh my feeble carcass. If I went to their Wigwam at any time, they would always give me something, and yet they were strangers that I never saw before. Another Squaw gave me a piece of fresh Pork and a little Salt with it, and lent me her Pan to Fry it in, and I cannot but remember what a sweet, pleasant and delightful relish that bit had to me, to this day. So little do we prize common mercies, when we have them to the full.

THE TWENTIETH REMOVE

It was their usual manner to remove when they had done any mischief lest they should be found out, and so they did at this time. We went about three or four miles, and there they built a great Wigwam, big enough to hold an hundred Indians, which they did in preparation to a great day of Dancing. They would say now amongst themselves that the Governor[1] would be so angry for his loss at Sudbury that he would send no more about the Captives, which made me grieve and tremble.

My Sister, being not far from the place where we now were and hearing that I was here, desired her master to let her come and see me, and he was willing to it and would go with her, but she, being ready before him, told him she would go before and was come within a Mile or two of the place. Then he overtook her and began to rant as if he had been mad and made her go back again in the Rain; so that I never saw her till I saw her in Charlestown.[2] But the Lord requited many of their ill doings, for this Indian her Master was hanged afterward at Boston.

The Indians now began to come from all quarters against their merry dancing day. Among some of them came one Good-wife Kettle. I told her my heart was so heavy that it was ready to break. "So is mine too," said she, but yet said, "I hope we shall hear some good news shortly." I could hear how earnestly my Sister desired to see me, and I as earnestly desired to see her, and yet neither of us could get an opportunity. My Daughter was also now about a mile off, and I had not seen her in nine or ten weeks, as I had not seen my Sister since our first taking. I earnestly desired them to let me go and see them; yea, I en-treated, begged, and persuaded them but to let me see my Daughter, and yet so hard-hearted were they, that they would not suffer it. They made use of their tyrannical power whilst they had it, but through the Lord's wonderful mercy, their time was now but short.

On a Sabbath day, the Sun being about an hour high in the afternoon, came Mr. John Hoar[3] (the Council permitting him, and his own forward spirit inclining him) together with the two forementioned Indians, Tom and Peter, with their third Letter from the Council. When they came near, I was abroad. Though I saw them not, they [her captors] presently called me in and bade me sit down and not stir. Then they caught up their Guns and away they ran, as if an Enemy had been at hand; and the Guns went off apace. I manifested some great trouble, and they asked me what was the matter. I told them I thought they had killed the Englishman (for they had in the meantime informed me that an Englishman was come). They said no, they shot over his Horse and under and before his Horse; and they pushed him this way and that way at their pleasure, showing what they could do. Then they let them come to their Wigwams. I begged of them to let me see the Englishman, but they would not. But there was I fain to sit their pleasure.

When they had talked their fill with him, they suffered me to go to him. We asked each other of our welfare, and how my Husband did and all my Friends. He told me they were all well and would be glad to see me. Amongst other things which my Husband sent me, there came a pound of Tobacco, which I sold for nine shillings in Money, for many of the Indians for want of Tobacco smoked Hemlock and Ground-Ivy. It was a great mistake in any who thought I sent for Tobacco, for through the favor of God, that desire was overcome. I now asked them whether I should go home with Mr. Hoar. They answered no, one and another of them, and it being night, we lay down with that answer. In the morning, Mr. Hoar invited the Sagamores to Dinner, but when we went to get it ready, we found that they had stolen the greatest part of the Provision Mr. Hoar had brought out of his Bags in the night.

And we may see the wonderful power of God in that one passage, in that when there was such a great number of the Indians together and so greedy of a little good food; and no English there but Mr. Hoar and myself, that there they did not knock us in the head and take what we had, there being not only some Provision but also Trading-cloth, a part of the twenty pounds agreed upon. But instead of doing us any mischief, they seemed to be ashamed of the fact, and said it were some Matchit[4] Indian that did it. . . .

Mr. Hoar called them betime to Dinner, but they ate very little, they being so busy in dressing themselves and getting ready for their Dance, which was carried on by eight of them, four Men and four Squaws, my master and mistress being two. He was dressed in his Holland shirt, with great Laces sewed at the tail of it. He had his silver Buttons, his white Stockings; his Garters were hung round with Shillings, and he had Girdles of

Wampum upon his head and shoulders. She had a Kersey[5] Coat, and covered with Girdles of Wampum from the Loins upward. Her arms from her elbows to her hands were covered with Bracelets; there were handfuls of Necklaces about her neck, and several sorts of Jewels in her ears. She had fine red Stockings and white Shoes, her hair powdered and face painted Red, that was always before Black. And all the Dancers were after the same manner.

There were two other[s] singing and knocking on a Kettle for their music. They kept hopping up and down one after another, with a Kettle of water in the midst standing warm upon some Embers to drink of when they were dry. They held on till it was almost night, throwing out Wampum to the standers by. At night I asked them again if I should go home. They all as one said no except my Husband would come for me. When we were lain down, my Master went out of the Wigwam, and by and by sent in an Indian called James the Printer,[6] who told Mr. Hoar that my Master would let me go home tomorrow, if he would let him have one pint of Liquors. Then Mr. Hoar called his own Indians, Tom and Peter, and bid them go and see whether he would promise it before them three, and if he would, he should have it; which he did, and he had it.

Then Philip, smelling the business, called me to him, and asked me what I would give him to tell me some good news, and speak a good word for me. I told him I could not tell what to give him, I would anything I had, and asked him what he would have. He said two Coats and twenty shillings in Money, and half a bushel of seed Corn, and some Tobacco. I thanked him for his love, but I knew the good news as well as the crafty Fox.

My Master, after he had had his drink, quickly came ranting into the Wigwam again and called for Mr. Hoar, drinking to him and saying he was a good man, and then again he would say, "Hang him, Rogue." Being almost drunk, he would drink to him, and yet presently say he should be hanged. Then he called for me. I trembled to hear him, yet I was fain to go to him, and he drank to me, showing no incivility. He was the first Indian I saw drunk all the while that I was amongst them. At last his Squaw ran out, and he after her, round the Wigwam, with his money jingling at his knees, but she escaped him. But having an old Squaw, he ran to her, and so through the Lord's mercy, we were no more troubled that night.

Yet I had not a comfortable night's rest, for I think I can say I did not sleep for three nights together. The night before the Letter came from the Council, I could not rest, I was so full of fears and troubles, God many times leaving us most in the dark when deliverance is nearest; yea, at this time I could not rest night nor day. The next night I was overjoyed, Mr. Hoar being come, and that with such good tidings. The third night I was even swallowed up with the thoughts of things, *viz.* that ever I should go home again; and that I must go leaving my Children behind me in the Wilderness, so that sleep was now almost departed from mine eyes.

On Tuesday morning they called their General Court (as they call it) to consult and determine whether I should go home or no. And they all as one man did seemingly consent to it, that I should go home; except Philip, who would not come among them.

But before I go any further, I would take leave to mention a few remarkable passages of providence, which I took special notice of in my afflicted time.

1. Of the fair opportunity lost in the long March, a little after the Fort-fight, when our English Army was so numerous, and in pursuit of the Enemy, and so near as to take several and destroy them, and the Enemy in such distress for food that our men might track them by their rooting in the earth for Ground-nuts, whilst they were flying for their lives. I say that then our Army should want Provision, and be forced to leave their pursuit and return homeward, and the very next week the Enemy came upon our Town like Bears bereft of their whelps, or so many ravenous Wolves, rending us and our Lambs to death. But what shall I say? God seemed to leave his People to themselves, and order all things for his own holy ends. . . .

2. I cannot but remember how the Indians derided the slowness and dullness of the English Army in its setting out. For after the desolations at Lancaster and Medfield, as I went along with them, they asked me when I thought the English Army would come after them. I told them I could not tell. It may be they will come in May, said they. Thus did they scoff at us, as if the English would be a quarter of a year getting ready.

3. Which also I have hinted before, when the English Army with new supplies were sent forth to pursue after the enemy, and they, understanding it, fled before them till they came to Bacquag River, where they forthwith went over safely, that that River should be impassable to the English. I can but admire to see the wonderful providence of God in preserving the heathen for farther affliction to our poor Country. They could go in great numbers over, but the English must stop. God had an over-ruling hand in all those things.

4. It was thought, if their Corn were cut down, they would starve and die with hunger. And all their Corn that could be found was destroyed, and they driven from that little they had in store into the Woods in the midst of Winter; and yet how to admiration did the Lord preserve them for his holy ends, and the destruction of many still amongst the English! Strangely did the Lord provide for them, that I did not see (all the time I was among them) one Man, Woman, or Child die with hunger.

Though many times they would eat that, that a Hog or a Dog would hardly touch; yet by that God strengthened them to be a scourge to his People. The chief and commonest food was Ground-nuts. They ate also Nuts and Acorns, Artichokes, Lilly roots, Ground-beans, and several other weeds and roots that I know not. They would pick up old bones, and cut them to pieces at the joints, and if they were full of worms and maggots, they would scald them over the fire to make the vermin come out, and then boil them and drink up the Liquor, and

then beat the great ends of them in a Mortar, and so eat
them. They would eat Horses' guts and ears, and all sorts
of wild Birds which they could catch; also Bear, Venison,
Beaver, Tortoise, Frogs, Squirrels, Dogs, Skunks, Rattle-
snakes, yea, the very Bark of Trees; besides all sorts of
creatures and provision which they plundered from the
English.

I can but stand in admiration to see the wonderful
power of God, in providing for such a vast number of
our Enemies in the Wilderness, where there was nothing to be seen but from hand to mouth. Many times in
a morning, the generality of them would eat up all they
had and yet have some further supply against they
wanted. It is said, Psalm 81:13–14, "Oh, that my People had hearkened to me, and Israel had walked in my
ways, I should soon have subdued their Enemies, and
turned my hand against their Adversaries." But now
our perverse and evil carriages in the sight of the Lord
have so offended him that instead of turning his hand
against them, the Lord feeds and nourishes them up to
be a scourge to the whole Land.

5. Another thing that I would observe is the strange providence of God in turning things about when the Indians
was at the highest, and the English at the lowest. I was
with the Enemy eleven weeks and five days, and not one
Week passed without the fury of the Enemy and some
desolation by fire and sword upon one place or other.
They mourned (with their black faces) for their own
losses, yet triumphed and rejoiced in their Inhumane and
many times devilish cruelty to the English. They would
boast much of their Victories; saying that in two hours
time they had destroyed such a Captain and his Company at such a place; and such a Captain and his Company in such a place; and such a Captain and his
Company in such a place, and boast how many Towns
they had destroyed; and then scoff and say they had done
them a good turn to send them to Heaven so soon.
Again, they would say this Summer that they would

knock all the Rogues in the head, or drive them into the
Sea, or make them fly the Country, thinking surely,
Agag-like, "The bitterness of Death is past."[7]

Now the Heathen begins to think all is their own,
and the poor Christians' hopes to fail (as to man), and
now their eyes are more to God, and their hearts sigh
heavenward, and to say in good earnest, "Help, Lord,
or we perish."[8] When the Lord had brought his people
to this, that they saw no help in any thing but himself,
then he takes the quarrel into his own hand, and though
they had made a pit in their own imaginations as deep
as hell for the Christians that Summer, yet the Lord
hurled themselves into it. And the Lord had not so
many ways before to preserve them, but now he hath as
many to destroy them.

But to return again to my going home, where we may see a
remarkable change of Providence. At first they were all against
it, except my Husband would come for me; but afterwards they
assented to it, and seemed much to rejoice in it. Some asked me
to send them some Bread, others some Tobacco, others shaking
me by the hand, offering me a Hood and Scarf to ride in, not
one moving hand or tongue against it. Thus hath the Lord answered my poor desire, and the many earnest requests of others
put up unto God for me. In my travels an Indian came to me
and told me, if I were willing, he and his Squaw would run
away and go home along with me. I told him no, I was not willing to run away, but desired to wait God's time that I might go
home quietly and without fear. And now God hath granted me
my desire.

Oh, the wonderful power of God that I have seen, and the
experience that I have had. I have been in the midst of those
roaring Lions and Savage Bears, that feared neither God, nor
Man, nor the Devil, by night and day, alone and in company;
sleeping all sorts together, and yet not one of them ever offered
me the least abuse of unchastity to me in word or action.
Though some are ready to say I speak it for my own credit, but

I speak it in the presence of God, and to his Glory. . . . Let the Redeemed of the Lord say so, whom he hath redeemed from the hand of the Enemy, especially that I should come away in the midst of so many hundreds of Enemies quietly and peaceably, and not a Dog moving his tongue.

So I took my leave of them, and in coming along my heart melted into tears more than all the while I was with them, and I was almost swallowed up with the thoughts that ever I should go home again. About the Sun going down, Mr. Hoar and myself and the two Indians came to Lancaster, and a solemn sight it was to me. There had I lived many comfortable years amongst my Relations and Neighbors, and now not one Christian to be seen, nor one house left standing. We went on to a Farm house that was yet standing, where we lay all night, and a comfortable lodging we had, though nothing but straw to lie on. The Lord preserved us in safety that night, and raised us up again in the morning, and carried us along that before noon we came to Concord.

Now was I full of joy, and yet not without sorrow; joy to see such a lovely sight, so many Christians together, and some of them my Neighbors. There I met with my Brother and my Brother-in-Law, who asked me if I knew where his Wife was. Poor heart! he had helped to bury her and knew it not; she being shot down by the house [that] was partly burned, so that those who were at Boston at the desolation of the Town and came back afterward and buried the dead did not know her. Yet I was not without sorrow to think how many were looking and longing, and my own Children amongst the rest, to enjoy that deliverance that I had now received, and I did not know whether ever I should see them again.

Being recruited with food and raiment we went to Boston that day, where I met with my dear Husband, but the thoughts of our dear Children, one being dead and the other we could not tell where, abated our comfort each to other. I was not before so much hemmed in with the merciless and cruel Heathen, but now as much with pitiful, tender-hearted, and compassionate Christians. In that poor and distressed and beggarly condition I was received in, I was kindly entertained in several Houses. So much love I received from several (some of whom I knew, and others I knew not) that I am not capable to declare it. But the Lord knows them all by name. . . . The twenty pounds the price of my redemption was raised by some Boston Gentlemen and Mrs. Usher, whose bounty and religious charity, I would not forget to make mention of. Then Mr. Thomas Shepard of Charlestown received us into his House, where we continued eleven weeks; and a Father and Mother they were to us. And many more tenderhearted Friends we met with in that place.

We were now in the midst of love, yet not without much and frequent heaviness of heart for our poor Children and other Relations who were still in affliction. The week following after my coming in, the Governor and Council sent forth to the Indians again, and that not without success, for they brought in my Sister and Goodwife Kettle. Their not knowing where our Children were was a sore trial to us still, and yet we were not without secret hopes that we should see them again. That which was dead lay heavier upon my spirit than those which were alive and amongst the Heathen; thinking how it suffered with its wounds and I was no way able to relieve it, and how it was buried by the Heathen in the Wilderness from among all Christians. We were hurried up and down in our thoughts. Sometime we should hear a report that they were gone this way, and sometimes that; and that they were come in, in this place or that. We kept inquiring and listening to hear concerning them, but no certain news as yet.

About this time the Council had ordered a day of public Thanksgiving, though I thought I had still cause of mourning, and being unsettled in our minds, we thought we would ride toward the Eastward to see if we could hear any thing concerning our Children. And as we were riding along (God is the wise disposer of all things) between Ipswich and Rowley we met with Mr. William Hubbard,[9] who told us that our Son Joseph was come in to Major Waldron's,[10] and another with him, which was my Sister's Son. I asked him how he knew it. He said the Major himself told him so. So along we went till we came to

Newbury, and their Minister being absent, they desired my Husband to Preach the Thanksgiving for them; but he was not willing to stay there that night, but would go over to Salisbury to hear further, and come again in the morning; which he did, and Preached there that day.

At night, when he had done, one came and told him that his Daughter was come in at Providence. Here was mercy on both hands. . . . Now we were between them, the one on the East, and the other on the West. Our Son being nearest, we went to him first to Portsmouth, where we met with him, and with the Major also, who told us he had done what he could, but could not redeem him under seven pounds; which the good People thereabouts were pleased to pay. The Lord reward the Major and all the rest, though unknown to me, for their labor of Love. My Sister's Son was redeemed for four pounds, which the Council gave order for the payment of.

Having now received one of our Children, we hastened toward the other. . . . On Monday we came to Charlestown, where we heard that the Governor of Rhode Island[11] had sent over for our Daughter to take care of her, being now within his Jurisdiction, which should not pass without our acknowledgments. But she being nearer Rehoboth than Rhode Island, Mr. Newman[12] went over and took care of her, and brought her to his own House. And the goodness of God was admirable to us in our low estate, in that he raised up passionate Friends on every side to us, when we had nothing to recompense any for their love. The Indians were now gone that way, that it was apprehended dangerous to go to her. But the Carts which carried Provision to the English Army, being guarded, brought her with them to Dorchester,[13] where we received her safe. Blessed be the Lord for it, for great is his Power, and he can do whatsoever seemeth him good.

Her coming in was after this manner. She was traveling one day with the Indians with her basket at her back. The company of Indians were got before her and gone out of sight, all except one Squaw. She followed the Squaw till night, and then both of them lay down, having nothing over them but the heavens, and under them but the earth. Thus she traveled three days together, not knowing whither she was going, having nothing to eat or drink but water and green Hurtleberries. At last they came into Providence, where she was kindly entertained by several of that Town. The Indians often said that I should never have her under twenty pounds. But now the Lord hath brought her in upon free-cost and given her to me the second time. . . . Thus hath the Lord brought me and mine out of that horrible pit, and hath set us in the midst of tender-hearted and compassionate Christians. It is the desire of my soul that we may walk worthy of the mercies received, and which we are receiving.

Our Family being now gathered together (those of us that were living) the South Church in Boston hired an House for us. Then we removed from Mr. Shepard's, those cordial Friends, and went to Boston, where we continued about three-quarters of a year. Still the Lord went along with us and provided graciously for us. I thought it somewhat strange to set up House-keeping with bare walls; but as Solomon says, "Money answers all things,"[14] and that we had through the benevolence of Christian friends, some in this Town, and some in that, and others, and some from England, that in a little time we might look and see the House furnished with love. The Lord hath been exceeding good to us in our low estate in that when we had neither house nor home, nor other necessaries; the Lord so moved the hearts of these and those towards us, that we wanted neither food nor raiment for ourselves or ours. . . .

I can remember the time, when I used to sleep quietly without workings in my thoughts, whole nights together, but now it is other ways with me. When all are fast about me, and no eye open but his who ever waketh, my thoughts are upon things past, upon the awful dispensation of the Lord towards us; upon his wonderful power and might in carrying of us through so many difficulties, in returning us in safety, and suffering none to hurt us. I remember in the night season how the other day I was in the midst of thousands of enemies, and nothing but death before me. It is then hard work to persuade myself that ever I should be satisfied with bread again. But now we are fed with the finest of the Wheat, and, as I may say, with honey out of the rock.[15] . . . Oh! the wonderful power of God that mine eyes have seen, affording matter enough for my thoughts to run in, that when others are sleeping mine eyes are weeping. . . .

From Benjamin Church
and Thomas Church,
Entertaining Passages
Relating to Philip's War, 1716

No better account of the war that engulfed New England in 1675 and 1676 exists than that of Benjamin Church (1639–1718). Church, a carpenter and farmer turned Indian fighter, was a leading participant in the combat and an eye-witness to many of its most important phases. Again and again responding to Plymouth Colony's calls to arms, he was instrumental in changing the course of war in favor of the English during the late spring and summer of 1676. If his account of the struggle is sometimes colored by an old soldier's prideful memory of his glory days, it is nonetheless un-rivalled among the narratives of colonial American warfare in immediacy and authenticity. The curiously titled Entertaining Passages *came into being forty years after the event, when Church's son Thomas assembled it from his father's recollections and field notebooks. It is thus what one might call a colonial "as-told-to" book, one in which the pitch and rhythm of Church's speech still seem audible through his son's transcription.*

Entertaining Passages Relating to Philip's War,
Which began in the Year 1675,
With the Proceedings of Benjamin Church, Esquire

TO THE READER

The Subject of this following Narrative offering itself to your friendly Perusal relates to the Former and Later Wars of New

England, which I myself was not a little concerned in, for in the Year 1675, that unhappy and bloody Indian War broke out in Plymouth Colony, where I was then building and beginning a Plantation at a Place called by the Indians Sakonnet; and since by the English, Little Compton.[1] I was the first Englishman that built upon that Neck, which was full of Indians. My head and hands were full about Settling a New Plantation, where nothing was brought to; no preparation of Dwelling House, or Out-Housing or Fencing made. Horses and Cattle were to be provided, Ground to be cleared and broken up, and the uttermost caution to be used to keep myself free from offending my Indian Neighbors all round about me.

While I was thus busily Employed, and all my Time and Strength laid out in this Laborious Undertaking, I Received a Commission from the Government to engage in their Defense. And with my Commission I received another heart, inclining me to put forth my Strength in Military Service. And through the Grace of God I was Spirited for that work, and Direction in it was renewed to me day by day. And although many of the Actions that I was concerned in were very Difficult and Dangerous, yet myself and those that went with me Voluntarily in the Service had our Lives, for the most part, wonderfully preserved by the over-ruling Hand of the Almighty, from first to last; which doth aloud bespeak our Praises. And to declare His Wonderful Works is our Indispensable Duty. I was ever very sensible of my own Littleness and Unfitness to be employed in such Great Services; but calling to mind that God is Strong, I Endeavored to put all my Confidence in Him, and by His Almighty Power was carried through every difficult Action, and my desire is that His Name may have the Praise.

It was ever my Intent, having laid myself under a Solemn promise, that the many and Repeated Favors of God to myself and those with me in the Service might be published for Generations to come. And now my great Age requiring my Dismission from Service in the Militia, and to put off my Armor, I am willing that the Great and Glorious works of Almighty God to us Children of Men should appear to the World. And having my Minutes by me, my Son has taken the care and pains to

Collect from them the Ensuing Narrative of many passages relating to the Former and Later Wars, which I have had the perusal of and find nothing amiss as to the Truth of it, and with as
little Reflection upon any particular person as might be, either
alive or dead.

And seeing every particle of historical Truth is precious, I
hope the Reader will pass a favorable Censure upon an Old Soldier telling of the many Rencounters he has had, and yet is
come off alive. It is a pleasure to Remember what a great Number of Families in this and the Neighboring Provinces in New
England did during the War enjoy a great measure of Liberty
and Peace by the hazardous Stations and Marches of those Engaged in Military Exercises, who were a Wall unto them on this
side and on that side. I desire Prayers that I may be enabled Well
to accomplish my Spiritual Warfare, and that I may be more
than Conqueror through Jesus Christ loving of me.

Benjamin Church.

[THE OUTBREAK]

In the Year 1674, Mr. Benjamin Church of Duxbury, being
providentially at Plymouth in the time of the Court,[1] fell into
acquaintance with Captain John Almy of Rhode Island.[2] Captain Almy with great importunity invited him to ride with him
and view that part of Plymouth Colony that lay next to Rhode
Island, known then by their Indian Names of Pocasset[3] and
Sakonnet. Among other arguments to persuade him, he told
him the Soil was very rich and the Situation pleasant. Persuades
him by all means to purchase of the Company some of the
Court grant rights.[4] He accepted his invitation, views the Country, and was pleased with it; makes a purchase, settled a Farm,
found the Gentlemen of the Island very Civil and obliging. And
being himself a Person of uncommon Activity and Industry, he
soon erected two buildings upon his Farm, and gained a good
acquaintance with the Natives, got much into their favor, and
was in a little time in great esteem among them.

The next Spring advancing, while Mr. Church was diligently

Settling his new Farm, stocking, leasing, and disposing of his Affairs, and had a fine prospect of doing no small things; and hoping that his good success would be inviting unto other good Men to become his Neighbors, behold! the rumor of a War between the English and the Natives gave check to his projects. People began to be very jealous of the Indians, and indeed they had no small reason to suspect that they had formed a design of War upon the English. Mr. Church had it daily suggested to him that the Indians were plotting a bloody design. That Philip, the great Mount Hope Sachem,⁵ was Leader therein, and so it proved. He was sending his Messengers to all the Neighboring Sachems to engage them in a Confederacy with him in the War.

Among the rest he sent Six Men to Awashonks, Squaw-Sachem of the Sakonnet Indians, to engage her in his Interests. Awashonks so far listened unto them as to call her Subjects together to make a great Dance, which is the custom of that Nation when they advise about Momentous Affairs. But what does Awashonks do but sends away two of her Men that well understood the English Language (Sassamon and George by Name) to invite Mr. Church to the Dance. Mr. Church upon the Invitation immediately takes with him Charles Hazelton, his Tenant's Son, who well understood the Indian Language, and rode down to the Place appointed, where they found hundreds of Indians gathered together from all Parts of her Dominion.

Awashonks herself, in a foaming Sweat, was leading the Dance. But she was no sooner sensible of Mr. Church's arrival, but she broke off, sat down, calls her Nobles round her, orders Mr. Church to be invited into her presence, Compliments being passed, and each one taking Seats. She told him King Philip had sent Six Men of his with two of her People that had been over at Mount Hope to draw her into a confederacy with him in a War with the English, desiring him to give her his advice in the case, and to tell her the Truth whether the Umpame⁶ Men (as Philip had told her) were gathering a great Army to invade Philip's Country.

He assured her he would tell her the Truth and give her his best advice. Then he told her 'twas but a few days since he came from Plymouth, and the English were then making no Preparations for

War; that he was in Company with the Principal Gentlemen of the Government, who had no Discourse at all about War, and, he believed, no thoughts about it. He asked her whether she thought he would have brought up his Goods to Settle in that Place, if he apprehended an entering into War with so near a Neighbor. She seemed to be somewhat convinced by his talk and said she believed he spoke the Truth.

Then she called for the Mount Hope Men, who made a formidable appearance, with their Faces Painted, and their Hair Trimmed up in Comb-fashion, with their Powder horns and Shot-bags at their backs; which among that Nation is the posture and figure of preparedness for War. She told Mr. Church, these were the Persons that had brought her the Report of the English preparation for War. And then told them what Mr. Church had said in answer to it.

Upon this began a warm talk among the Indians, but 'twas soon quashed, and Awashonks proceeded to tell Mr. Church that Philip's Message to her was that unless she would forthwith enter into a confederacy with him in a War against the English, he would send his Men over privately to kill the English Cattle and burn their Houses on that side the River,[7] which would provoke the English to fall upon her, whom they would without doubt suppose the author of the Mischief. Mr. Church told her he was sorry to see so threatening an aspect of Affairs; and stepping to the Mount Hopes, he felt of their bags, and finding them filled with Bullets, asked them what those Bullets were for. They scoffingly replied to shoot Pigeons with.

Then Mr. Church turned to Awashonks and told her if Philip were resolved to make War, her best way would be to knock those Six Mount Hopes on the head and shelter herself under the Protection of the English, upon which the Mount Hopes were for the present Dumb. But those two of Awashonks's Men who had been at Mount Hope expressed themselves in a furious manner against his advice.

And Little Eyes, one of the Queen's Council, joined with them, and urged Mr. Church to go aside with him among the bushes that he might have some private Discourse with him, which other Indians immediately forbid, being sensible of his ill design, but the Indians began to side[8] and grow very warm. Mr. Church with undaunted Courage told the Mount Hopes they were bloody wretches, and thirsted after the blood of their English Neighbors, who had never injured them but had always abounded in their kindness to them; that for his own part, though he desired nothing more than Peace, yet if nothing but War would satisfy them, he believed he should prove a sharp thorn in their sides; bid the Company observe those Men that were of such bloody dispositions, whether Providence would suffer them to Live to see the event[9] of the War, which others more Peaceably disposed might do.

Then he told Awashonks he thought it might be most advisable for her to send to the Governor of Plymouth[10] and shelter herself and People under his Protection. She liked his advice and desired him to go on her behalf to the Plymouth Government, which he consented to, and at parting advised her whatever she did, not to desert the English Interest to join with her Neighbors in a Rebellion which would certainly prove fatal to her. (He moved none of his Goods from his House that there might not be the least umbrage from such an Action.) She thanked him for his advice, and sent two of her Men to guard him to his House; which, when they came there, urged him to take care to secure his Goods, which he refused for the reasons before mentioned. But desired the Indians that if what they feared should happen, they would take care of what he left, and directed them to a Place in the woods where they should dispose them; which they faithfully observed.

He took his leave of his guard and bid them tell their Mistress, if she continued steady in her dependence on the English, and kept within her own limits of Sakonnet, he would see her again quickly; and then hastened away to Pocasset, where he met with Peter Nunnuit, the Husband of the Queen of Pocasset[11] who was just then come over in a Canoe from Mount Hope. Peter told him that there would certainly be War, for Philip had held a Dance of several Weeks' continuance and had entertained the Young Men from all Parts of the Country. And added that Philip expected to be sent for to Plymouth to be examined about Sassamon's death, who was Murdered at Assawompsett Ponds;[12]

knowing himself guilty of contriving that Murder. The same Peter told him that he saw Mr. James Brown of Swansea[13] and Mr. Samuel Gorton, who was an Interpreter, and two other Men, who brought a Letter from the Governor of Plymouth to Philip. He observed to him further that the Young Men were very eager to begin the War, and would fain have killed Mr. Brown, but Philip prevented it; telling them that his Father had charged him to show kindness to Mr. Brown. In short, Philip was forced to promise them that on the next Lord's Day, when the English were gone to Meeting, they should rifle their Houses and from that time forward kill their Cattle.

Peter desired Mr. Church to go and see his Wife, who was but up the hill; he went and found but few of her People with her. She said they were all gone against her Will to the Dances; and she much feared there would be a War. Mr. Church advised her to go to the Island and secure herself, and those that were with her; and send to the Governor of Plymouth, who she knew was her friend; and so left her, resolving to hasten to Plymouth and wait on the Governor; and he was so expeditious that he was with the Governor early next Morning, though he waited on some of the Magistrates by the way who were of the Council of War and also met him at the Governor's. He gave them an account of his observations and discoveries, which confirmed their former intelligences, and hastened their preparation for Defense.

Philip, according to his promise to his People, permitted them to March out of the Neck[14] on the next Lord's Day, when they plundered the nearest Houses that the Inhabitants had deserted, but as yet offered no violence to the People, at least none were killed. However, the alarm was given by their Numbers and hostile Equipage, and by the Prey they made of what they could find in the forsaken Houses.

An express came the same day to the Governor, who immediately gave orders to the Captains of the Towns to March the greatest Part of their Companies, and to rendezvous at Taunton on Monday Night, where Major Bradford[15] was to receive them, and dispose them under Captain (now made Major) Cudworth of Scituate. The Governor desired Mr. Church to give them his Company, and to use his interest in their behalf with the Gentlemen of Rhode Island. He complied with it, and they Marched the next day. Major Bradford desired Mr. Church with a commanded party consisting of English and some Friend-Indians to March in the Front at some distance from the Main body. Their orders were to keep so far before, as not be in sight of the Army. And so they did, for by the way they killed a Deer, flayed, roasted, and ate the most of him before the Army came up with them. But the Plymouth Forces soon arrived at Swansea and were posted at Major Brown's and Mr. Miles's Garrisons chiefly; and were there soon joined with those that came from Massachusetts,[16] who had entered into a Confederacy with their Plymouth Brethren against the Perfidious Heathen.

The Enemy, who began their Hostilities with plundering and destroying Cattle, did not long content themselves with that game. They thirsted for English blood, and they soon broached it, killing two Men in the way not far from Mr. Miles's Garrison. And soon after, eight more at Mattapoisett,[17] upon whose bodies they exercised more than brutish barbarities; beheading, dismembering, and mangling them, and exposing them in the most inhumane manner, which gashed and ghostly objects struck a damp[18] on all beholders.

The Enemy, flushed with these exploits, grew yet bolder, and skulking everywhere in the bushes, shot at all Passengers and killed many that ventured abroad. They came so near as to shoot down two Sentinels at Mr. Miles's Garrison under the very Noses of most of our Forces. These provocations drew out the resentments of some of Captain Prentice's Troop,[19] who desired they might have liberty to go out and seek the Enemy in their own quarters. Quartermasters Gill and Belcher commanded the Parties drawn out, who earnestly desired Mr. Church's company. They provided him a Horse and Furniture[20] (his own being out of the way); he readily complied with their desires and was soon Mounted.

This party were no sooner over Miles's Bridge, but were fired on by an Ambuscade of about a dozen Indians, as they were afterwards discovered to be. When they drew off, the Pilot[21] was

Mortally wounded; Mr. Belcher received a shot in his knee, and his Horse was killed under him; Mr. Gill was struck with a Musket-ball on the side of his belly; but being clad with a buff Coat[22] and some thickness of Paper under it, it never broke his skin.

The Troopers were surprised to see both their Commanders wounded, and wheeled off. But Mr. Church persuaded, at length stormed and stamped, and told them 'twas a shame to run and leave a wounded Man there to become a Prey to the barbarous Enemy. For the Pilot yet sat his Horse, though so mazed with the Shot as not to have sense to guide him. Mr. Gill seconded him and offered, though much disenabled, to assist in bringing him off. Mr. Church asked a Stranger who gave them his company in that action if he would go with him and fetch off the wounded Man. He readily consented; they with Mr. Gill went, but the wounded Man fainted and fell off his Horse before they came to him; but Mr. Church and the Stranger dismounted, took up the Man dead, and laid him before Mr. Gill on his Horse.

Mr. Church told the other two if they would take care of the dead Man, he would go and fetch his Horse back, which was going off the Causeway toward the Enemy; but before he got over the Causeway, he saw the Enemy run to the right into the Neck. He brought back the Horse, and called earnestly and repeatedly to the Army to come over and fight the Enemy; and while he stood calling and persuading, the skulking Enemy returned to their old stand, and all discharged their Guns at him at one clap. Though every shot missed him, yet one of the Army on the other side of the river received one of the balls in his foot. Mr. Church now began (no succor coming to him) to think it time to retreat, saying, "The Lord have Mercy on us, if such a handful of Indians shall thus dare such an Army!"

Upon this 'twas immediately resolved, and orders were given to March down into the Neck, and having passed the Bridge and Causeway, the direction was to extend both wings, which being not well heeded by those that remained in the Center, some of them mistook their Friends for their Enemies and made a fire upon them on the right wing, and wounded that noble

Heroic Youth Ensign Savage in the thigh; but it happily proved but a flesh wound. They Marched until they came to the narrow of the Neck, at a Place called Kickemuit,[23] where they took down the heads of Eight Englishmen that were killed at the head of Mattapoisett Neck, and set upon Poles after the barbarous manner of those Savages.

There Philip had staved all his Drums and conveyed all his Canoes to the East side of Mattapoisett River.[24] Hence it was concluded by those that were acquainted with the Motions of those People that they had quitted the Neck. Mr. Church told 'em that Philip was doubtless gone over to Pocasset side to engage those Indians in Rebellion with him, which they soon found to be true. The Enemy were not really beaten out of Mount Hope Neck, though 'twas true they fled from thence; yet it was before any pursued them. 'Twas but to strengthen themselves and to gain a more advantageous Post. However, some and not a few pleased themselves with the fancy of a Mighty Conquest.

A grand Council was held and a Resolve passed to build a Fort there to maintain the first ground they had gained by the Indians leaving it to them. And to speak the Truth, it must be said that as they gained not that Field by their Sword nor their Bow; so 'twas rather their fear than their courage that obliged them to set up the marks of their Conquest. Mr. Church looked upon it and talk[ed?] of it with contempt, and urged hard the pursuing the Enemy on Pocasset side, and with the greater earnestness because of his promise made to Awashonks, before mentioned.

The Council adjourned themselves from Mount Hope to Rehoboth,[25] where Mr. Treasurer Southworth,[26] being weary of his charge of Commissary General (Provision being scarce and difficult to be obtained, for the Army, that now lay still to Cover the People from nobody, while they were building a Fort for nothing), retired, and the Power and Trouble of that Post was left with Mr. Church, who still urged the Commanding Officers to move over to Pocasset side to pursue the Enemy and kill Philip, which would in his opinion be more probable to keep possession of the Neck than to tarry to build a Fort. He was still restless on that side of the River, and the rather because of his promise to the Squaw Sachem of Sakonnet. And Captain Fuller also urged the same, until at length there came further order concerning the Fort. And with all, an order for Captain Fuller with Six files to cross the River to the side so much insisted on, and to try if he could get Speech with any of the Pocasset or Sakonnet Indians, and that Mr. Church should go his Second.

Upon the Captain's receiving his orders, he asked Mr. Church whether he was willing to engage in this enterprise. To whom 'twas indeed too agreeable to be declined; though he thought the enterprise was hazardous enough for them to have more Men assigned them. Captain Fuller told him that for his own part he was grown Ancient and heavy, he feared the travel and fatigue would be too much for him. But Mr. Church urged him, and told him he would cheerfully excuse him his hardship and travel, and take that part to himself if he might but go; for he had rather do anything in the World than stay there to build the Fort.

Then they drew out the Number assigned them and Marched the same Night to the Ferry and were transported to Rhode Island, from whence the next Night they got a passage over to Pocasset-side in Rhode Island Boats, and concluded there to dispose themselves in two Ambuscades before day, hoping to surprise some of the Enemy by their falling into one or other of their Ambushments. But Captain Fuller's party, being troubled with the Epidemical plague of lust after Tobacco, must needs strike fire to Smoke it, and thereby discovered themselves to a party of the Enemy coming up to them, who immediately fled with great precipitation.

This Ambuscade drew off about break of day, perceiving they were discovered; the other continued in their Post until the time assigned them, and the light and heat of the Sun rendered their Station both insignificant and troublesome, and then returned unto the place of Rendezvous, where they were acquainted with the other party's disappointment, and the occasion of it. Mr. Church calls for the breakfast he had ordered to be brought over in the Boat, but the Man that had the charge of it confessed that he was asleep when the Boatsmen called him, and in haste came away and never thought of it. It happened that Mr. Church had a few Cakes of Rusk[27] in his Pocket, that Madam Cranston (the Governor of Rhode Island's Lady) gave him, when he came off the Island, which he divided among the Company, which was all the Provision they had.

[THE PEASE FIELD FIGHT]

Mr. Church after their slender breakfast proposed to Captain Fuller that he would March in quest of the Enemy with such of the Company as would be willing to March with him; which he complied with, though with a great deal of scruple because of his small Number and the extreme hazard he foresaw must attend them. But some of the Company had reflected upon Mr. Church that, notwithstanding his talk on the other side of the River, he had not shown them any Indians since they came over. Which now moved him to tell them that if it was their desire to see Indians, he believed he should now soon show them what they should say was enough.

The Number allowed him soon drew off to him, which could not be many because their whole Company listed of no more than Thirty-Six. They moved towards Sakonnet until they came to the brook that runs into Nannaquaket Neck,[1] where they discovered a fresh and plain Track, which they concluded to be from the great Pine Swamp about a Mile from the Road that leads to Sakonnet. Now says Mr. Church to his Men, "If we follow this Track no doubt but we shall soon see Indians enough." They expressed their willingness to follow the Track, and moved in it, but had not gone far before one of them narrowly escaped being bit with a Rattlesnake. And the Woods that the Track led them through was haunted much with those Snakes, which the little Company seemed more to be afraid of than the black Serpents they were in quest of, and therefore bent their course another way to a Place where they thought it probable to find some of the Enemy. Had they kept the Track to the Pine Swamp they had been certain of meeting Indians enough, but not so certain that any of them should have returned to give account how many.

Now they passed down into Punkatest Neck,[2] and in their March discovered a large Wigwam full of Indian Truck, which the Soldiers were for loading themselves with until Mr. Church forbid it; telling them they might expect soon to have their hands full, and business without caring for Plunder. Then crossing the head of the Creek into the Neck, they again discovered fresh Indian Tracks, very lately passed before them into the Neck. They then got privately and undiscovered unto the Fence of Captain Almy's Pease field, and divided into two Parties. Mr. Church, keeping the one Party with himself, sent the other with Lake,[3] that was acquainted with the ground, on the other side.

Two Indians were soon discovered coming out of the Pease field towards them when Mr. Church and those that were with him concealed themselves from them by falling flat on the ground. But the other division, not using the same caution, were seen by the Enemy, which occasioned them to run; which when Mr. Church perceived, he showed himself to them and called, telling them he desired but to speak with them and would not hurt them. But they ran, and Church pursued. The Indians climbed over a Fence and one of them facing about discharged his Piece, but without effect on the English. One of the English Soldiers ran up to the Fence and fired upon him that had discharged his Piece; and they concluded by the yelling they heard that the Indian was wounded; but the Indians soon got into the thickets, whence they saw them no more for the present.

Mr. Church, then Marching over a plain piece of Ground where the Woods were very thick on one side, ordered his little Company to March at double distance to make as big a show (if they should be discovered) as might be. But before they saw anybody, they were Saluted with a Volley of fifty or sixty Guns. Some Bullets came very surprisingly near Mr. Church, who, starting, looked behind him to see what was become of his Men, expecting to have seen half of them dead, but seeing them all upon their Legs and briskly firing at the Smokes of the Enemy's Guns (for that was all that was then to be seen), he Blessed God and called to his Men not to discharge all their Guns at once, lest the Enemy should take the advantage of such an opportunity to run upon them with their Hatchets.

Their next Motion was immediately into the Pease field. When they came to the Fence, Mr. Church bid as many as had not discharged their Guns to clap under the Fence and lie close, while the other at some distance in the Field stood to charge,[4] hoping that if the Enemy should creep to the Fence to gain a shot at those that were charging their Guns, they might be surprised by those that lay under the Fence. But casting his Eyes to the side of the Hill above them; the hill seemed to move, being covered over with Indians with their bright Guns glittering in the Sun, and running in a circumference with a design to surround them.

Seeing such Multitudes surrounding him and his little Company, it put him upon thinking what was become of the Boats that were ordered to attend him. And looking up, he spied them ashore at Sandy Point on the Island side of the River with a number of Horse and Foot by them, and wondered what should be the occasion; until he was afterwards informed that the Boats had been over that Morning from the Island and had landed a Party of Men at Fogland[5] that were designed in Punkatest Neck to fetch off some Cattle and Horses, but were Ambuscaded and many of them wounded by the Enemy.

Now our Gentleman's Courage and Conduct were both put to the Test. He encourages his Men, and orders some to run and take a Wall to shelter before the Enemy gained it. 'Twas time for them now to think of escaping if they knew which way. Mr. Church orders his Men to strip to their white Shirts, that the Islanders might discover them to be Englishmen. and then orders Three Guns to be fired distinct, hoping it might be observed by their friends on the opposite Shore. The Men that were ordered to take the Wall, being very hungry, stopped a while among the Peas to gather a few. Being about four Rod from the Wall, the Enemy from behind it hailed them with a Shower of Bullets, but soon all but one came tumbling over an old hedge down the bank where Mr. Church and the rest were, and told him that his Brother B. Southworth,[6] who was the Man that was missing, was killed, that they saw him fall; and so they did indeed see him fall, but 'twas without a Shot, and lay no longer than till he had opportunity to clap a Bullet into one of the Enemy's Forehead, and then came running to his Company.

The meanness[7] of the English's Powder was now their greatest misfortune; when they were immediately upon this beset with Multitudes of Indians, who possessed themselves of every Rock, Stump, Tree, or Fence that was in sight, firing upon them without ceasing; while they had no other shelter but a small bank and bit of a water Fence. And yet to add to the disadvantage of this little handful of distressed Men, the Indians also possessed themselves of the Ruins of a Stone house that overlooked them, and of the black Rocks to the Southward of them; so that now they had no way to prevent lying quite open to some or other of the Enemy but to heap up Stones before them, as they did, and still bravely and wonderfully defended themselves against all the numbers of the Enemy.

At length came over one of the Boats from the Island Shore, but the Enemy plied their Shot so warmly to her as made her keep at some distance. Mr. Church desired them to send their Canoe ashore to fetch them on board; but no persuasions nor arguments could prevail with them to bring their Canoe to shore. Which some of Mr. Church's Men perceiving, began to cry out for God's sake to take them off, for their Ammunition was spent, etc. Mr. Church, being sensible of the danger of the Enemy's hearing their Complaints and being made acquainted with the weakness and scantiness of their Ammunition, fiercely called to the Boat's master and bid either send his Canoe ashore or else begone presently, or he would fire upon him.

Away goes the Boat and leaves them still to shift for themselves. But then another difficulty arose; the Enemy, seeing the Boat leave them, were reanimated and fired thicker and faster than ever. Upon which some of the Men that were lightest of foot began to talk of attempting an escape by flight, until Mr. Church solidly convinced them of the impracticableness of it; and encouraged them yet, told them that he had observed so much of the remarkable and wonderful Providence of God hitherto preserving them, that encouraged him to believe with much confidence that God would yet preserve them; that not a hair of their head should fall to the ground; bid them be Patient,

Courageous, and Prudently sparing of their Ammunition, and he made no doubt but they should come well off yet, etc., until his little Army again resolve one and all to stay with and stick by him. One of them by Mr. Church's order was pitching a flat Stone up on end before him in the Sand, when a Bullet from the Enemy with a full force struck the Stone while he was pitching it on end; which put the poor fellow to a miserable start, till Mr. Church called upon him to observe how God directed the Bullets that the Enemy could not hit him when in the same place, yet could hit the Stone as it was erected.

While they were thus making the best Defense they could against their numerous Enemies that made the Woods ring with their constant yelling and shouting and Night coming on, somebody told Mr. Church they spied a Sloop up the River as far as Gould Island that seemed to be coming down towards them. He looked up and told them Succor was now coming, for he believed it was Captain Golding, whom he knew to be a man for business, and would certainly fetch them off if he came. The Wind being fair, the Vessel was soon with them, and Captain Golding it was. Mr. Church (as soon as they came to Speak one with another) desired him to come to Anchor at such a distance from the Shore that he might veer out his Cable and ride afloat, and let slip his Canoe that it might drive ashore. Which directions Captain Golding observed; but the Enemy gave him such a warm Salute, that his Sails, Color[s], and Stern were full of Bullet holes.

The Canoe came ashore, but was so small that she would not bear above two Men at a time; and when two were got aboard, they turned her loose to drive ashore for two more, and the Sloop's company kept the Indians in play the while. But when at last it came to Mr. Church's turn to go aboard, he had left his Hat and Cutlass at the Well where he went to drink when he first came down. He told his Company he would never go off and leave his Hat and Cutlass for the Indians; they would never have that to reflect upon him. Though he was much dissuaded from it, yet he would go fetch them. He put all the Powder he had left into his Gun (and a poor charge it was) and went, presenting his Gun at the Enemy, until he took up what he went for. At his return he discharged his Gun at the Enemy to bid them farewell for that time; but had not Powder enough to carry the Bullet half way to them. Two Bullets from the Enemy struck the Canoe as he went on Board, one grazed the hair of his Head a little before, another struck in a small Stake that stood right against the middle of his Breast.

Now this Gentleman with his Army, making in all twenty Men (himself, and his Pilot being numbered with them), got all safe aboard after Six hours' engagement with 300 Indians, whose Number we were told afterwards by some of themselves. A deliverance which that good Gentleman often mentions to the Glory of God, and His Protecting Providence.

[THE PURSUIT OF WEETAMOO AND THE GREAT SWAMP FIGHT]

The next day,[1] meeting with the rest of their little Company whom he had left at Pocasset (that had also a small skirmish with the Indians and had two Men Wounded), they returned to the Mount Hope Garrison; which Mr. Church used to call the losing Fort. Mr. Church, then returning to the Island to seek Provision for the Army, meets with Alderman, a noted Indian that was just come over from the Squaw Sachem's Cape of Pocasset, having deserted from her, and had brought over his Family, who gave him an account of the State of the Indians, and where each of the Sagamore's headquarters were. Mr. Church then discoursed with some who knew the Spot well where the Indians said Weetamoo's headquarters were, and offered their Service to Pilot him. With this News he hastened to the Mount Hope Garrison. The Army expressed their readiness to embrace such an opportunity.

All the ablest Soldiers were now immediately drawn off, equipped, and dispatched upon this design under the Command of a certain Officer, and having Marched about two Miles, viz. until they came to the Cove that lies southwest from the Mount, where orders was given for an halt. The Commander-in-Chief told them he thought it proper to take advice before he went any further, called Mr. Church and the Pilot, and asked them how they knew that Philip and all his Men were not by that time got to Weetamoo's Camp, or that all her own Men were not by that time returned to her again, with many more frightful questions. Mr. Church told him they had acquainted him with as much as they knew, and that for his part he could discover nothing that need to discourage them from Proceeding; that he thought it so practicable that he with the Pilot would willingly lead the way to the Spot and hazard the brunt.

But the Chief Commander insisted on this, that the Enemy's number were so great, and he did not know what numbers more might be added unto them by that time. And his Company so small that he could not think it practicable to attack them. Added, moreover, that if he was sure of killing all the Enemy and knew that he must lose the Life of one of his Men in the action, he would not attempt it. "Pray, Sir, then (Replied Mr. Church), please to lead your Company to yonder Windmill on Rhode Island, and there they will be out of danger of being killed by the Enemy, and we shall have less trouble to supply them with Provisions." But return he would and did unto the Garrison until more strength came to them, and a Sloop to transport them to the Fall River[2] in order to visit Weetamoo's Camp.

Mr. Church, one Baxter, and Captain Hunter (an Indian) proffered to go out on the discovery on the left Wing; which was accepted. They had not Marched above a quarter of a Mile before they started Three of the Enemy. Captain Hunter wounded one of them in his knee, whom when he came up he discovered to be his near kinsman. The Captive desired favor for his Squaw, if she should fall into their hands, but asked none for himself, excepting the liberty of taking a Whiff of Tobacco, and while he was taking his Whiff, his kinsman with one blow of his Hatchet dispatched him.

Proceeding to Weetamoo's Camp, they were discovered by one of the Enemy, who ran in and gave Information, upon which a lusty Young Fellow left his Meat upon his Spit, running hastily out told his companions he would kill an Englishman before he ate his dinner, but failed of his design, being no sooner out but shot down. The Enemy's fires, and what shelter they had was by the Edge of a thick Cedar Swamp, into which on this Alarm they betook themselves, and the English as nimbly pursued, but were soon commanded back by their Chieftain after they were come within hearing of the Cries of their Women and Children, and so ended that Exploit. But returning to their Sloop the Enemy pursued them and wounded two of their Men. The next day [they] returned to the Mount Hope Garrison.

Soon after this was Philip's headquarters visited by some other English Forces, but Philip and his gang had the very fortune to escape that Weetamoo and hers (but now mentioned) had; they took into a Swamp and their pursuers were commanded back. After this Dartmouth's distresses[3] required Succor, great Part of the Town being laid desolate, and many of the Inhabitants killed; the most of Plymouth Forces were ordered thither.

And coming to Russell's Garrison at Apponagansett, they met with a Number of the Enemy that had surrendered themselves Prisoners on terms promised by Captain Eels of the Garrison and Ralph Earl that persuaded them (by a friend Indian he had employed) to come in. And had their promises to the Indians been kept, and the Indians fairly treated, 'tis probable that most if not all the Indians in those Parts had soon followed the Example of those that had now surrendered themselves; which would have been a good step towards finishing the War. But in spite of all that Captain Eels, Church, or Earl could say, argue, plead, or beg, somebody else that had more Power in their hands improved[4] it; and without any regard to the promises made them on their surrendering themselves, they were carried away to Plymouth, there sold, and transported out of the Country;[5] being about Eight-score Persons. An action so hateful to Mr. Church that he opposed it to the loss of the good Will and Respects of some that before were his good Friends.

But while these things were acting at Dartmouth, Philip made his escape, leaving his Country, fled over Taunton River, and Rehoboth Plain, and Patuxet River,[6] where Captain Edmunds

of Providence made some spoil upon; and had probably done
more but was prevented by the coming up of a Superior Officer[7] that put him by. And now another Fort was built at Pocasset that proved as troublesome and chargeable[8] as that at Mount
Hope; and the remainder of the Summer was improved in providing for the Forts and Forces there maintained, while our Enemies were fled some hundreds of Miles into the Country, near
as far as Albany.

And now strong Suspicions began to arise of the Narragansett Indians that they were ill affected and designed mischief; and so the event soon discovered.[9] The next Winter they
began their Hostilities upon the English. The United Colonies[10]
then agreed to send an Army to suppress them, Governor
Winslow to command the Army. He, undertaking the Expedition, invited Mr. Church to command a Company in the Expedition, which he declined. Craving excuse from taking
Commission, he promised to wait upon him as a Reformado[11]
through the Expedition. Having ridden with the General to
Boston and from thence to Rehoboth, upon the General's request he went thence the nearest way over the Ferries with Major Smith to his Garrison in the Narragansett Country to
prepare and provide for the coming of General Winslow, who
Marched round through the Country with his Army, proposing
by Night to surprise Pumham (a certain Narragansett Sachem)
and his Town;[12] but being aware of the approach of our Army
made their escape into the deserts.

But Mr. Church, meeting with fair Winds, arrived safe at the
Major's Garrison in the evening,[13] and soon began to inquire
after the Enemy's Resorts, Wigwams or Sleeping Places. And
having gained some intelligence, he proposed to the Eldridges
and some other brisk hands that he met with to attempt the Surprising of some of the Enemy to make a Present of to the General, when he should arrive; which might advantage his design.
Being brisk blades, they readily complied with the motion and
were soon upon their March.

The Night was very cold but blessed with the Moon. Before
the day broke, they effected their exploit, and by the rising of
the Sun arrived at the Major's Garrison, where they met the

General and presented him with Eighteen of the Enemy, they had Captived. The General, pleased with the exploit, gave them thanks, particularly to Mr. Church, the mover and chief actor of the business; and sending two of them (likely Boys) a present to Boston. Smiling on Mr. Church, told him that he made no doubt but his Faculty would supply them with Indian Boys enough before the War was ended.

Their next move was to a Swamp[14] which the Indians had Fortified with a Fort. Mr. Church rode in the General's guard when the bloody engagement began; but being impatient of being out of the heat of the action, importunately begged leave of the General that he might run down to the assistance of his friends. The General yielded to his request, provided he could rally some hands to go with him. Thirty Men immediately drew out and followed him.

They entered the Swamp and passed over the Log that was the passage into the Fort, where they saw many Men and several Valiant Captains lie slain. Mr. Church, spying Captain Gardner of Salem amidst the Wigwams in the East end of the Fort, made towards him, but on a sudden, while they were looking each other in the Face, Captain Gardner settled down. Mr. Church stepped to him and seeing the blood run down his cheek, lifted up his Cap, and calling him by his Name. He looked up in his Face, but spoke not a Word, being Mortally Shot through the head. And observing his Wound, Mr. Church found the ball entered his head on the side that was next the Upland, where the English entered the Swamp. Upon which, having ordered some care to be taken of the Captain, he dispatched information to the General that the best and forwardest of his Army, that hazarded their lives to enter the Fort upon the muzzle of the Enemy's Guns, were Shot in their backs and killed by them that lay behind.

Mr. Church with his small Company hastened out of the Fort (that the English were now possessed of) to get a Shot at the Indians that were in the Swamp and kept firing upon them. He soon met with a broad bloody track, where the Enemy had fled with their Wounded men. Following hard in the trac[k], he soon spied one of the Enemy, who clapped his Gun across his breast, made towards Mr. Church, and beckoned to him with his hand. Mr. Church immediately commanded no Man to hurt him, hoping by him to have gained some intelligence of the Enemy that might be of advantage. But it unhappily fell out that a Fellow that had lagged behind coming up, shot down the Indian to Mr. Church's great grief and disappointment.

But immediately they heard a great shout of the Enemy which seemed to be behind them, or between them and the Fort; and discovered them running from tree to tree to gain advantages of firing upon the English that were in the Fort. Mr. Church's great difficulty now was how to discover himself to his Friends in the Fort, using several inventions, till at length gained an opportunity to call to and inform a Sergeant in the Fort, that he was there and might be exposed to their Shots unless they observed it.

By this time he discovered a number of the Enemy almost within Shot of him, making towards the Fort. Mr. Church and his Company were favored by a heap of brush that was between them and the Enemy and prevented their being discovered to them. Mr. Church had given his Men their particular orders for firing upon the Enemy; and as they were rising up to make their Shot, the aforementioned Sergeant in the Fort called out to them for God's sake not to fire, for he believed they were some of their Friend Indians. They clapped down again, but were soon sensible of the Sergeant's mistake. The Enemy got to the top of the Tree, the body whereof the Sergeant stood upon, and there clapped down out of sight of the Fort, but all this while never discovered Mr. Church, who observed them to keep gathering unto that Place, until there seemed to be a formidable black heap of them.

"Now brave boys (said Mr. Church to his Men), if we mind our hits, we may have a brave Shot. and let our sign for firing on them be their rising up to fire into the Fort." It was not long before the Indians r[ose] up as one body, designing to pour a Volley into the Fort, when our Church nimbly started up and gave them such a round Volley and unexpected clap on their backs, that they who escaped with their Lives were so surprised that they scampered, they knew not whither themselves. About a dozen of them ran right over the Log into the Fort and took into a sort of a Hovel that was built with Poles after the manner of a corn crib. Mr. Church's Men, having their Cartridges fixed, were soon ready to obey his order, which was immediately to charge and run on upon the Hovel, and overset it, calling as he run on to some that were in the Fort to assist him in oversetting of it.

They no sooner came to Face the Enemy's shelter, but Mr. Church discovered that one of them had found a hole to point his Gun through right at him; but however encouraged his Company, and ran right on, till he was struck with Three Bullets, one in his Thigh, which was near half of it cut off as it glanced on the joint of the Hip bone; another through the gatherings of his Breeches and Draws, with a small flesh Wound; a third pierced his Pocket and wounded a pair of Mittens that he had borrowed of Captain Prentice; being wrapped up together had the misfortune of having many holes cut through them with one Bullet. But however he made shift to keep on his Legs and nimbly discharged his Gun at them that wounded him. Being disenabled now to go a step, his Men would have carried him off, but he forbid their touching of him until they had perfected their project of oversetting the Enemy's shelter; bid them run, for now the Indians had no Guns charged. While he was urging them to run on, the Indians began to shoot Arrows, and with one pierced through the Arm of an Englishman that had hold of Mr. Church's Arm to support him. The English, in short, were discouraged, and drew back.

And by this time the English People in the Fort had begun to set fire to the Wigwams and Houses in the Fort, which Mr. Church labored hard to prevent. They told him they had orders from the General to burn them. He begged them to forbear until he had discoursed the General, and hastening to him, he begged to spare the Wigwams, etc., in the Fort from fire; told him the Wigwams were Musket-proof, being all lined with Baskets and Tubs of Grain and other Provisions, sufficient to supply the whole Army until the Spring of the Year, and every wounded Man might have a good warm House to lodge in, which otherwise would necessarily perish with the Storms and

Cold. And moreover, that the Army had no other Provision to trust unto or depend upon; that he knew that Plymouth Forces had not so much as one Biscuit left, for he had seen their last dealt out, etc.

The General, advising a few Words with the Gentlemen that were about him, Moved towards the Fort, designing to ride in himself and bring in the whole Army. But just as he was entering the Swamp, one of his Captains[15] met him and asked him whither he was going. He told him into the Fort; the Captain laid hold of his Horse and told him his Life was worth an hundred of theirs, and he should not expose himself. The General told him that he supposed the brunt was over, and that Mr. Church had informed him that the Fort was taken, etc., and as the case was circumstanced, he was of the Mind that it was most practicable for him, and his Army to shelter themselves in the Fort.

The Captain in a great heat replied that Church lied and told the General that if he moved another step towards the Fort he would shoot his Horse under him. Then brusled[16] up another Gentleman, a certain Doctor, and opposed Mr. Church's advice, and said if it were complied with, it would kill more Men than the Enemy had killed; for (said he) "by tomorrow the wounded Men will be so stiff that there will be no moving of them." And looking upon Mr. Church and seeing the blood flowing apace from his Wounds, told him that if he gave such advice as that was, he should bleed to Death like a Dog before they would endeavor to staunch his blood. Though after they had prevailed against his advice, they were sufficiently kind to him.

And burning up all the Houses and Provisions in the Fort, the Army returned the same Night in the Storm and Cold. And I Suppose everyone that is acquainted with the circumstances of that Night's March deeply laments the miseries that attended them, especially the wounded and dying Men. But it mercifully came to pass that Captain Andrew Belcher arrived at Mr. Smith's that very Night from Boston, with a Vessel laden with Provisions for the Army, who must otherwise have perished for want.

Some of the Enemy that were then in the Fort have since in-

formed us that near a third of the Indians belonging to all that
Narragansett Country were killed by the English and by the
Cold that Night; that they fled out of their Fort so hastily that
they carried nothing with them; that if the English had kept in
the Fort, the Indians had certainly been necessitated either to
surrender themselves to them, or to have perished by Hunger
and the severity of the Season. Some time after this Fort-fight a
certain Sakonnet Indian, hearing Mr. Church relate the manner
of his being wounded, told him that he did not know but he
himself was the Indian that wounded him, for that he was one
of that company of Indians that Mr. Church made a Shot upon
when they were rising up to make a Shot into the Fort. They
were in number about sixty or seventy that just then came down
from Pumham's Town, and never before then fired a Gun against
the English; that when Mr. Church fired upon them, he killed
fourteen dead in the Spot and wounded a greater number than he
killed, many of which died afterwards with their wounds in the
Cold and Storm the following Night.

[THE VICISSITUDES OF WAR]

Mr. Church was moved with other wounded men over to Rhode
Island, where in about a Month's time he was in some good
measure recovered of his Wounds and the Fever that attended
them. And then went over to the General to take his leave of
him, with a design to return home. But the General's great importunity again persuaded him to accompany him in a long
March into the Nipmuck Country,[1] though he had then Tents[2]
in his Wounds, and so Lame as not able to Mount his Horse
without two Men's assistance.

In this March the first thing remarkable was they came to an
Indian Town where there were many Wigwams in sight, but an
Icy Swamp lying between them and the Wigwams prevented
their running at once upon it, as they intended. There was much
firing upon each side before they passed the Swamp. But at
length the Enemy all fled, and a certain Mohegan that was a
friend Indian pursued and seized one of the Enemy that had a

small wound in his Leg, and brought him before the General, where he was examined. Some were for torturing of him to bring him to a more ample confession of what he knew concerning his Countrymen. Mr. Church, verily believing he had been ingenuous in his confession, interceded and prevailed for his escaping torture.

But the Army being bound forward in their March, and the Indian's wound somewhat disenabling him for Traveling, 'twas concluded he should be knocked on the Head. Accordingly, he was brought before a great fire, and the Mohegan that took him was allowed, as he desired, to be the Executioner. Mr. Church, taking no delight in the Sport, framed an errand at some distance among the baggage Horses, and when he had got some Ten Rods or thereabouts from the fire, the Executioner fetching a blow with his Hatchet at the head of the Prisoner, he being aware of the blow, dodged his [head] aside, and the Executioner missing his stroke, the Hatchet flew out of his hand and had like to have done execution where 'twas not designed.

The Prisoner upon his narrow escape broke from them that held him, and, notwithstanding his Wound, made use of his Legs, and happened to run right upon Mr. Church, who laid hold on him, and a close scuffle they had, but the Indian, having no Clothes on, slipped from him, and ran again. And Mr. Church pursued the Indian, although being Lame, there was no great odds in the Race until the Indian stumbled and fell. And they closed again, scuffled and fought pretty smartly, until the Indian by the advantage of his nakedness slipped from his hold again, and set out on his third Race with Mr. Church close at his heels, endeavoring to lay hold on the hair of his Head, which was all the hold could be taken of him. And running through a Swamp that was covered with hollow Ice, it made so loud a noise that Mr. Church expected (but in vain) that some of his English friends would follow the noise and come to his assistance.

But the Indian happened to run athwart a mighty Tree that lay fallen near breast-high, where he stopped and cried out aloud for help; but Mr. Church being soon upon him again, the Indian seized him fast by the hair of his Head and endeavoring by twisting to break his Neck. But though Mr. Church's wounds had somewhat weakened him, and the Indian a stout fellow, yet he held him well in play and twisted the Indian's Neck as well, and took the advantage of many opportunities while they hung by each other's hair [to give] him notorious bunts[3] in the face with his head. But in the heat of this scuffle they heard the Ice break with somebody's coming apace to them, which when they heard, Church concluded there was help for one or other of them, but was doubtful which of them must now receive the fatal stroke.

Anon somebody comes up to them, who proved to be the Indian that had first taken the Prisoner. Without speaking a word, he felt them out (for 'twas so dark he could not distinguish them by light), the one being clothed, and the other naked. He felt where Mr. Church's hands were fastened in the Netop's[4] hair, and with one blow settled his Hatchet in between them, and ended the strife. He then spoke to Mr. Church and hugged him in his Arms, and thanked him abundantly for catching his Prisoner; and cut off the head of his Victim, and carried it to the Camp. And giving an account to the rest of the friend Indians in the Camp how Mr. Church had seized his Prisoner, etc., they all joined [in] a mighty shout.

Proceeding in this March, they had the success of killing many of the Enemy until at length their Provision failing, they returned home.

King Philip (as was before hinted) was fled to a Place called Schaghticoke,[5] between York and Albany, where the Mohawks made a descent upon him and killed many of his Men, which moved him from thence. His next kennelling Place was at the falls of Connecticut River, where sometime after, Captain Turner found him, came upon him by Night, killed him a great many Men, and frighted many more into the River, that were hurled down the falls and drowned.[6] Philip got over the River, and on the back side of the Wachusett hills[7] meets with all the Remnants of the Narragansett and Nipmuck Indians that were there gathered together, and became very numerous; and made their descent on Sudbury, and the Adjacent Parts of the

Country, where they met with and swallowed up Valiant Captain Wadsworth and his Company, and many other doleful desolations in those Parts.

The News whereof coming to Plymouth, and they expecting probably the Enemy would soon return again into their Colony, the Council of War were called together; and Mr. Church was sent for to them, being observed by the whole Colony to be a Person extraordinarily qualified for and adapted to the Affairs of War. 'Twas proposed in Council that lest the Enemy in their return should fall on Rehoboth or some other of their Out-Towns, a Company consisting of sixty or seventy Men should be sent into those Parts; and Mr. Church invited to take the Command of them.

He told them that if the Enemy returned into that Colony again, they might reasonably expect that they would come very numerous; and that if he should take the Command of Men, he should not lie in any Town or Garrison with them, but would lie in the Woods as the Enemy did. And that to send out such small Companies against such Multitudes of the Enemy that were now Mustered together would be but to deliver so many Men into their hands to be destroyed, as the Worthy Captain Wadsworth and his Company were. His advice upon the whole was that if they sent out any Forces, to send not less than 300 Soldiers; and that the other Colonies should be asked to send out their Quotas also; adding that if they intended to make an end of the War by subduing the Enemy, they must make a business of the War as the Enemy did; and that for his own part, he had wholly laid aside all his own private business and concerns, ever since the War broke out.

He told them that if they would send forth such Forces as he would direct to, he would go with them for Six weeks' March, which was long enough for Men to be kept in the Woods at once; and if they might be sure of Liberty to return in such a space, Men would go out cheerfully. And he would engage 150 of the best Soldiers should immediately List Voluntarily to go with him, if they would please to add fifty more, and 100 of the Friend Indians. And with such an Army he made no doubt but he might do good Service, but on other terms he did not incline to be concerned.

Their reply was that they were already in debt, and so big an Army would bring such charge upon them that they should never be able to pay. And as for sending out Indians, they thought it no ways advisable, and in short, none of his advice practicable.

Now Mr. Church's Consort and his then only Son were till this time remaining at Duxbury, and his fearing their safety there (unless the War were more vigorously engaged in) resolved to move to Rhode Island, though it was much opposed both by the Government and by Relations. But at length, the Governor, considering that he might be no less Serviceable by being on that side of the Colony, gave his permit and wished he had Twenty more as good Men to send with him.

Then preparing for his Removal, he went with his small Family to Plymouth to take leave of their Friends; where they met with his Wife's Parents, who much persuaded that She might be left at Mr. Clark's Garrison,[8] (which they supposed to be a mighty safe Place) or at least that She might be there until her soon expected lying-in was over (being near her time). Mr. Church, no ways inclining to venture her any longer in those Parts, and no arguments prevailing with him, he resolutely set out for Taunton and many of their Friends accompanied them. There they found Captain Pierce with a commanded Party, who offered Mr. Church to send a Relation of his with some others to guard him to Rhode Island. But Mr. Church thanked him for his Respectful offer, but for some good reasons refused to accept it. In short, they got safe to Captain John Almy's house upon Rhode Island, where they met with friends and good entertainment. But by the way, let me not forget this remarkable Providence, viz., that within Twenty-four hours or thereabouts after their arrival at Rhode Island, Mr. Clark's Garrison that Mr. Church was so much importuned to leave his Wife and Child at, was destroyed by the Enemy.[9]

Mr. Church, being at present disenabled from any particular Service in the War, began to think of some other employ; but he no sooner took a tool to cut a small stick, but he cut off the top of his Forefinger, and the next to it, half off; upon which he smilingly said that he thought he was out of his way to leave the War and resolved he would to War again. Accordingly his Second Son being born on the 12th of May and his Wife and Son like to do well, Mr. Church embraces the opportunity of a passage in a Sloop bound to Barnstable, who landed him at Saconnesset,[10] from whence he rode to Plymouth; arrived there on the first Tuesday in June.

The General Court, then sitting, welcomed him, told him they were glad to see him Alive. He replied he was as glad to see them Alive, for he had seen so many fires and smokes towards their side of the Country since he left them, that he could scarce eat or sleep with any comfort, for fear they had been all destroyed. For all Traveling was stopped, and no News had passed for a long time together. He gave them account that the Indians had made horrid desolations at Providence, Warwick, Pawtuxet,[11] and all over the Narragansett Country, and that they prevailed daily against the English on that side of the Country; told them he longed to hear what Methods they designed in the War.

They told him they were particularly glad that Providence had brought him there at that juncture. For they had concluded the very next day to send out an Army of 200 Men, two-thirds English, and one-third Indians, in some measure agreeable to his former proposal; expecting Boston and Connecticut to join with their Quotas. In short, it was so concluded. And that Mr. Church should return to the Island and see what he could Muster there of those that had moved from Swansea, Dartmouth, etc.[12] So, returning the same way he came, when he came to Sogkonesset, he had a sham put upon him about a Boat he had bought to go home in, and was forced to hire two of the friend Indians to paddle him in a Canoe from Elizabeth's[13] to Rhode Island.

It fell out that as they were in their Voyage passing by Sakonnet-point, some of the Enemy were upon the Rocks a-fishing. He bid the Indians that managed the Canoe to paddle so near to the Rocks as that he might call to those Indians; told them that he had a great mind ever since the War broke out to

speak with some of the Sakonnet Indians, and that they were
their Relations, and therefore they need not fear their hurting
of them. And he added that he had a mighty conceit that if he
could gain a fair Opportunity to discourse them, that he could
draw them off from Philip, for he knew they never heartily
loved him.

The Enemy hallooed and made signs for the Canoe to come
to them, but when they approached them, they skulked and hid
in the clefts of the Rocks. Then Mr. Church ordered the Canoe
to be paddled off again, lest if he came too near they should fire
upon him. Then the Indians appearing again, beckoned and
called in the Indian Language, and bid them come ashore, they
wanted to speak with them. The Indians in the Canoe answered
them again; but they on the Rocks told them that the surf made
such a noise against the Rocks, they could not hear anything
they said.

Then Mr. Church by signs with his hands gave to understand
that he would have two of them go down upon the point of the
beach (a place where a Man might see who was near him). Accordingly, two of them ran along the beach and met him there
without their Arms, excepting that one of them had a Lance in
his hand. They urged Mr. Church to come ashore, for they had
a great desire to have some discourse with him. He told them if
he that had his weapon in his hand would carry it up some distance upon the beach and leave it, he would come ashore and
discourse them. He did so, and Mr. Church went ashore, hailed
up his Canoe, ordered one of his Indians to stay by it, and the
other to walk above on the beach, as a Sentinel to see that the
Coasts were clear.

And when Mr. Church came up to the Indians, one of them
happened to be honest George, one of the two that Awashonks
formerly sent to call him to her Dance, and was so careful to
guard him back to his House again; the last Sakonnet Indian he
spoke with before the War broke out. He spoke English very
well. Mr. Church asked him where Awashonks was. He told
him in a Swamp about three Miles off. Mr. Church again asked
him what it was he wanted that he hallooed and called him
ashore. He answered that he took him for Church as soon as he

heard his Voice in the Canoe, and that he was very glad to see him alive, and he believed his Mistress would be as glad to see him and speak with him. He told him further that he believed she was not fond of maintaining a War with the English, and that she had left Philip and did not intend to return to him anymore. He was mighty earnest with Mr. Church to tarry there while he would run and call her. But he told him no, for he did not know but the Indians would come down and kill him before he could get back again. He said if Mount Hope or Pocasset Indians could catch him, he believed they would knock him on the head, but all Sakonnet Indians knew him very well, and he believed would none of them hurt him. In short, Mr. Church refused then to tarry, but promised that he would come over again and speak with Awashonks and some other Indians that he had a mind to talk with.

Accordingly, he appointed him to notify Awashonks, her Son Peter, their Chief Captain, and one Nompash (an Indian that Mr. Church had formerly a particular respect for) to meet him two days after at a Rock at the lower end of Captain Richmond's Farm, which was a very noted place; and if that day should prove Stormy or Windy, they were to expect him the next moderate day, Mr. Church telling George that he would have him come with the Persons mentioned, and no more. They giving each other their hand upon it parted, and Mr. Church went home, and the next Morning to Newport and informed the Government what had passed between him and the Sakonnet Indians. And desired their permit for him and Daniel Wilcocks (a Man that well understood the Indian Language) to go over to them. They told him they thought he was mad after such Service as he had done and such dangers that he escaped now to throw away his Life, for the Rogues would as certainly kill him as ever he went over, and utterly refused to grant his permit or to be willing that he should run the risk.

Mr. Church told them that it had ever been in his thoughts since the War broke out, that if he could discourse the Sakonnet Indians, he could draw them off from Philip and employ them against him, but could, till now, never have an Opportunity to speak with any of them and was very loath to lose it, etc. At length, they told him if he would go, it should be only with the two Indians that came with him; but they would give him no permit under their hands. He took his leave of them, Resolving to prosecute his design. They told him they were sorry to see him so Resolute, nor if he went did they ever expect to see his face again.

He bought a Bottle of Rum and a small roll of Tobacco to carry with him, and returned to his Family. The next Morning, being the day appointed for the Meeting, he prepared two light Canoes for the design, and his own Man with the two Indians for his company. He used such arguments with his tender and now almost broken-hearted Wife, from the experience of former preservations and the prospect of the great Service he might do, might it please God to succeed his design, etc., that he obtained her consent to his attempt. And committing her, his Babes, and himself to Heaven's protection, he set out.

They had from the Shore about a League to paddle. Drawing near the place, they saw the Indians sitting on the bank, waiting for their coming. Mr. Church sent one of the Indians ashore in one of the Canoes to see whither it were the same Indians whom he had appointed to meet him, and no more; and if so, to stay ashore and send George to fetch him. Accordingly, George came and fetched Mr. Church ashore, while the other Canoe played off to see the event, and to carry tidings if the Indians should prove false.

Mr. Church asked George whether Awashonks and the other Indians he appointed to meet him were there. He answered they were. He then asked him if there were no more than they whom he appointed to be there. To which he would give him no direct answer. However, he went ashore, where he was no sooner landed, but Awashonks and the rest that he had appointed to meet him there rose up and came down to meet him; and each of them successively gave him their hands, and expressed themselves glad to see him, and gave him thanks for exposing himself to visit them. They walked together about a Gunshot from the water to a convenient place to sit down. Where at once arose up a great body of Indians, who had lain hid in the grass (that was as high as a Man's waist) and gathered round them till they had closed them in, being all armed with Guns, Spears, Hatchets, etc., with their hair trimmed and faces painted in their Warlike appearance.

It was doubtless somewhat surprising to our Gentleman at first, but without any visible discovery of it, after a small silent pause on each side he spoke to Awashonks, and told her that George had informed him that she had a desire to see him, and discourse about making peace with the English. She answered, "Yes." Then said Mr. Church, "it is customary when People meet to treat of Peace to lay aside their Arms, and not to appear in such Hostile form as your People do"; desired of her that if they might talk about Peace, which he desired they might, her men might lay aside their Arms and appear more treatable. Upon which there began a considerable noise and murmur among them in their own Language. Till Awashonks asked him what Arms they should lay down, and where. He (perceiving the Indians looked very surly, and much displeased) Replied, "Only their Guns at some small distance, for formality['s] sake." Upon which with one consent they laid aside their Guns, and came and sat down.

Mr. Church pulled out his Calabash and asked Awashonks whether she had lived so long at Wachusett as to forget to drink Occapeches;[14] and drinking to her, he perceived that she watched him very diligently to see (as he thought) whether he swallowed any of the Rum. He offered her the Shell, but she desired him to drink again first. He then told her there was no poison in it, and pouring some into the Palm of his hand, supped[15] it up, and took the Shell and drank to her again, and drank a good Swig which indeed was no more than he needed. Then they all standing up, he said to Awashonks, "You won't drink for fear there should be poison in it." And then handed it to a little ill-looked fellow, who caught it readily enough, and as greedily would have swallowed the Liquor when he had it at his mouth. But Mr. Church caught him by the throat and took it from him, asking him whether he intended to swallow Shell and all, and then handed it to Awashonks. She ventured to take a good hearty dram and passed it among her Attendants.

The Shell being emptied, he pulled out his Tobacco, and having distributed it, they began to talk. Awashonks demanded of him the Reason why he had not (agreeable to his promise when she saw him last) been down at Sakonnet before now, Saying that probably if he had come then according to his promise, they had never joined with Philip against the English.

He told her he was prevented by the War's breaking out so suddenly. And yet he was afterwards coming down and came as far as Punkatest, where a great many Indians set upon him and fought him a whole afternoon, though he did not come prepared to fight, had but Nineteen Men with him, whose chief design was to gain an Opportunity to discourse some Sakonnet Indians. Upon this there at once arose a mighty Murmur, confused noise, and talk among the fierce-looked Creatures, and all rising up in an hubbub; and a great surly looked fellow took up his Tomahawk, or wooden Cutlass, to kill Mr. Church, but some others prevented him.

The Interpreter asked Mr. Church if he understood what it was that the great fellow (they had hold of) said. He answered him, "No." "Why," said the Interpreter, "he says you killed his Brother at Punkatest, and therefore he thirsts for your blood." Mr. Church bid the Interpreter tell him that his Brother began first; that if he had kept at Sakonnet according to his desire and order, he should not have hurt him.

Then the chief Captain commanded Silence, and told them that they should talk no more about old things, etc., and quelled the tumult, so that they sat down again and began upon a discourse of making Peace with the English. Mr. Church asked them what Proposals they would make, and on what terms they would break their League with Philip, desiring them to make some Proposals that he might carry to his Masters, telling them that it was not in his Power to conclude a Peace with them, but that he knew that if their Proposals were reasonable, the Government would not be unreasonable, and that he would use his Interest in the Government for them.

And to encourage them to proceed, put them in mind that the Pequots once made War with the English,[16] and that after they subjected themselves to the English, the English became their Protectors and defended them against other Nations that would otherwise have destroyed them, etc. After some further discourse and debate, he brought them at length to consent that if the Government of Plymouth would firmly engage to them that they, and all of them and their Wives and Children should have their Lives spared and none of them transported out of the Country, they would subject themselves to them and serve them in what they were able.

Then Mr. Church told them that he was well satisfied the Government of Plymouth would readily concur with what they proposed, and would sign their Articles; and complimenting them upon it, how pleased he was with the thoughts of their return and of the former friendship that had been between them, etc.

The chief Captain rose up and expressed the great value and respect he had for Mr. Church; and bowing to him, said, "Sir, if you'll please to accept of me and my men, and will head us, we'll fight for you, and will help you to Philip's head before Indian Corn be ripe." And when he had ended, they all expressed their consent to what he said, and told Mr. Church they loved him and were willing to go with him and fight for him, as long as the English had one Enemy left in the Country. Mr. Church assured them that if they proved as good as their word, they should find him theirs and their Children's fast friend. And (by the way) the friendship is maintained between them to this day.

Then he proposed unto them that they should choose five men to go straight with him to Plymouth. They told him, No; they would not choose, but he should take which five he pleased. Some compliments passed about it; at length it was agreed they should choose Three, and he Two. Then he agreed with that he would go back to the Island that Night and would come to them the next Morning, and go through the Woods to Plymouth. But they afterwards objected that this traveling through the Woods would not be safe for him; the Enemy might meet with them and kill him, and then they should lose their friend and the whole design ruined beside. And therefore proposed that he should come in an English Vessel, and they would meet him and come on board at Sakonnet point and Sail from thence to Sandwich, which, in fine, was concluded upon.

So Mr. Church promising to come as soon as he could possibly obtain a Vessel, and then they parted. He returned to the Island and was at great pains and charge to get a Vessel, but with unaccountable disappointments, sometimes by the falseness, and sometimes by the faint-heartedness of Men that he bargained with, and something by Wind and Weather, etc.

Until at length Mr. Anthony Lowe put into the Harbor with a laden Vessel bound to the Westward, and being made acquainted with Mr. Church's case, told him that he had so much kindness for him, and was so pleased with the business that he was engaged in, that he would run the venture of his Vessel and Cargo to wait upon him. Accordingly, next Morning they set Sail with a Wind that soon brought them to Sakonnet point; but coming there they met with a contrary wind and a great swelling Sea. The Indians were there waiting upon the Rocks, but had nothing but a miserable broken Canoe to get aboard in. Yet Peter Awashonks ventured off in it, and with a great deal of difficulty and danger got aboard. And by this time it began to Rain and Blow exceedingly, and forced them away up the Sound; and then went away through Bristol Ferry, round the Island to Newport, carrying Peter with them.

Then Mr. Church dismissed Mr. Lowe, and told him that inasmuch as Providence opposed his going by Water, and he expected that the Army would be up in a few days, and probably if he should be gone at that juncture, it might ruin the whole design; would therefore yield his Voyage. Then he wrote the account of his transactions with the Indians, and drew up the Proposals and Articles of Peace, and dispatched Peter with them to Plymouth, that his Honor the Governor, if he saw cause, might sign them.

Peter was set over to Sakonnet on the Lord's day Morning with orders to take those men that were chosen to go down, or some of them at least, with him. The time being expired that was appointed for the English Army to come, there was great looking for them. Mr. Church on the Monday Morning (partly to divert himself after his fatigue, and partly to listen for the Army) Rode out with his Wife and some of his friends to Portsmouth[17] under a pretence of Cherrying, but came home without any News from the Army. But by Midnight, or sooner, he was roused with an Express from Major Bradford, who was arrived with the Army at Pocasset. To whom he forthwith repaired, and informed him of the whole of his proceedings with the Sakonnet Indians.

With the Major's consent and advice, he returned again next Morning to the Island in order to go over that way to Awashonks to inform her that the Army was arrived, etc. Accordingly, from Sachueset Neck[18] he went in a Canoe to Sakonnet; told her Major Bradford was arrived at Pocasset with a great Army, whom he had informed of all his proceedings with her. That if she would be advised and observe order, she nor her People need not to fear being hurt by them. Told her she should call all her People down into the Neck,[19] lest if they should be found straggling about, mischief might light on them. That on the Morrow they would come down and receive her, and give her further orders. She promised to get as many of her People together as possibly she could, desiring Mr. Church to consider that it would be difficult for [her] to get them together at such short warning. Mr. Church returned to the Island and to the Army the same Night.

The next Morning[20] the whole Army Marched towards Sakonnet as far as Punkatest, and Mr. Church with a few Men went down to Sakonnet to call Awashonks and her People to come up to the English Camp. As he was going down, they met with a Pocasset Indian who had killed a Cow and got a Quarter of her on his back and her Tongue in his Pocket; who gave them an account that he came from Pocasset two days since in company with his Mother and several other Indians now hid in a Swamp above Nonquit.[21] Disarming of him, he sent him by two Men to Major Bradford and proceeded to Sakonnet. They saw several Indians by the way skulking about, but let them pass.

Arriving at Awashonk's Camp, told her he was come to invite her and her People up to Punkatest, where Major Bradford now was with the Plymouth Army, expecting her and her Subjects to receive orders, until further order could be had from the Government. She complied and soon sent out orders for such of her Subjects as were not with her immediately to come in; and by Twelve o'Clock of the next day, she with most of her Number appeared before the English Camp at Punkatest. Mr. Church tendered the Major to Serve under his Commission, provided the Indians might be accepted with him, to fight the Enemy. The Major told him his Orders were to improve[22] him, if he pleased, but as for the Indians, he would not be concerned with them. And presently gave forth orders for Awashonks and all her Subjects, both Men, Women, and Children, to repair to Sandwich,[23] and to be there upon Peril in Six days.

Awashonks and her chiefs gathered round Mr. Church (where he was walked off from the rest), expressed themselves concerned that they could not be confided in, nor improved. He told them 'twas best to obey Orders, and that if he could not accompany them to Sandwich, it should not be above a Week before he would meet them there; that he was confident the Governor would Commission him to improve them. The Major hastened to send them away with Jack Havens (an Indian who had never been in the Wars) in the Front with a flag of Truce in his hand.

They being gone, Mr. Church by the help of his Man Toby (the Indian whom he had taken Prisoner, as he was going down to Sakonnet) took said Toby's Mother, and those that were with her, Prisoners. Next Morning, the whole Army moved back to Pocasset. This Toby informed them that there were a great many Indians gone down to Wepoiset[24] to eat Clams (other Provisions being very scarce with them); that Philip himself was expected within three or four days at the same Place. Being asked what Indians they were, he answered some Weetamoo's Indians, some Mount Hope Indians, some Narragansett Indians, and some other Upland Indians, in all about 300.

The Rhode Island Boats by the Major's order meeting them at Pocasset, they were soon embarked. It being just in the dusk of the Evening, they could plainly discover the Enemy's fires at the Place the Indian directed to. And the Army concluded no other but they were bound directly thither, until they came to the North End of the island, and heard the word of Command for the Boats to bear away. Mr. Church was very fond of having this probable opportunity of surprising that whole Company of Indians embraced. But Orders, 'twas said, must be obeyed, which was to go to Mount Hope and there to fight Philip. This with some other good opportunities of doing spoil upon the Enemy, being unhappily missed.

Mr. Church obtained the Major's Consent to meet the Sakonnet Indians, according to his promise. He was offered a Guard to Plymouth, but chose to go with one Man only, who was a good Pilot. About Sunset he with Sabin, his Pilot, mounted their Horses at Rehoboth, where the Army now was, and by two Hours by Sun next Morning arrived safe at Plymouth. And by that time they had refreshed themselves, the Governor and Treasurer came to Town, Mr. Church giving them a short account of the Affairs of the Army, etc. His Honor was pleased to give him thanks for the good and great Service he had done at Sakonnet, told him he had confirmed all that he promised Awashonks, and had sent the Indian back again that brought his Letter. He asked his Honor whether he had anything later from Awashonks. He told him he had not. Whereupon he gave his Honor account of the Major's orders relating to her and hers, and what discourse had passed pro and con about them; and that he had promised to meet them, and that he had encouraged them that he thought he might obtain of his Honor a Commission to lead them forth to fight Philip. His Honor smilingly told him that he should not want Commission if he would accept it, nor yet good Englishmen enough to make up a good Army.

But in short, he told his Honor the time was expired that he had appointed to meet the Sakonnets at Sandwich. The Governor asked him, when he would go. He told him that afternoon, by his Honor's leave. The Governor asked him how many Men he would have with him. He answered, not above half a dozen, with an order to take more at Sandwich, if he saw cause; and Horses provided. He no sooner moved it but had his number of Men tendering to go with him, among which was Mr. Jabez Howland and Nathaniel Southworth. They went to Sandwich that Night, where Mr. Church (with need enough) took a Nap of Sleep.

The next Morning with about sixteen or eighteen Men proceeded as far as Agawam,[25] where they had great expectation of meeting the Indians, but met them not. His Men being discouraged, about half of them returned. Only half a dozen stuck by him, and promised so to do until they should meet with the Indians. When they came to Sippican River,[26] Mr. Howland began to tire, upon which Mr. Church left him and two more for a Reserve at the River, that if he should meet with Enemies and be forced back, they might be ready to assist them in getting over the River.

Proceeding in their March, they crossed another River and opened a great Bay, where they might see many Miles alongshore, where were Sands and Flats. And hearing a great noise below them towards the Sea, they dismounted their Horses, left them, and creeped among the bushes, until they came near the bank and saw a vast company of Indians of all Ages and Sexes, some on Horseback running races, some at Football, some catching Eels and Flatfish in the water, some Clamming, etc. But which way with safety to find out what Indians they were, they were at a loss.

But at length, retiring into a thicket, Mr. Church hallooed to them. They soon answered him, and a couple of smart young Fellows, well mounted, came upon a full Career to see who it might be that called, and came just upon Mr. Church before they discovered him. But when they perceived themselves so near Englishmen, and Armed, were much surprised, and tacked short about to run as fast back as they came forward, until one of the Men in the bushes called to them, and told them his Name was Church, and need not fear his hurting of them. Upon which, after a small pause, they turned about their Horses and came up to him. One of them that could speak English, Mr. Church took aside and examined, who informed him that the Indians below were Awashonks and her company, and that Jack Havens was among them; whom Mr. Church immediately sent for to come to him and ordered the Messenger to inform Awashonks that he was come to meet her.

Jack Havens soon came, and by that time Mr. Church had asked him a few Questions and had been satisfied by him that it was Awashonks and her company that were below and that Jack had been kindly treated by them, a company of Indians, all

Mounted on Horseback and well Armed, came riding up to Mr. Church, but treated him with all due respects. He then ordered Jack to go tell Awashonks that he designed to Sup with her in the Evening and to lodge in her Camp that Night. Then taking some of the Indians with him, he went back to the River to take care of Mr. Howland.

Mr. Church, being a Mind to try what Mettle he was made of, imparted his notion to the Indians that were with him, and gave them directions how to act their parts. When he came pretty near the Place, he and his Englishmen pretendedly fled, firing on their retreat towards the Indians that pursued them, and they firing as fast after them. Mr. Howland, being upon his guard, hearing the Guns, and by and by seeing the motion both of the English and Indians, concluded his friends were distressed, was soon on the full Career on Horseback to meet them, until he, perceiving their laughing, mistrusted the Truth. As soon as Mr. Church had given him the News, they hasted away to Awashonks.

Upon their arrival, they were immediately conducted to a shelter, open on one side, whither Awashonks and her chiefs soon came and paid their Respects, and the Multitudes gave shouts as made the heavens to ring. It being now about Sun-setting, or near the dusk of the Evening, the Netops came running from all quarters laden with the tops of dry Pines and the like combustible matter, making a huge pile thereof near Mr. Church's shelter on the open side thereof. But by this time Supper was brought in, in three dishes, viz., a curious young Bass in one dish, Eels and Flat-fish in a second, and Shellfish in a third, but neither Bread nor Salt to be seen at Table.

But by that time Supper was over, the mighty pile of Pine Knots and Tops, etc., was fired, and all the Indians great and small gathered in a ring round it. Awashonks with the oldest of her People, Men and Women mixed, kneeling down, made the first ring next the fire, and all the lusty stout Men standing up made the next; and then all the Rabble in a confused Crew surrounded on the outside. Then the chief Captain stepped in between the rings and the fire, with a Spear in one hand and an

Hatchet in the other, danced round the fire, and began to fight with it, making mention of all the several Nations and Companies of Indians in the Country that were Enemies to the English; and at naming of every particular Tribe of Indians, he would draw out and fight a new firebrand. And at his finishing his fight with each particular firebrand, would bow to him and thank him; and when he had named all the several Nations and Tribes and fought them all, he stuck down his Spear and Hatchet and came out; and another stepped in and acted over the same dance with more fury, if possible, than the first.

And when about half a dozen of their chiefs had thus acted their parts, the Captain of the Guard stepped up to Mr. Church and told him they were making Soldiers for him, and what they had been doing was all one Swearing of them and having in that manner engaged all the lusty stout men. Awashonks and her chiefs came to Mr. Church and told him that now they were all engaged to fight for the English, and he might call forth all or any of them at any time as he saw occasion to fight the Enemy, and presented him with a very fine Firelock.[27] Mr. Church accepts their offer, drew out a number of them, and set out next Morning before day for Plymouth, where they arrived safe the same day.

[A NEW COMMISSION]

The Governor being informed of [Church's arrival], came early to Town next Morning, and by that time he had Englishmen enough to make up a good Company, when joined with Mr. Church's Indians, that offered their Voluntary Service to go under his Command in quest of the Enemy. . . . Receiving Commission, he Marched the same Night into the Woods, got to Middleboro before day,[1] and as soon as the light appeared, took into the Woods and Swampy thickets towards a place where they had some reason to expect to meet with a parcel of Narragansett Indians, with some others that belonged to Mount Hope.

Coming near to where they expected them, Captain Church's

Indian Scout discovered the Enemy, and well observing their fires and postures, returned with the intelligence to their Captain, who gave such directions for the surrounding of them, as had the direct effect; surprising them from every side so unexpectedly, that they were all taken; not so much as one escaped. And upon a strict examination, they gave intelligence of another parcel of the Enemy at a Place called Monponsett Pond.[2] Captain Church hastening with his Prisoners through the Woods to Plymouth, disposed of them all, excepting only one Jeffery, who, proving very ingenious and faithful to him in informing where other parcels of the Indians harbored, Captain Church promised him that if he continued to be faithful to him, he should not be Sold out of the Country, but should be his waiting man, to take care of his Horse, etc., and accordingly he Served him faithfully as long as he lived.

But Captain Church was forthwith sent out again; and the Terms for his encouragement being concluded on, viz., that the Country should find them Ammunition and Provision and have half the Prisoners and Arms they took; the Captain and his English Soldiers to have the other half of the Prisoners and Arms, and the Indian Soldiers the loose Plunder. Poor encouragement! But after some time it was mended.

They soon Captivated the Monponsetts and brought [them] in, not one escaping. This stroke he held several Weeks, never returning empty handed. When he wanted intelligence of their Kennelling Places, he would March to some place likely to meet with some travelers or ramblers, and scattering his Company, would lie close; and seldom lay above a day or two, at the most, before some of them would fall into their hands, whom he would compel to inform where their Company was; and so by his method of secret and sudden surprises took great Numbers of them Prisoners.

The Government observing his extraordinary courage and conduct, and the success from Heaven added to it, saw cause to enlarge his Commission; gave him power to raise and dismiss his Forces as he should see occasion; to Commissionate Officers under him, and to March as far as he should see cause within the limits of the three United Colonies; to receive to mercy,[3] give quarter or not; excepting some particular and noted Murderers, viz., Philip, and all that were at the destroying of Mr. Clark's Garrison,[4] and some few others.

Major Bradford being now at Taunton with his Army and wanting Provisions, some Carts were ordered from Plymouth for their supply, and Captain Church to guard them. But he, obtaining other guards for the Carts as far as Middleboro, ran before with a small Company, hoping to meet with some of the Enemy, appointing the Carts and their guards to meet them at Nemasket[5] about an hour after the Sun's rising next Morning. He arrived there about the breaking of the daylight, discovered a company of the Enemy; but his time was too short to wait for gaining advantage; and therefore ran right in upon them, Surprised and Captivated about sixteen of them, who upon examination informed that Tuspaquin,[6] a very famous Captain among the Enemy was at Assawompsett,[7] with a numerous Company.

But the Carts must now be guarded, and the opportunity of visiting Tuspaquin must now be laid aside. The Carts are to be faithfully guarded, lest Tuspaquin should attack them.

Coming towards Taunton, Captain Church, taking two Men with him, made all speed to the Town; and coming to the River side,[8] he hallooed, and inquiring of them that came to the River for Major Bradford or his Captains, he was informed they were in the Town, at the Tavern. He told them of the Carts that were coming, that he had the cumber[9] of guarding of them, which had already prevented his improving opportunities of doing Service. Prayed therefore that a guard might be sent over to receive the Carts, that he might be at liberty. Refusing all invitations and persuasions to go over to the Tavern to visit the Major, he at length obtained a guard to receive the Carts; by whom also he sent his Prisoners to be conveyed with the Carts to Plymouth, directing them not to return by the way they came, but by Bridgewater.[10]

Hastening back, he purposed to Camp that Night at Assawompsett Neck.[11] But as soon as they came to the River that runs into the great Pond through the thick Swamp at the entering of the Neck, the Enemy fired upon them, but hurt not a

Man. Captain Church's Indians ran right into the Swamp and fired upon them, but it being in the dusk of the Evening, the Enemy made their escape in the thickets. The Captain then moving about a Mile into the Neck, took the advantage of a small Valley to feed his Horses. Some held the Horses by the Bridles; the rest on the guard looked sharp out for the Enemy, within hearing on every side, and some very near.

But in the dead of the Night, the Enemy being out of hearing or still, Captain Church moved out of the Neck (not the same way he came in, least he should be Ambuscaded) toward Acushnet,[12] where all the Houses were burnt. And crossing Acushnet River, being extremely fatigued with two Nights' and one Day's ramble without Rest or Sleep; and observing good forage for their Horses, the Captain concluded upon bating,[13] and taking a Nap, setting Six Men to watch the passage of the River, two to watch at a time while the other[s] slept, and so to take their turns; while the rest of the Company went into a thicket to Sleep under the guard of two Sentinels more. But the whole Company, being very drowsy, soon forgot their danger and were fast a-sleep, Sentinels, and all. The Captain first awakes, looks up, and judges he had slept four Hours, which being longer than he designed, immediately rouses his Company, and sends away a file to see what were become of the watch at the passage of the River, but they no sooner opened the River in sight, but they discovered a company of the Enemy viewing of their tracks, where they came into the Neck.

Captain Church and those with him soon dispersed into the brush on each side of the way, while the file sent got undiscovered to the passage of the River, and found their watch all fast asleep, but these Tidings thoroughly awakened the whole Company. But the Enemy giving them no present disturbance, they examined their Snapsacks,[14] and taking a little refreshment, the Captain orders one party to guard the Horses, and the other to Scout, who soon met with a Track. And following of it, they were brought to a small company of Indians, who proved to be Little Eyes and his Family and near Relations, who were of Sakonnet, but had forsaken their Countrymen upon their making Peace with the English.

Some of Captain Church's Indians asked him if he did not know that Fellow, [and] told him, "This is the Rogue that would have killed you at Awashonks's Dance," and signified to him that now he had an opportunity to be revenged on him. But the Captain told them it was not Englishman's fashion to seek revenge, and that he should have the same quarter the rest had. Moving to the River side, they found an old Canoe, with which the Captain ordered Little Eyes and his company to be carried over to an Island; telling him he would leave him on that Island until he returned. And lest the English should light on them and kill them, he would leave his cousin Light-foot (whom the English knew to be their Friend) to be his guard. Little Eyes expressed himself very thankful to the Captain.

He, leaving his orders with Light-foot, returns to the River's side towards Apponagansett to Russell's Orchard.[15] Coming near the Orchard, they clapped into a thicket and there lodged the rest of the Night without any fire; and upon the Morning light appearing, moves towards the Orchard, discovers some of the Enemy, who had been there the day before, and had beat down all the Apples, and carried them away. Discovered also where they had lodged that Night, and saw the ground where they set their baskets bloody, being as they supposed and as it was afterwards discovered to be with the flesh of Swine, etc., which they had killed that day. They had lain under the Fences without any fires; and seemed by the marks they left behind them to be very numerous, perceived also by the dew on the grass that they had not been long gone; and therefore moved apace in pursuit of them. Traveling three Miles or more, they came into the Country Road, where the track parted, one parcel sheered towards the West end of the great Cedar Swamp,[16] and the other to the East end.

The Captain halted and told his Indian Soldiers that they had heard as well as he what some Men had said at Plymouth about them, etc.; that now was a good opportunity for each party to prove themselves. The Track being divided, they should follow one and the English the other, being equal in number. The Indians declined the Motion, and were not willing to move anywhere without him; said they should not think themselves safe without him. But the Captain insisting upon it, they submitted. He gave the Indians their choice to follow which track they pleased. They replied they were light and able to Travel; therefore if he pleased, they would take the West Track. And appointing the Ruins of John Cook's House at Acushnet for the place to meet at, each Company set out briskly to try their Fortunes.

Captain Church with his English Soldiers followed their Track until they came near entering a miry Swamp, when the Captain heard a Whistle in the Rear (which was a note for a halt). Looking behind him, he saw William Fobes start out of the Company and made towards him, who hastened to meet him as fast as he could. Fobes told him they had discovered abundance of Indians, and if he pleased to go a few steps back he might see them himself. He did so and saw them across the Swamp. Observing them, he perceived they were gathering of Hurtleberries, and that they had no apprehensions of their being so near them.

The Captain supposed them to be chiefly Women, and therefore calling one Mr. Delano, who was acquainted with the ground and the Indian Language, and another named Mr. Barnes; with these two Men he takes right through the Swamp as fast as he could, and orders the rest to hasten after them. Captain Church with Delano and Barnes, having good Horses, spurred on and were soon among the Thickest of the Indians and out of sight of their own Men.

Among the Enemy was an Indian Woman who with her Husband had been driven off from Rhode Island. Notwithstanding they had an House upon Mr. Sanford's Land and had planted an Orchard before the War; yet the Inhabitants would not be satisfied till they were sent off. And Captain Church, with his Family living then at the said Sanford's, came acquainted with them, who thought it very hard to turn off such old, quiet People; but in the end it proved a Providence and an advantage to him and his Family, as you may see afterwards.

This Indian Woman knew Captain Church, and as soon as she saw him, held up both her hands and came running towards him, crying aloud, "Church, Church, Church." Captain Church bid her stop the rest of the Indians and tell them the way to save their Lives was not to run, but yield themselves Prisoners, and he would not kill them. So with her help and Delano's, who could call to them in their own Language, many of them stopped and surrendered themselves. Others, scampering and casting away their baskets, etc., betook themselves to the thickets, but Captain Church, being on Horseback, soon came up with them and laid hold on a Gun that was in the hand of one of the foremost of the company, pulled it from him, and told him he must go back.

And when he had turned them, he began to look about him to see where he was and what was become of his Company, hoping they might be all as well employed as himself, but could find none but Delano, who was very busy gathering up Prisoners. The Captain drove his that he had stopped to the rest, inquiring of Delano for their Company, but could have no news of them. But, moving back, picked up now and then a skulking Prisoner by the way. When they came near the place where they first started the Indians, they discovered their Company standing in a body together, and had taken some few Prisoners. When they saw their Captain, they hastened to meet him. They told him they found it difficult getting through the Swamp, and neither seeing nor hearing anything of him, they concluded the Enemy had killed him, and were at a great loss what to do. Having brought their Prisoners together, they found they had taken and killed sixty-six of the Enemy.

Captain Church then asked the old Squaw what company they belonged unto. She said they belonged part to Philip and part to Quinnapin and the Narragansett-Sachem;[17] discovered also upon her declaration that both Philip and Quinnapin were about two Miles off in the great Cedar Swamp. He inquired of her what company they had with them. She answered, "Abundance of Indians." The Swamp, she said, was full of Indians from one end unto the other that were settled there; that there were near an 100 men came from the Swamp with them and left them upon that plain to gather Hurtleberries, and promised to call them as they came back out of Sconticut Neck,[18] whither they went to kill Cattle and Horses for Provisions for the company.

She, perceiving Captain Church move towards the Neck, told him if they went that way, they would all be killed. He asked her whereabout they crossed the River. She pointed to the upper passing place. Upon which Captain Church passed over so low down as he thought it not probable they should meet with his Track in their return and hastened towards the Island where he left Little Eyes with Light-foot. Finding a convenient place by the River side for the Securing their Prisoners, Captain Church and Mr. Delano went down to see what was become of Captain Light-foot and the Prisoners left in his charge. Light-foot, seeing and knowing them, soon came over with his broken Canoe and informed them that he had seen that day about 100 Men of the Enemy go down into Sconticut Neck, and that they were now returning again.

Upon which they three ran down immediately to a Meadow where Light-foot said the Indians had passed; where they not only saw their Tracks, but also them. Whereupon they lay close until the Enemy came into the said Meadow, and the foremost set down his load and halted, until all the company came up, and then took up their loads and marched again the same way that they came down into the Neck, which was the nearest way unto their Camp. Had they gone the other way along the River, they could not have missed Captain Church's Track, which would doubtless have exposed them to the loss of their Prisoners, if not of their lives.

But as soon as the Coast was clear of them, the Captain sends his Light-foot to fetch his Prisoners from the Island, while he and Mr. Delano returns to the company; sent part of them to conduct Light-foot and his company to the aforesaid Meadow, where Captain Church and his company met them. Crossing the Enemy's Track, they made all haste until they got over Mattapoisett River[19] near about four Miles beyond the ruins of Cook's House, where he appointed to meet his Indian company, whither he sent Delano, with two more to meet them, ordering them that if the Indians were not arrived, to wait for them. Accordingly, finding no Indians there, they waited until late in the Night, when they arrived with their booty. They dispatched a Post to their Captain to give him an account of their Success; but the day broke before they came to him.

And when they had compared Successes, they very remarkably found that the number that each Company had taken and slain was equal. The Indians had killed three of the Enemy, and taken sixty-three Prisoners, as the English had done before them. Both English and Indians were surprised at this remarkable Providence, and were both parties rejoicing at it; being both before afraid of what might have been the event of the unequal Success of the parties. But the Indians had the fortune to take more Arms than the English.

They told the Captain that they had missed a brave Opportunity by parting. They came upon a great Town of the Enemy, viz., Captain Tyasks's company (Tyasks was the next man to Philip). They fired upon the Enemy before they were discovered and ran upon them with a shout. The Men ran and left their Wives and Children and many of them their Guns. They took Tyasks's Wife and Son, and thought that if their Captain and the English company had been with them, they might have taken some hundreds of them. And now they determined not to part any more.

That Night Philip sent (as afterwards they found out) a great Army to waylay Captain Church at the entering on of Assawompsett Neck, expecting he would have returned the same way he went in; but that was never his method to return the same way that he came; and at this time, going another way, he escaped falling into the hands of his Enemies. The next day they went home by Sippican, and got well with their Prisoners to Plymouth.

He soon went out again, and this stroke he drove many Weeks. And when he took any number of Prisoners, he would pick out some that he took a fancy to, and would tell them he took a particular fancy to them, and had chosen them for himself to make Soldiers of; and if any would behave themselves well, he would do well by them, and they should be his men and not Sold out of the Country. If he perceived they looked surly, and his Indian Soldiers called them treacherous Dogs, as some of them would sometimes do, all the notice he would take of it would only be to clap them on the back and tell them, "Come, come, you look wild and surly, and mutter, but that Signifies nothing. These my best Soldiers were a little while ago as wild and surly as you are now. By that time you have been but one day along with me, you'll love me too, and be as brisk as any of them." And it proved so. For there was none of them but (after they had been a little while with him, and seen his behavior, and how cheerful and successful his Men were) would be as ready to Pilot him to any place where the Indians dwelt or haunted (though their own Fathers or nearest Relations should be among them) or to sight for him, as any of his own Men.

Captain Church was in two particulars much advantaged by the great English Army that was now abroad. One was, that they drove the Enemy down to that part of the Country, viz., to the Eastward of Taunton River by which means his business was nearer home. The other was that whenever he fell on with a push upon any body of the Enemy (were they never so many), they fled expecting the great Army. And his manner of Marching through the Woods was such as, if he were discovered, they appeared to be more than they were. For he always Marched at a wide distance one from another, partly for their safety. And this was an Indian custom, to March thin and scattered.

Captain Church inquired of some of the Indians that were become his Soldiers how they got such advantage often of the English in their Marches through the Woods. They told him that the Indians gained great advantage of the English by two things. The Indians always took care in their Marches and Fights not to come too thick together. But the English always kept in a heap together, that it was as easy to hit them as to hit an House. The other was, that if at any time they discovered a company of English Soldiers in the Woods, they knew that there was all, for the English never scattered; but the Indians always divided and scattered.

[THE HUNT FOR PHILIP AND TOTOSON]

Captain Church [being] now at Plymouth, something or other happened that kept him at home a few days until a Post came to Marshfield on the Lord's day Morning,[1] informing the Governor that a great army of Indians were discovered, who it was supposed were designing to get over the River[2] towards Taunton or Bridgewater to Attack those Towns that lay on that side the River. The Governor hastened to Plymouth, raised what Men he could by the way, came to Plymouth in the beginning of the forenoon Exercise; sent for Captain Church out of the Meeting-house, gave him the News, and desired him immediately to Rally what of his Company he could; and what Men he had raised should join them.

The Captain bestirs himself, but found no Bread in the Store-house, and so was forced to run from House to House to get Household Bread for their March; but this nor anything else prevented his Marching by the beginning of the afternoon Exercise. Marching with what Men were ready, he took with him the Post that came from Bridgewater to Pilot him to the Place, where he thought he might meet with the Enemy.

In the Evening they heard a smart firing at a distance from them, but it being near Night and the firing but of short continuance, they missed the place and went into Bridgewater Town. It seems the occasion of the firing was that Philip, finding that Captain Church made that side of the Country too hot for him, designed to return to the other side of the Country that he came last from. And coming to Taunton River with his company, they felled a great Tree across the River for a Bridge to pass over on; and just as Philip's old Uncle Akkompoin and some other of his chiefs were passing over the Tree, some brisk Bridgewater Lads had Ambushed them, fired upon them and killed the old man and several others, which put a stop to their coming over the River that Night.

Next Morning, Captain Church moved very early with his Company which was increased by many of Bridgewater that listed under him for that Expedition, and by their Piloting, he soon came very still to the top of the great Tree which the Enemy had fallen across the River; and the Captain spied an Indian sitting upon the stump of it on the other side of the river. And he clapped his Gun up and had doubtless dispatched him, but that one of his own Indians called hastily to him not to fire, for he believed it was one of his own men; upon which the Indian upon the stump looked about. And Captain Church's Indian, seeing his face, perceived his mistake, for he knew him to be Philip; clapped up his Gun and fired, but it was too late, for Philip immediately threw himself off the stump, leaped down a bank on the side of the River, and made his escape.

Captain Church as soon as possible got over the River and scattered in quest of Philip and his company; but the Enemy scattered and fled every way. But he picked up a considerable many of their Women and Children, among which was Philip's Wife and Son of about Nine Years Old.[3] Discovering a considerable new Track along the River and examining the Prisoners, found that it was Quinnapin and the Narragansetts, that were drawing off from those parts towards the Narragansett Country. He inquired of the Prisoners whether Philip were gone in the same Track. They told him they did not know, for he fled in a great fright when the first English Gun was fired, and they had none of them seen or heard anything of him since.

Captain Church left part of his Company there to secure the Prisoners they got and to pick up what more they could find, and with the rest of his company hastened in the Track of the Enemy to overtake them, if it might be, before they got over the River; and ran some Miles along the River until he came unto a place where the Indians had waded over. And he with his Company waded over after them up to the Armpits, being almost as wet before with Sweat as the River could make them. Following about a Mile further and not overtaking them, and the Captain being under a necessity to return that Night to the Army, came to an halt, told his Company he must return to his other men.

His Indian Soldiers moved for leave to pursue the Enemy (though he returned); said the Narragansetts were great Rogues, and they wanted to be revenged on them for killing some of their Relations; named Takanumma (Awashonks's Brother) and some others. Captain Church bade them go and prosper, and made Light-foot their chief and gave him the title of Captain; bid them go and quit[4] themselves like men. And away they scampered like so many Horses. Next Morning early, they returned to their Captain and informed him that they had come up with the Enemy and killed several of them, and brought him Thirteen of them Prisoners; were mighty proud of their Exploit, and rejoiced much at the opportunity of avenging themselves.

Captain Church sent the Prisoners to Bridgewater and sent out his Scouts to see what Enemies or Tracks they could. Discovering some small Tracks, he follows them, found where the Enemy had kindled some fires, and roasted some flesh, etc., but had put out their fires and were gone. The Captain followed them by the Track, putting his Indians in the Front, some of which were such as he had newly taken from the Enemy and added to his Company. Gave them order to March softly, and upon hearing a whistle in the Rear, to sit down till further order. Or upon discovery of any of the Enemy to stop, for his design was, if he could discover where the Enemy were, not to fall upon them (unless necessitated to do it) until next Morning.

The Indians in the Front came up with many Women and Children and others that were faint and tired and so not able to keep up with the Company. These gave them an account that Philip with a great number of the Enemy were a little before. Captain Church's Indians told the others they were their Prisoners, but if they would submit to order and be still, no one should hurt them. They being their old acquaintance, they were easily persuaded to conform. A little before Sunset there was a halt in the Front until the Captain came up, and they told him they discovered the Enemy. He ordered them to dog them, and watch their motion till it was dark.

But Philip soon came to a stop and fell to breaking and chopping Wood to make fires, and a great noise they made. Captain Church draws his company up into a ring and sat down in the Swamp without any noise or fire. The Indian Prisoners were much surprised to see the English Soldiers; but the Captain told them if they would be quiet and not make any disturbance or noise, they should meet with civil treatment, but if they made any disturbance or offered to run or make their escape, he would immediately kill them all; so they were very submissive and obsequious.

When the day broke, Captain Church told his Prisoners that his Expedition was such at this time that he could not afford them any guard. Told them they would find it to be their interest to attend the orders he was now about to give them; which was that when the fight was over which they now expected, or as soon as the firing ceased, they must follow the Tracks of his Company and come to them. (An Indian is next to a bloodhound to follow a Track.) He said to them it would be in vain for them to think of disobedience, or to gain any thing by it, for he had taken and killed a great many of the Indian Rebels, and should in a little time kill and take all the rest, etc.

By this time it began to be so light as the time that he usually chose to make his onset. He moved sending two Soldiers before to try if they could privately discover the Enemy's postures. But very unhappily it fell out that the very same time Philip had sent two of his as a Scout upon his own Track to see if none dogged them; who spied the two Indian men and turned short about and fled with all speed to their Camp. And Captain Church pursued as fast as he could. The two Indians set a-yelling and howling, and made the most hideous noise they could invent. [They] soon gave the Alarm to Philip and his Camp; who all fled at the first tidings, left their Kettles boiling and Meat roasting upon their wooden Spits, and run into a Swamp with no other Breakfast than what Captain Church afterwards treated them with.

Captain Church, pursuing, sent Mr. Isaac Howland with a party on one side of the Swamp, while himself with the rest ran on the other side, agreeing to run on each side, until they met on the further end; placing some men in secure Stands at that end of the Swamp where Philip entered, concluding that if they headed him and beat him back, that he would take back in his own Track. Captain Church and Mr. Howland soon met at the further end of the Swamp (it not being a great one), where they

met with a great number of the Enemy, well armed, coming out
of the Swamp. But on sight of the English they seemed very much
surprised, and tacked short. Captain Church called hastily to
them, and said if they fired one Gun they were all dead men; for
he would have them know that he had them hemmed in with a
force sufficient to command them, but if they peaceably surrendered they should have good quarter, etc.

They, seeing both Indians and English come so thick upon
them, were so surprised that many of them stood still and let the
English come and take the Guns out of their hands, when they
were both charged and cocked. Many, both Men, Women and
Children, of the Enemy were imprisoned at this time, while
Philip, Tuspaquin, Totoson,[5] etc., concluded that the English
would pursue them upon their Tracks, so were waylaying their
Tracks at the first end of the Swamp, hoping thereby to gain a
shot upon Captain Church, who was now better employed in
taking his Prisoners and running them into a Valley, in form
something shaped like a Punch-bowl, and appointing a guard of
two files triple armed with Guns taken from the Enemy.

But Philip having waited all this while in vain, now moves on
after the rest of his company to see what was become of them.
And by this time Captain Church was got into the Swamp
ready to meet him; and, as it happened, made the first discovery,
clapped behind a Tree until Philip's company came pretty near,
and then fired upon them, killed many of them, and a close
skirmish followed. Upon this, Philip, having grounds sufficient
to suspect the event of his company that went before them, fled
back upon his own Track, and coming to the place where the
Ambush lay, they fired on each other, and one Lucus of Plymouth, not being so careful as he might have been about his
Stand, was killed by the Indians.

In this Swamp skirmish, Captain Church, with his two men
which always ran by his side as his guard, met with three of the
Enemy, two of which surrendered themselves, and the Captain's guard seized them, but the other being a great stout, surly
fellow, with his two locks tied up with red and a great Rattlesnake skin hanging to the back part of his head (whom Captain
Church concluded to be Totoson), ran from them into the

Swamp. Captain Church in person pursued him close, till coming pretty near up with him, presented his Gun between his Shoulders, but it missing fire, the Indian perceiving it, turned and presented at Captain Church, and missing fire also; their Guns taking wet with the Fog and Dew of the Morning. But the Indian turning short for another run, his foot tripped in a small grapevine, and he fell flat on his face. Captain Church was by this time up with him, and struck the Muzzle of his Gun an inch and half into the back part of his head, which dispatched him without another blow.

But Captain Church, looking behind him, saw Totoson, the Indian whom he thought he had killed, come flying at him like a dragon. But this happened to be fair in sight of the guard that were set to keep the Prisoners, who, spying Totoson and others that were following of him, in the very seasonable juncture made a shot upon them and rescued their Captain; though he was in no small danger from his friends' bullets, for some of them came so near him that he thought he felt the wind of them. The skirmish being over, they gathered their Prisoners together and found the number that they had killed and taken was 173, the Prisoners which they took over Night included, who, after the skirmish, came to them as they were ordered.

Now having no Provisions but what they took from the Enemy, they hastened to Bridgewater, sending an express before to provide for them, their Company being now very numerous. The Gentlemen of Bridgewater met Captain Church with great expression of honor and thanks, and received him and his Army with all due respect and kind treatment. Captain Church drove his Prisoners that Night into Bridgewater Pound,[6] and set his Indian Soldiers to guard them. They being well treated with Victuals and drink, they had a merry Night; and the Prisoners laughed as loud as the Soldiers, not being so treated a long time before.

Some of the Indians now said to Captain Church, "Sir, You have now made Philip ready to die, for you have made him as poor and miserable as he used to make the English; for you have now killed or taken all his Relations." That they believed he would now soon have his head, and that this bout had almost broke his heart.

The next day, Captain Church moved and arrived with all his Prisoners safe at Plymouth.[7] The great English army were now at Taunton, and Major Talcott with the Connecticut Forces, being in these parts of the Country, did considerable spoil upon the Enemy. Now Captain Church, being arrived at Plymouth, received thanks from the Government for his good Service, etc. Many of his Soldiers were disbanded; and he thought to rest himself awhile, being much fatigued and his health impaired by excessive heats and colds, and wading through Rivers, etc. But it was not long before he was called upon to Rally, upon advice that some of the Enemy were discovered in Dartmouth woods.

He took his Indians and as many English Volunteers as presented to go with him, and scattering into small parcels. Mr. Jabez Howland (who was now, and often his Lieutenant and a worthy good Soldier) had the fortune to discover and imprison a parcel of the Enemy. In the Evening they met together at an appointed place, and by examining the Prisoners, they gained intelligence of Totoson's haunt; and being brisk in the Morning, they soon gained an advantage of Totoson's company, though he himself with his Son of about Eight Years old made their escape, and one old Squaw with them, to Agawam, his own Country.

But Sam Barrow,[8] as noted a Rogue as any among the Enemy, fell into the hands of the English at this time. Captain Church told him that because of his inhumane Murders and Barbarities, the Court had allowed him no quarter, but was to be forthwith put to Death, and therefore he was to prepare for it. Barrow replied that the Sentence of death against him was just, and that indeed he was ashamed to live any longer, and desired no more favor than to Smoke a Whiff of Tobacco before his Execution. When he had taken a few Whiffs, he said he was ready; upon which one of Captain Church's Indians sunk his Hatchet into his Brains.

The famous Totoson arriving at Agawam, his Son, which was the last which was left of his Family (Captain Church having destroyed all the rest), fell sick. The wretch reflecting upon the miserable condition he had brought himself into, his heart became as a stone within him, and he died. The old Squaw slung a few leaves and brush over him, and came into Sandwich and gave this account of his death, and offered to show them where she left his body; but never had the opportunity, for she immediately fell sick and died also.

[PHILIP'S END]

Captain Church, being now at Plymouth again weary and worn, would have gone home to his Wife and Family, but the Government being Solicitous to engage him in the Service until Philip was slain, and promising him satisfaction and redress for some mistreatment that he had met with, he fixes for another Expedition. He had soon Volunteers enough to make up the Company he desired and Marched through the Woods, until he came to Pocasset.

And not seeing nor hearing of any of the Enemy, they went over the Ferry to Rhode Island to refresh themselves. The Captain with about half a dozen in his company took Horse and rode about eight Miles down the Island to Mr. Sanford's, where he had left his Wife; who no sooner saw him but fainted with the surprise; and by that time she was a little revived, they spied two Horsemen coming a great pace. Captain Church told his company that those men (by their riding) came with Tidings.

When they came up they proved to be Major Sanford and Captain Golding, who immediately asked Captain Church what he would give to hear some News of Philip. He replied, that was what he wanted. They told him they had ridden hard with some hopes of overtaking of him, and were now come on purpose to inform him that there was just now Tidings from Mount Hope. An Indian came down from thence (where Philip's Camp now was) on to Sandy Point over against Tripp's,[1] and hallooed, and made signs to be fetched over; and being fetched over, he reported that he was fled from Philip, who (said he) "has killed my Brother just before I came away, for giving some advice that displeased him." And said he was fled for fear of meeting with the same his Brother had met with. Told them also that Philip was now in Mount Hope Neck. Captain Church thanked them for their good News and said he hoped by tomorrow Morning to have the Rogue's head.

The Horses that he and his company came on standing at the door (for they had not been unsaddled), his Wife must content herself with a short visit, when such game was ahead. They immediately Mounted, set Spurs to their Horses, and away. The two Gentlemen that brought him the Tidings told him they would gladly wait upon him to see the event of this Expedition. He thanked them and told them he should be as fond of their company as any Men's; and (in short) they went with him.

And they were soon at Tripp's Ferry (with Captain Church's company) where the deserter was; who was a fellow of good sense and told his story handsomely. He offered Captain Church to Pilot him to Philip and to help to kill him that he might revenge his Brother's death. Told him that Philip was now upon a little spot of Upland that was in the South end of the miry Swamp just at the foot of the Mount, which was a spot of ground that Captain Church was well acquainted with.

By that time they were got over the Ferry and came near the ground, half the Night was spent. The Captain commands a halt, and bringing the company together, he asked Major Sanford and Captain Golding's advice what method was best to take in making the onset, but they declining giving any advice, telling him that his great Experience and Success forbid their taking upon them to give advice. Then Captain Church offered Captain Golding that he should have the honor (if he would please accept of it) to beat up[2] Philip's headquarters. He accepted the offer and had his allotted number drawn out to him, and the Pilot. Captain Church's instructions to him were to be very careful in his approach to the Enemy, and be sure not to show himself until by daylight they might see and discern their own men from the Enemy. Told him also that his custom in the like cases was to creep with his company on their bellies until they came as near as they could; and that as soon as the Enemy discovered them they would cry out; and that was the word for his Men to fire and fall on. Directed him when the Enemy should start and take into the Swamp, they should pursue with speed, every man shouting and making what noise they could; for he would give orders to his Ambuscade to fire on any that should come silently.

Captain Church, knowing it was Philip's custom to be foremost in the flight, went down to the Swamp and gave Captain Williams of Scituate the command of the right wing of the Ambush, and placed an Englishman and an Indian together behind such shelters of Trees, etc., that he could find, and took care to place them at such distance as none might pass undiscovered between them. Charged 'em to be careful of themselves and of hurting their friends, and to fire at any that should come silently through the Swamp. But it being somewhat further through the Swamp than he was aware of, he wanted men to make up his Ambuscade. Having placed what men he had, he took Major Sanford by the hand, said, "Sir, I have so placed them that 'tis scarce possible Philip should escape them."

The same moment a Shot whistled over their heads, and then the noise of a Gun towards Philip's camp. Captain Church at first thought it might be some Gun fired by accident, but before he could speak, a whole Volley followed, which was earlier than he expected. One of Philip's gang going forth to ease himself, when he had done, looked round him, and Captain Golding thought the Indian looked right at him (though probably 'twas but his conceit) so fired at him, and upon his firing, the whole company that were with him fired upon the Enemy's shelter, before the Indians had time to rise from their sleep, and so overshot them. But their shelter was open on that side next the Swamp, built so on purpose for the convenience of flight on occasion.

They were soon in the Swamp and Philip the foremost, who, starting at the first Gun, threw his Petunk[3] and Powder horn over his head, caught up his Gun, and ran as fast as he could scamper, without any more clothes than his small breeches and stockings, and ran directly upon two of Captain Church's Ambush. They let him come fair within shot, and the Englishman's Gun missing fire, he bid the Indian fire away, and he did so to purpose; sent one Musket Bullet through his heart, and another not above two inches from it. He fell upon his face in the Mud and Water with his Gun under him.

By this time, the Enemy perceived they were waylaid on the east side of the Swamp, [and] tacked short about. One of the Enemy, who seemed to be a great surly old fellow, hallooed with a loud voice, and often called out, "Iootash, iootash." Captain Church called to his Indian Peter and asked him who that was that called so. He answered it was old Annawon, Philip's great Captain, calling on his Soldiers to stand to it and fight stoutly.

Now the Enemy finding that place of the Swamp which was not Ambushed, many of them made their escape in the English Tracks. The Man that had shot down Philip ran with all speed to Captain Church and informed him of his exploit, who commanded him to be Silent about it, and let no man more know it until they had drove the Swamp clean. But when they had drove the Swamp through and found the Enemy had escaped, or at least the most of them; and the Sun now up and so the dew gone that they could not so easily Track them, the whole Company met together at the place where the Enemy's Night shelter was. And then Captain Church gave them the news of Philip's death, upon which the whole Army gave Three loud Huzzahs. Captain Church ordered his body to be pulled out of the mire on to the Upland, so some of Captain Church's Indians took hold of him by his Stockings, and some by his small Breeches, (being otherwise naked) and drew him through the Mud unto the Upland, and a doleful, great, naked, dirty beast, he looked like.

Captain Church then said that forasmuch as he had caused many an Englishman's body to lie unburied and rot above ground, that not one of his bones should be buried. And calling his old Indian Executioner, bid him behead and quarter him. Accordingly, he came with his Hatchet and stood over him, but before he struck he made a small Speech, directing it to Philip, and said he had been a very great Man, and had made many a man afraid of him, but so big as he was he would now chop his Ass for him; and so went to work, and did as he was ordered. Philip having one very remarkable hand being much scarred, occasioned by the splitting of a Pistol in it formerly, Captain Church gave the head and that hand to Alderman, the Indian who shot him, to show to such Gentlemen as would bestow gratuities upon him; and accordingly he got many a Penny by it.

This being on the last day of the Week,[4] the Captain with his Company returned to the Island, tarried there until Tuesday, and then went off and ranged through all the Woods to Plymouth and received their Premium, which was Thirty Shillings per head for the Enemies which they had killed or taken, instead of all Wages; and Philip's head went at the same price. Methinks it's scanty reward, and poor encouragement; though it was better than what had been sometime before. For this March they received Four Shillings and Six Pence a Man, which was all the Reward they had, except the honor of killing Philip. This was in the latter end of August, 1676.

[ANNAWON]

Captain Church had been but a little while at Plymouth before a Post from Rehoboth came to inform the Government that old Annawon, Philip's chief Captain, was with his company ranging about their Woods, and was very offensive and pernicious to Rehoboth and Swansea. Captain Church was immediately sent for again, and treated with to engage one Expedition more. He told them their encouragement was so poor he feared his Soldiers would be dull about going again. But being a hearty friend to the cause, he Rallies again, goes to Mr. Jabez Howland, his old Lieutenant, and some of his Soldiers that used to go out with him; told them how the case was circumstanced, and that he had intelligence of old Annawon's walk and haunt, and wanted hands to hunt him. They did not want much entreating, but told him they would go with him as long as there was an Indian left in the Woods.

He moved and ranged through the Woods to Pocasset. It being the latter end of the Week, he proposed to go on to Rhode Island and rest until Monday. But early on the Lord's day Morning, there came a Post to inform the Captain that early the same Morning a Canoe with several Indians in it passed from Prudence Island to Poppasquash Neck.[1] Captain Church thought if he could possibly surprise them, he might probably gain some intelligence of more game. Therefore he made all possible speed after them. The Ferry-boat being out of the way, he made use of Canoes. But by that time they had made two freights and had got over the Captain and about fifteen or sixteen of his Indians, the Wind sprung up with such violence that Canoes could no more pass.

The Captain seeing it was impossible for any more of his Soldiers to come to him, he told his Indians if they were willing to go with him, he would go to Poppasquash and see if they could catch some of those Enemy Indians. They were willing to go, but were sorry they had no English Soldiers. So they Marched through the thickets that they might not be discovered, until they came unto the Salt Meadow to the Northward of Bristol Town that now is. Then they heard a Gun; the Captain looked about, not knowing but it might be some of his own Company in the rear. So halting till they all came up, he found 'twas none of his own Company that fired.

Now though he had but a few Men, [he] was minded to send some of them out on a Scout. He moved it to Captain Lightfoot to go with three more on a Scout. He said he was willing provided the Captain's man Nathaniel (which was an Indian that they had lately taken) might be one of them, because he was well acquainted with the Neck, and, coming lately from among them, knew how to call them. The Captain bid him choose his three companions and go; and if they came across any of the Enemy, not to kill them if they could possibly take them alive, that they might gain intelligence concerning Annawon.

The Captain with the rest of his company moved but a little way further toward Poppasquash before they heard another Gun, which seemed to be the same way with the other, but further off. But they made no halt until they came unto the narrow of Poppasquash Neck, where Captain Church left three men more to watch if any should come out of the Neck, and to inform the Scout when they returned which way he was gone. He parted the remainder of his company, half on one side of the

Neck, and the other with himself went on the other side of the Neck until they met; and meeting neither with Indians nor Canoes returned big with expectations of Tidings by their Scout.

But when they came back to the three men at the narrow of the Neck, they told their Captain the Scout was not returned, had heard nor seen anything of them. This filled them with thoughts what should become of them. By that time they had sat down and waited an hour longer, it was very dark, and they despaired of their returning to them. Some of the Indians told their Captain they feared his new man Nathaniel had met with his old Mount Hope friends and was turned Rogue. They concluded to make no fires that Night, and indeed they had no great need of any for they had no Victuals to cook, had not so much as a morsel of Bread with them. They took up their lodging scattering, that if possibly their Scout should come in the Night, and whistle (which was their sign) some or other of them might hear them.

They had a very solitary, hungry Night; and as soon as the day broke, they drew off through the brush to a hill without the Neck, and, looking about them, they espied one Indian man come running somewhat towards them. The Captain ordered one man to step out of the brush and show himself. Upon which the Indian ran right to him, and who should it be but Captain Lightfoot, to their great joy. Captain Church asked him, "What News?" He answered, "Good News." They were all well and had caught Ten Indians, and that they guarded them all Night in one of the Flankers[2] of the old English Garrison; that their prisoners were part of Annawon's company; and that they had left their Families in a Swamp above Mattapoisett Neck.

And as they were Marching towards the old Garrison, Lightfoot gave Captain Church a particular account of their Exploit, viz., that presently after they left him, they heard another Gun, which seemed to be towards the Indian burying place. And moving that way, they discovered two of the Enemy flaying of an Horse. The Scout clapping into the brush, Nathaniel bid them Sit down, and he would presently call all the Indians thereabout unto him. They hid, and he went a little distance back from them and set up his note and howled like a Wolf. One of the two immediately left his Horse and came running to see who was there; but Nathaniel, howling lower and lower, drew him in between those that lay in wait for him, who seized him. Nathaniel continuing the same note, the other left the Horse, also following his mate, and met with the same.

When they caught these two, they examined them apart and found them to agree in their Story that there were Eight more of them come down into the Neck to get Provisions, and had agreed to meet at the burying place that evening. These two being some of Nathaniel's old acquaintance, he had great influence upon them, and with his enticing Story (telling what a brave Captain he had, how bravely he lived Since he had been with him, and how much they might better their condition by turning to him, etc.) persuaded and engaged them to be on his Side, which indeed now began to be the better Side of the hedge. They waited but a little while before they espied the rest of theirs coming up to the burying place, and Nathaniel soon howled them in as he had done their mates before.

When Captain Church came to the Garrison, he met his Lieutenant[3] and the rest of his company; and then making up good fires they fell to roasting their Horse-beef, enough to last them the whole day, but had not a morsel of Bread; though Salt they had which they always carried in their Pockets, which at this time was very acceptable to them. Their next motion was towards the place where the Prisoners told them they had left their Women and Children, and surprised them all, and some others that were newly come to them. And upon examination they held to one Story, that it was hard to tell where to find Annawon, for he never roosted twice in a place.

Now a certain Indian Soldier that Captain Church had gained over to be on his side prayed that he might have liberty to go and fetch in his Father, who he said was about four Miles from that place in a Swamp with no other than one Young Squaw. Captain Church inclined to go with him, thinking it might be in his way to gain some intelligence of Annawon; and so taking one Englishman and a few Indians with him, leaving the rest there, he went with his new Soldier to look [for] his Father.

When he came to the Swamp, he bid the Indian go see if he could find his Father.

He was no sooner gone but Captain Church discovered a Track coming down out of the Woods, upon which he and his little company lay close, some on one side of the Track and some on the other. They heard the Indian Soldier make a howling for his Father; and at length somebody answered him, but while they were listening, they thought they heard somebody coming towards them, presently saw an old man coming up with a Gun on his Shoulder, and a young Woman following of him in the Track which they lay by. They let them come up between them and then started up and laid hold on them both.

Captain Church immediately examined them apart, telling them what they must trust to if they told false Stories. He asked the young Woman what company they came last from. She said from Captain Annawon's. He asked her how many were in company with him when she left him. She said fifty or sixty. He asked her how many Miles it was to the place where She left him. She said she did not understand Miles, but he was up in Squannakonk Swamp.[4] The old man, who had been one of Philip's Council, upon examination gave exactly the same account. Captain Church asked him if they could get there that Night. He said if they went presently and traveled stoutly, they might get there by Sunset. He asked whither he was going. He answered that Annawon had sent him down to look for some Indians that were gone down into Mount Hope Neck to kill Provisions. Captain Church let him know that those Indians were all his Prisoners.

By this time came the Indian Soldier and brought his Father and one Indian more. The Captain was now in great strait of mind what to do next. He had a mind to give Annawon a visit, now knew where to find him, but his company was very small, but half a dozen men beside himself, and was under a necessity to send somebody back to acquaint his Lieutenant and company with his proceedings. However, he asked his small company that were with him whether they would willingly go with him and give Annawon a visit. They told him they were always ready to obey his commands, etc. But withal told him that they knew this Captain Annawon was a great Soldier; that he had been a valiant Captain under Asuhmequin,[5] Philip's Father, and that he had been Philip's Chieftain all this War; a very subtle man and of great resolution, and had often said, that he would never be taken alive by the English. And, moreover, they knew that the men that were with him were resolute fellows, some of Philip's chief Soldiers, and therefore feared whether it was practicable to make an attempt upon him with so small a handful of assistants as now were with him. Told him further that it would be a pity that after all the Great Things he had done, he should throw away his Life at last, etc.

Upon which he replied that he doubted not Annawon was a subtle and valiant Man; that he had a long time but in vain sought for him, and never till now could find his quarters and he was very loath to miss of the opportunity; and doubt not but that if they would cheerfully go with him, the same Almighty Providence that had hitherto protected and befriended them would do so still, etc. Upon this with one consent they said they would go. Captain Church then turned to one Cook of Plymouth (the only Englishman then with him) and asked him what he thought of it. Who replied, "Sir, I am never afraid of going anywhere when you are with me."

Then Captain Church asked the old Indian if he could carry his Horse with him (for he conveyed a Horse thus far with him). He replied that it was impossible for an Horse to pass the Swamps. Therefore he sent away his new Indian Soldier with his Father and the Captain's Horse to his Lieutenant, and orders for him to move to Taunton with the Prisoners, to secure them there, and to come out in the Morning in the Rehoboth Road, in which he might expect to meet him, if he were alive and had success. The Captain then asked the old fellow if he would Pilot him unto Annawon. He answered that he having given him his life, he was obliged to serve him. He bid him move on then, and they followed. The old man would out-travel them, so far sometimes that they were almost out of sight. Looking over his Shoulder and seeing them behind, he would halt.

Just as the Sun was setting, the old man made a full stop and sat down; the company coming up also sat down, being all weary. Captain Church asked what news. He answered that about that time in the Evening Captain Annawon sent out his Scouts to see if the Coast were clear, and as soon as it began to grow dark the Scouts return. And then (said he) we may move again securely. When it began to grow dark the old man stood up again. Captain Church asked him if he would take a Gun and fight for him. He bowed very low and prayed him not to impose such a thing upon him as to fight against Captain Annawon, his old friend. But says he, "I will go along with you, and be helpful to you, and will lay hands on any man that shall offer to hurt you."

It being now pretty dark, they moved close together. Anon they heard a noise. The Captain stayed the old man with his hand, and asked his own men what noise they thought it might be. They concluded it to be the pounding of a Mortar. The old man had given Captain Church a description of the Place where Annawon now lay, and of the Difficulty of getting at him. Being sensible that they were pretty near them, with two of his Indians he creeps to the edge of the Rocks, from whence he could see their Camps.

He saw three companies of Indians at a little distance from each other, being easy to be discovered by the light of their fire. He saw also the great Annawon and his company, who had formed his Camp or Kenneling-place by felling a Tree under the side of the great cliffs of Rocks and setting a row of birch bushes up against it, where he himself and his Son and some of his chiefs had taken up the lodging, and made great fires without them, and had the Pots and Kettles boiling, and Spits roasting. Their Arms also he discovered, all set together in a place fitted for the purpose, standing up on end against a stick lodged in two crotches, and a Mat placed over them, to keep them from the wet or dew. The old Annawon's feet and his Forehead were so near the Arms as almost to touch them. But the Rocks were so steep that it was impossible to get down but as they lowered themselves by the boughs and the bushes that grew in the cracks of the Rock.

Captain Church, creeping back again to the old man, asked him if there was no possibility of getting at them some other

way. He answered no, that he and all that belonged to Annawon were ordered to come that way, and none could come any
other way without difficulty or danger of being shot. Captain
Church then ordered the old man and his daughter to go down
foremost with their baskets at their backs, that when Annawon
saw them with their baskets he should not mistrust the intrigue.
Captain Church and his handful of Soldiers crept down also
under the shadow of these two and their baskets, and the Captain himself crept close behind the old man, with his Hatchet in
his hand, and stepped over the young man's head to the Arms.

The young Annawon, discovering of him, whipped his blanket over his head and shrunk up in a heap. The old Captain
Annawon started up on his breech, and cried out, "Howok,"[6]
and, despairing of escape, threw himself back again, and lay
silent until Captain Church had secured all the Arms, etc. And
having secured that company, he sent his Indian Soldiers to the
other fires and companies, giving them instructions what to do
and say. Accordingly, they went into the midst of them, when
they discovered themselves who they were, told them that their
Captain Annawon was taken, and it would be best for them
quietly and peaceably to surrender themselves, which would
procure good quarter for them. Otherwise if they should pretend to resist or make their escape, it would be in vain, and they
could expect no other but that Captain Church with his great
Army, who had now entrapped them, would cut them to pieces.
Told them also if they would submit themselves and deliver up
all their Arms unto them, and keep every man his place until it
was day, they would assure them that their Captain Church
who had been so kind to themselves when they surrendered to
him, should be as kind unto them.

Now they being old acquaintance, and many of them Relations, did much the readier give heed to what they said, and
complied and surrendered up their Arms unto them, both their
Guns and Hatchets, etc., and were forthwith carried to Captain
Church. Things being so far settled, Captain Church asked Annawon what he had for Supper, "for (said he) I am come to Sup
with you." "Taubut,"[7] said Annawon with a big voice; and looking about upon his Women, bid them hasten and get Captain

Church and his company some Supper; then turned to Captain Church and asked him whether he would eat Cow-beef or Horse-beef. The Captain told him Cow-beef would be most acceptable. It was soon got ready, and pulling his little bag of Salt out of his Pocket, which was all the Provision he brought with him; this seasoned his Cow-beef so that with it and the dried green-corn, which the old Squaw was pounding in the Mortar while they were sliding down the Rocks, he made a very hearty Supper. And this pounding in the Mortar proved lucky for Captain Church's getting down the Rocks, for when the old Squaw pounded, they moved, and when she ceased to turn the corn, they ceased creeping; the noise of the Mortar prevented the Enemy's hearing their creeping. And the corn, being now dressed, supplied the want of Bread, and gave a fine relish with the Cow-beef.

Supper being over, Captain Church sent two of his men to inform the other companies that he had killed Philip and had taken their friends in Mount Hope Neck, but had spared their lives, and that he had subdued now all the Enemy (he supposed) excepting this company of Annawon's, and now if they would be orderly and keep their places until Morning, they should have good quarter, and that he would carry them to Taunton, where they might see their friends again, etc. The Messengers returned that the Indians yielded to his proposals.

Captain Church thought it was now time for him to take a Nap, having had no sleep in two days and one night before; told his men that if they would let him sleep two hours, they should sleep all the rest of the night. He laid himself down and endeavored to sleep, but all disposition to sleep departed from him. After he had lain a little while he looked up to see how his Watch managed, but found them all fast asleep. Now Captain Church had told Captain Annawon's company, as he had ordered his Indians to tell the others, that their lives should all be spared, excepting Captain Annawon's, and it was not in his power to promise him his life, but he must carry him to his Masters at Plymouth, and he would entreat them for his life.

Now when Captain Church found not only his own men, but all the Indians fast asleep, Annawon only excepted, whom he

perceived was as broad awake as himself; and so they lay looking one upon the other perhaps an hour. Captain Church said
nothing to him, for he could not speak Indian and thought Annawon could not speak English. At length Annawon raised himself up, cast off his blanket, and with no more clothes than his
small breeches, walked a little way back from the company. Captain Church thought no other but that he had occasion to ease
himself, and so walked to some distance rather than offend him
with the stink. But by and by he was gone out of sight and hearing; and then Captain Church began to suspect some ill design
in him, and got all the Guns close to him, and crowded himself
close under young Annawon, that if he should anywhere get a
Gun, he should not make a shot at him without endangering
his Son.

Lying very still a while waiting for the event, at length he
heard somebody coming the same way that Annawon went. The
Moon now shining bright, he saw him at a distance coming with
something in his hands, and coming up to Captain Church, he
fell upon his knees before him, and offered him what he had
brought. And speaking in plain English, said, "Great Captain,
you have killed Philip, and conquered his Country, for I believe
that I and my company are the last that War against the English,
so suppose the War is ended by your means; and therefore these
things belong unto you." Then opening his pack, he pulled out
Philip's belt, curiously wrought with Wampum, being Nine inches
broad, wrought with black and white Wampum in various figures and flowers and pictures of many birds and beasts. This
when hung upon Captain Church's shoulders it reached his ankles. And another belt of Wampum he presented him with,
wrought after the former manner, which Philip was wont to put
upon his head. It had two flags on the back part which hung
down on his back; and another small belt with a Star upon the
end of it, which he used to hang on his breast. And they were all
edged with red hair, which Annawon said they got in the Mohawks' Country. Then he pulled out two horns of glazed Powder, and a red cloth Blanket.

He told Captain Church these were Philip's Royalties which
he was wont to adorn himself with when he sat in State. That he

thought himself happy that he had an opportunity to present them to Captain Church, who had won them, etc.; spent the remainder of the night in discourse; and gave an account of what mighty success he had formerly in Wars against many Nations of Indians, when served Asuhmequin, Philip's Father, etc.

In the Morning, as soon as it was light, the Captain Marched with his Prisoners out of that Swampy Country towards Taunton, met his Lieutenant and Company about four Miles out of Town, who expressed a great deal of joy to see him again, and said 'twas more than ever he expected. They went into Taunton, were civilly and kindly treated by the Inhabitants, refreshed and rested themselves that night. Early next Morning, the Captain took old Annawon and half a dozen of his Indian Soldiers and his own man, and went to Rhode Island, sending the rest of his Company and his Prisoners by his Lieutenant to Plymouth. Tarrying two or three days upon the Island, he then went to Plymouth and carried his Wife and his two Children with him.

[LAST CAMPAIGNS]

Captain Church had been but a little while at Plymouth before he was informed of a parcel of Indians that haunted the Woods between Plymouth and Sippican, that did great damage to the English in killing their Cattle, Horses, and Swine; and the Captain was soon in pursuit of them. Went out from Plymouth the next Monday in the afternoon. Next Morning early they discovered a Track. The Captain sent two Indians on the Track to see what they could discover, while he and his Company followed gently after, but the two Indians soon returned with Tidings that they had discovered the Enemy sitting round their fires in a thick place of brush. When they came pretty near the place, the Captain ordered every man to creep as he did and surround them by creeping as near as they could, till they should be discovered, and then to run on upon them and take them alive, if possible (for their Prisoners were their pay).

They did so, took everyone that was at the fires, not one escaping. Upon examination they agreed in their Story that they belonged to Tuspaquin, who was gone with John Bump and one more to Agawam and Sippican to kill Horses, and were not expected back in two or three days. This same Tuspaquin had been a great Captain, and the Indians reported that he was such a great Powow[1] that no bullet could enter him, etc. Captain Church said he would not have him killed, for there was a War broke out in the Eastern Part of the Country, and he would have him saved to go with them to fight the Eastern Indians. Agreeably, he left two old Squaws of the Prisoners and bid them tarry there until their Captain Tuspaquin returned, and to tell him that Church had been there and had taken his Wife, Children, and company, and carried them down to Plymouth; and would spare all their lives, and his, too, if he would come down to them and bring the other two that were with him, and they should be his Soldiers, etc.

Captain Church then returned to Plymouth, leaving the old Squaws well provided for, and Biscuit for Tuspaquin when he returned, telling his Soldiers that he doubted not but he had laid a Trap that would take him. Captain Church two days after went to Boston (the Commissioners[2] then sitting), and waited upon the Honorable Governor Leverett,[3] who then lay Sick; who requested of Captain Church to give him some account of the War. Who readily obliged his Honor therein, to his great Satisfaction, as he was pleased to express himself; taking him by the hand and telling him if it pleased God he lived, he would make it a brace of a hundred pounds advantage to him out of the Massachusetts Colony, and would endeavor the rest of the Colonies should do Proportionably; but he died within a Fortnight after,[4] and so nothing was done of that nature.

The same day Tuspaquin came in and those that were with him, but when Captain Church returned from Boston, he found to his grief that the heads of Annawon, Tuspaquin, etc., cut off, which were the last of Philip's friends. The General Court of Plymouth then sitting sent for Captain Church who waited upon them accordingly, and received their Thanks for his good Service, which they Unanimously Voted, which was all that Captain Church had for his aforesaid Service.

Afterwards in the Year 1677 in the Month of January, Captain

Church received a Commission from Governor Winslow to Scour the Woods of some of the lurking Enemy, which they were well informed were there. . . . Accordingly, Captain Church, accompanied with several Gentlemen and others, went out and took divers parties of Indians. And in one of which Parties there was a certain old man whom Captain Church seemed to take particular notice of, and asking him where he belonged, who told him to Swansea. The Captain asked his name, who replied his name was Conscience. "Conscience," said the Captain (smiling), "then the War is over, for that was what [we] were searching for, it being much wanting;" and then returned the said Conscience to his Post again at Swansea to a certain person the said Indian desired to be Sold to, and so returned home.

Notes

William Bradford, *Of Plymouth Plantation*

The Fourth Chapter

1. *that famous truce:* A twelve-year truce signed in 1609.
2. *Orpah did her mother-in-law Naomi, or as those Romans Cato in Utica:* See Ruth 1:14; Cato the Younger (95–46 B.C.E.) committed suicide on Utica after the defeat of his side in the Roman Civil War.
3. *their pastor:* John Robinson (1576?–1625).
4. *beaten:* Experienced.

The Seventh Chapter

1. *A small ship:* The *Speedwell*, of sixty tons.
2. *Another:* The *Mayflower*.
3. *they knew they were pilgrims:* See Hebrews 11:13.

The Eighth Chapter

1. *Mr. Jones:* Christopher Jones, part-owner as well as master of the *Mayflower*.
2. *lets:* Hindrances.
3. *Gideon's army:* See Judges 7:4.

The Ninth Chapter

1. *lusty:* Strong, vigorous.
2. *shroudly:* Severely.

3. *to hull*: To lie to under little sail in order to ride out a storm.

4. *seel*: A sudden roll to leeward.

5. *the Cape harbor*: Now known as Provincetown Harbor.

6. *Seneca was . . . unto him*: Cicero *Ad Lucilium Epistulae Morales* 53. 85.

7. *scripture*: Acts 28:2.

8. *Pisgah*: The mountain ridge from which Moses saw the Promised Land; see Deuteronomy 34:1–4.

9. *shallop*: A large open boat, equipped with both sails and oars.

10. *hath already been declared*: Prior to their departure from England, the Pilgrims had quarreled with the merchants who were financing the voyage and now feared the investors might withdraw their support.

11. *Our fathers . . . their adversity*: Deuteronomy 26:5,7.

12. *Let them . . . of men*: Psalm 107: 1–2, 4, 5, 8.

The Remainder of *Anno* 1620

1. *combination*: An agreement of alliance.

2. *strangers*: Those who were not members of the Leyden group but taken along at the insistence of the investors who financed the venture.

3. *another Government*: The Great Council Of New England, a company of investors and colonizers headed by Sir Fernando Gorges (c.1566–1647), had been granted rights to the territory lying to the north of that controlled by the Virginia Company, by which the Pilgrim colony had been mistakenly patented. In 1621 and again in 1630 the Council granted the patents that legalized Plymouth Colony.

4. *Mr. John Carver*: Carver (c.1576–1621) had taken a major role in arranging the voyage to America.

5. *Mr. William Brewster, their reverend Elder*: The Cambridge-educated Brewster (1567–1644), though not ordained, was the religious leader of the Pilgrims in the early years of the settlement.

6. *Miles Standish*: (c.1584–1656), a former soldier of fortune.

7. *begin the year 1621*: The Julian or Old Style calendar, in use in Great Britain and its colonies until 1752, begins the year on March 25.

Anno 1621

1. *Squanto*: Originally from Pawtuxet (Plymouth), Squanto had been abducted and taken to England by the shipmaster Thomas

Hunt in 1614. He was one of the first Native Americans to establish contact with the colony and served as its guide and interpreter.

2. *set*: Plant.

3. *Isaac Allerton*: Allerton (c.1586–1659) was later to betray the trust of the colony by his failed speculations and his creative book-keeping.

4. *Massasoit*: (c. 1580–1661), chief of the Pokanoket (later Wampanoag) tribe, whose authority extended from the eastern shores of Narragansett Bay to Cape Cod, including Martha's Vineyard and Nantucket; he was the father of King Philip. Squanto arranged his first meeting with the Pilgrims.

5. *Mr. Edward Winslow and Mr. Hopkins*: Winslow (1595–1655) served the colony with distinction as its representative to the Indians, as its agent in England, and as its governor; Stephen Hopkins (d. 1644) was later a tavern keeper and twice assistant governor of the colony.

6. *short commons*: Insufficient fare.

7. *his place*: Sowams, in present-day Warren, Rhode Island.

8. *Manomet*: In the present town of Bourne.

9. *Nauset*: The region corresponding to the present town of Eastham.

10. *Nemasket*: In present day Middleboro.

11. *Capawack*: Martha's Vineyard.

12. *Tarentines*: The Abnaki Indians of Maine.

13. *the Lord . . . their habitations*: Deuteronomy 32:8.

14. *Mr. Cushman*: Robert Cushman (1575–1625), a member of the Leyden congregation and one of the organizers of the voyage of the *Mayflower*.

15. *Birching-Lane*: A London street where cheap clothing was made.

16. *flankers*: Projections in a fortification from which cross-fires could be maintained.

17. *stool-ball*: A country game, something like cricket, in which a ball is batted from stool to stool.

Anno 1622

1. *jealousies*: Suspicions, mistrust.

2. *Mr. Weston*: Thomas Weston (d. 1646), a London ironmonger, headed the group of speculators who financed the Plymouth colony. Unscrupulous in his dealings, Weston long engendered anxiety and anger in the Pilgrim leadership.

3. *Damariscove*: An island off Boothbay, Maine.

4. *now seated at the Massachusetts*: At a place called Wessagussett in the present town of Weymouth.
5. *Manamoyick Bay*: Pleasant Bay, on the south coast of Cape Cod.

Anno Domini 1623

1. *ground nuts*: Edible tubers, once common in New England.
2. *discovers*: Reveals.
3. *a man's way . . . he fall*: Romans 14:4 and Corinthians 10:12.
4. *Piscataqua*: A settlement on the present site of Portsmouth, New Hampshire.
5. *bit in*: Restrained, curbed.
6. *adventurers*: The company of investors who financed the colony.
7. *for his own particular*: On his own behalf as an individual rather than in common.
8. *by course*: By regular alternation.
9. *pinnace*: A small vessel usually rigged with two masts and employed as a tender for a ship.

Anno Domini 1624

1. *pottle*: Two quarts.
2. *stage*: A rack for drying fish.

Anno Domini 1625

1. *Election Court*: The annual meeting for the election of the colony's officers.
2. *Reverend Mr. Hooker*: The noted Puritan preacher Thomas Hooker (1586–1647), who joined the Massachusetts Bay colony in 1633 and two years later founded Hartford, Connecticut.
3. *the composition*: The financial settlement between the colony and the English investors.
4. *old standers*: Original settlers.

Anno Domini 1626

1. *James Sherley*: Treasurer of the adventurers' company.
2. *Sagadahoc*: On the Kennebec River.

Anno Domini 1627

1. *oakum*: Hemp impregnated with pitch or tar and used for caulk-
   ing the hull seams of vessels.
2. *Namskaket*: In the present town of Orleans, on the Cape Cod Bay
   side.
3. *servants*: Indentured servants, to be employed as field hands.
4. *perpetuanes*: Woolen fabrics.

Anno Domini 1628

1. *Scusset*: A creek south of Plymouth that flows into Cape Cod Bay
   near the present eastern entrance to the Cape Cod Canal.
2. *Wampumpeag*: Wampum, or shell money.
3. *fort Orania*: Fort Orange, on the site of Albany, New York.
4. *Mount Wollaston*: In the present town of Quincy.
5. *Mr. Morton*: Thomas Morton, the author of the *New English
   Canaan* (1637), which paints a less than flattering picture of the
   Pilgrims.
6. *Furnival's Inn*: In his book Morton describes himself as a lawyer
   belonging to Clifford's Inn, not Furnival's.
7. *consociates*: Partners.
8. *John Endecott*: Endecott (c.1588–1665), one of the founders and
   governors of Massachusetts Bay Colony, the Puritan settlement
   centered at Boston that was eventually to overshadow Plymouth
   Colony.
9. *the broad seal*: The Great Seal of England, the symbol of royal au-
   thorization.
10. *Dagon*: The god of the Philistines; see Judges 16:23.
11. *screw-plates*: Devices for cutting the threads of screws.
12. *groat*: An English coin worth fourpence.
13. *Winnisimmet*: The present Chelsea, Massachusetts.

Anno Domini 1629

1. *to nose*: To defy in an insolent manner.

Anno Domini 1630

1. *Mr. Winthrop*: In 1630 John Winthrop (1588–1649) founded
   the settlement that became Boston and thereafter played a role in

the affairs of Massachusetts Bay equivalent to Bradford's at Plymouth.

Anno Domini 1631

1. *walte*: Unstable.
2. *congés*: Bows and other courtesies.
3. *the Ile of Rey gentlemen*: An allusion to the repulse of an English expedition against the Ile de Ré off La Rochelle on the French Atlantic coast in 1627.
4. *scapular*: A short cloak, worn by some religious orders.
5. *he showed his malice, but God prevented him*: Upon his return to England, Gardiner and others made complaints against Plymouth and Massachusetts Bay before the Privy Council, which rejected them.

Anno Domini 1632

1. *Green's Harbor*: Now Marshfield.

Anno Domini 1633

1. *Edward Winslow was chosen Governor*: Because Bradford refused the office; unless otherwise specified, as here, Bradford himself was governor.
2. *left that place*: Williams (c.1603–83), later the founder of Rhode Island, arrived at Massachusetts Bay in 1631, where his unorthodox views led to contention with the authorities of the colony.
3. *a slight fort*: Near the present site of Hartford.
4. *their place*: At the site of Windsor.
5. *by friends to have been thrust out*: By settlers from Massachusetts Bay Colony in 1635.
6. *a great sort of flies*: Cicadas.

Anno Domini 1634

1. *Thomas Prence*: Prence (1600–73) joined the Plymouth Colony in 1621 and quickly achieved a prominent role in its affairs.
2. *"Als 't u beleeft"*: "As you please."
3. *murderer*: A small cannon.
4. *a company of people* : A group of Indians.

Anno Domini 1637

1. *Mr. Vane*: Sir Henry Vane (1613–62), who soon after returned to England and played a prominent role in the Civil War.
2. *a sweet sacrifice*: Cf. Leviticus 2:2.
3. *the Mohawks*: Members of the Iroquois Confederacy, the Mohawks then occupied the region around Albany, New York.
4. *we sent the male children to Bermuda*: To be sold as slaves.
5. *Uncas*: (c.1588–c.1683), subchief of the Pequots who rebelled against Sassacus and with his followers founded the Mohegan tribe.

Anno Domini 1638

1. *drink tobacco*: A common seventeenth-century locution meaning to smoke or inhale tobacco.
2. *Aquidneck Island*: Later called Rhode Island, at the entrance to Narragansett Bay.
3. *cast*: Found guilty.
4. *make both . . . his hand*: Haggai 2:6 and Daniel 4:35.

Anno Domini 1642

1. *Scituate*: North of Plymouth and Duxbury, near the border with Massachusetts Bay Colony.

Anno Domini 1643

1. *confederation*: The New England Confederation, comprised of the colonies of Massachusetts, Plymouth, Connecticut, and New Haven.
2. *denouncing*: Declaring.

Anno Domini 1644

1. *Uncaway*: Present Fairfield, Connecticut.
2. *Niantics*: A tribe subordinate to the Narragansetts.

Anno Domini 1645

1. *Seekonk*: A settlement at the western edge of Plymouth Colony near the border with Providence Plantations.

2. *snaphance pieces*: Muskets fired by an early form of flintlock rather than by the clumsy matchlock with which the Pilgrims' weapons were fitted initially.

William Bradford and Edward Winslow, *Mourt's Relation*

Discovery

1. *Bay of Cape Cod*: Provincetown Harbor.
2. *shallop*: A large open boat, equipped with both sails and oars.
3. *Master*: Christopher Jones, part-owner as well as master of the *Mayflower*.
4. *cast and scour*: Vomit and empty the bowels.
5. *a spit's depth*: At the depth of the blade of a spade.
6. *much opened*: Leaking through the seams.
7. *a river*: As the explorers were to discover, their river was to turn out to consist of two creeks, now known as the Pamet and Little Pamet rivers in the present town of Truro.
8. *Miles Standish . . . Edward Tilley*: Standish (c.1584–1656), a former soldier of fortune, long served as the military leader of the Pilgrims; Bradford (1590–1657) was soon to become the chief figure in the colony; Hopkins (d.1644) was to play a lesser role as tavern keeper and assistant governor; while Tilley was to die a few months later in the spring of 1621.
9. *wood-gale*: Bayberry.
10. *whelmed*: Overturned.
11. *Match*: A cord impregnated with gunpowder, used for igniting the charge of a matchlock musket or a cannon.
12. *sprit*: Sapling.
13. *Carver*: John Carver (c.1576–1621) served as the first governor of Plymouth Colony until his death.
14. *helving*: Fitting with handles.
15. *Indian wheat*: Maize.
16. *towards*: At hand.
17. *broaches*: Skewers.
18. *a pack-needle*: a strong needle used for sewing canvas and other heavy materials.
19. *flight shot*: Bow shot.
20. *trunches*: Stakes.
21. *seethe*: Boil.

22. *truck*: Trade.
23. *Agawam*: Now Ipswich, Massachusetts.
24. *harping iron*: Harpoon.
25. *Thievish Harbor*: Soon after to be known as Plymouth Harbor.
26. *a Bay*: Wellfleet Harbor.
27. *becks*: Brooks.
28. *a grampus*: Probably a blackfish, a species of small, toothed whale that frequently strands itself on the Bay side of Cape Cod.
29. *an ell*: Forty-five inches.
30. *set*: Planted.
31. *spires*: Saplings.
32. *snaphance*: A weapon fired by an early form of flintlock, rather than by the clumsy matchlock with which most of the Pilgrims' firearms were fitted.
33. *"The First Encounter"*: In the present town of Eastham.
34. *the harbor*: Plymouth Harbor.

Settlement

1. *letted*: Delayed.
2. *This place*: The present Kingston, Massachusetts.
3. *the greater isle*: Clark's Island.
4. *point*: Determine.
5. *court of guard*: Guardhouse.
6. *rive*: Split.
7. *a Pole*: Sixteen and a half feet.
8. *a cable's length*: 600 feet.
9. *huckle-bone*: Hipbone.
10. *occasionally*: Accidentally.
11. *furniture*: Equipment.
12. *Minion*: A cannon that fired a shot weighing nearly four pounds.
13. *Saker*: A cannon firing a six pound shot.
14. *Bases*: Small cannons firing a half pound shot.
15. *neat's tongue*: cow's tongue.
16. *a savage*: Samoset, a sagamore from Pemaquid, Maine.
17. *Monhegan*: An island off the coast of Maine.
18. *a span*: Nine inches.
19. *the Massasoits*: The Pokanokets of the eastern shore of Narragansett Bay; their sachem was Massasoit.
20. *Sir Fernando Gorges's men*: Gorges (c.1566–1647), a British explorer and colonizer, had established a number of trading and fishing posts on the New England coast.

21. *antics*: Clowns or jesters.
22. *drank*: Smoked.
23. *listed*: Pleased.
24. *carried*: Escorted.
25. *sad*: Deep.
26. *murrey*: Mulberry.
27. *Isaac Allerton*: Allerton (c.1586–1659) was later to become the notoriously unreliable business agent of Plymouth Colony.
28. *the Narragansetts*: A powerful tribe on the western side of Narragansett Bay.

The First Thanksgiving

1. *our Governor . . . the Captain*: William Bradford, who had been chosen governor after the death of John Carver the previous April, and Miles Standish.
2. *a people without any religion*: Winslow, the author of this portion of *Mourt's Relation*, soon discovered his error on this account; as his *Good News from New England* (1624) makes clear:

   Whereas myself and others (in former Letters which came to the press against my will and knowledge) wrote that the Indians about us are a people without any religion, or knowledge of God, therein I erred, though we could then gather no better. For as they conceive of many Divine Powers, so of one, whom they call Kiehtan, to be the principal and maker of all the rest, and to be made by none. . . .

3. *trusty*: Trustworthy.

Edward Winslow, *Good News from New England*

An Errand of Mercy

1. *Massasoit*: The chief sachem of the several Indian groups living in what is now southeastern Massachusetts and eastern Rhode Island, later known as the Wampanoags.
2. *his dwelling*: At Sowams, in the present Warren, Rhode Island.
3. *myself having formerly been there*: In 1622, when he negotiated a peace treaty with Massasoit.

4. *Hobbamock*: A local warrior who early aided the Plymouth settlement.

5. *Namasket*: In Middleborough, Massachusetts.

6. *Corbitant's country*: Corbitant, a sachem subordinate to Massasoit, headed a group living near the present Rhode Island border in coastal Massachusetts.

7. *Mattapoisett*: In Swansea, Massachusetts.

8. *employed upon a service against him*: In the previous summer, when Corbitant was suspected of conspiring with the Narragansetts.

9. *Pokanoket*: Sowams.

10. *doubled*: Repeated.

11. *a confection of many comfortable conserves*: A mixture of many strengthening medicinal preparations.

12. *Patuxet*: Plymouth.

13. *stay*: Wait for.

14. *pottage*: A stew or thick soup.

15. *his stomach coming to him*: Recovering his appetite.

16. *take off the top thereof*: Skim the fat off the broth.

17. *blood stayed*: Bleeding stopped.

18. *chopped*: Thrust.

19. *motioned*: Proposed.

A Pilgrim Atrocity

1. Pnieses: Warriors having great physical and spiritual endowments.

2. *the Massachusetts*: Members of the Massachusett tribe living in the vicinity of modern Weymouth.

3. *Master Weston's Colony*: A plantation at Wessagussett (Weymouth, Massachusetts) established by Thomas Weston, a London promoter and speculator who led the group of investors that initially financed the Plymouth settlers.

4. *the ship*: The *Swan*, a thirty-ton vessel belonging to the English establishment at Wessagussett.

5. *John Sanders*: Sanders, the overseer of the plantation, was visiting the English fishing outpost on Monhegan Island on the Maine coast.

6. *discovered and crossed*: Revealed and thwarted.

Thomas Morton, *New English Canaan*

Chapter 5

1. *Wessagussett*: A trading post established by the English speculator and colonizer Thomas Weston in the present town of Weymouth, Massachusetts.
2. *Obtakiest*: Sachem of the the Neponset band of the Massachusett tribe; Morton calls him Checatawback.
3. *at the Massachusetts*: The headquarters of the tribe in the vicinity of what was soon to become Boston.
4. *relation to*: Consequence of.
5. *exigent*: Extremity, crisis.

Chapter 14

1. *Passonagessit*: In the present town of Quincy, Massachusetts.
2. *Ma-re Mount*: Morton's trading post is now generally known as Merrymount, a name which obscures the endless punning possibilities (in Latin as well as English) of Morton's spelling.
3. *the festival day of Philip and [James]*: May 1, in the calendar of the Anglican Church.
4. *mine Host of Ma-re Mount*: Morton's appellation for himself.
5. *separatists*: Unlike most English Protestant reformers of the time, the Pilgrims separated themselves from the Church of England, believing it to be beyond correction from within.
6. *Calf of Horeb*: See Exodus 32.
7. *Dagon:* The god of the Philistines; see Judges 16:23.
8. *Ganymede*: Cupbearer to Zeus/Jupiter, king of the gods, in Classical myth.
9. *Io to Hymen*: Io was beloved of Zeus; Hymen was the god of marriage.
10. Irish stuff nor Scotch: Irish or Scottish woolens.
11. *tithe of Mint and Cummin*: Matthew 23:23.

Chapter 15

1. *Hippeus's pine-tree horse*: The Trojan horse, constructed by the Greek Epeus; Morton's spelling of the name generates a small equine pun.

2. *the Geese kept in the Roman Capital*: According to tradition, geese served as watchdogs in early Rome, enabling the city's defenders to repel an attack by the Gauls in the fourth century B.C.E.

3. *give them a slip, instead of a tester*: Morton puns again: in addition to its other meanings, "slip" was a slang term for a counterfeit coin, while a tester was a sixpence.

4. *Captain Shrimp*: Miles Standish, who was notably short of stature.

5. *so short*: Close-cropped hair was the mark of Puritan men, who were soon to be dubbed "Roundheads" by the long-haired Royalists.

6. *Monatoquit*: The Fore River.

7. *rosa solis*: A liqueur flavored with the juice of the plant sundew.

8. *conclude*: Decide on a course of action.

9. *the nine Worthies*: Nine famous heroes of ancient or medieval history or legend, a group usually composed of three Jews, three pagans, and three Christians.

10. *Diogenes's tub*: According to tradition, the ancient Greek philosopher Diogenes showed his contempt for luxury by living in a tub.

11. *seven headed hydra*: In Greek myth, a monstrous water snake, eventually killed by Hercules.

12. *to beat a par[le]y*: To call for a conference by beating a drum. Morton errs in his reference to Cervantes's novel, for Don Quixote attacks the windmill that he mistakes for a giant without any preliminary parley.

Chapter 16

1. *the Monster Briareus*: In classical myth, one of the hundred-handed giants, the sons of Earth and Sky.

2. *Aeacus*: One of the three judges of the dead in the underworld of classical myth.

3. *pinnace*: A small vessel usually rigged with two masts and employed as a tender for a ship.

4. *a Plymouth ship*: A vessel belonging to the English seaport, not the New England colony.

5. *tax*: Accuse; Morton returned to Merrymount in 1629, only to be arrested and sent back to England the next year.

Mary Rowlandson, *The Sovereignty and Goodness of God*

The Attack

1. *Lancaster*: A town in Massachusetts, northeast of Worcester.
2. *Garrison*: A fortified house.
3. *Flankers*: Projections from which a crossfire could be maintained.
4. *Removes*: Movements from one place to another.

The First Remove

1. *in the Bay*: In the vicinity of Boston.
2. *profess*: Accept Christianity.
3. *One-eyed John . . . to Boston*: In August of 1675, the Nipmuck sachem Monoco (called One-eyed John) led an attack on Lancaster. Captain Samuel Moseley, a Massachusetts militia commander, claimed that the Christianized Indians of nearby Marlboro were implicated in the attack and brought fifteen of them to Boston for punishment.

The Second Remove

1. *furniture*: Saddle and other riding equipment.
2. *stopped*: Near the site of the present town of Princeton, south of Mount Wachusett. The party had moved westward about fifteen miles.

The Third Remove

1. *Wenimesset, northward of Quabaug*: The Nipmuck settlement of Wenimesset (or Menameset) was in the present town of New Braintree, north of Brookfield. The day's travel was in a south-westerly direction, again about fifteen miles in length.
2. *Captain Beers's Fight*: Richard Beers and most of his men were killed by Indians while attempting to relieve the garrison at North-field on September 4, 1675.
3. *King Philip*: Philip (or Metacom), son of Massasoit, was one of the prime movers of the Native uprising that swept New England in 1675–76.

4. *as he said*: As Job said (Job 16:2).
5. *Quinnapin*: A Narragansett sachem who had married Weetamoo, a sachem in her own right, whose slave Mary Rowlandson became.
6. *Medfield*: A town about fifteen miles southwest of Boston.

The Fourth Remove

1. *a desolate place in the Wilderness*: In the present town of Petersham, reached after a journey northward of some twelve miles.

The Fifth Remove

1. *Jehu*: See 2 Kings 9:20.
2. *Bacquag River*: Miller's River, a tributary of the Connecticut; the party crossed at the site of the town of Orange after traveling northward for fifteen miles from their previous encampment.
3. *my mistress*: Weetamoo.

The Sixth Remove

1. *Lot's Wife's Temptation, when she looked back*: See Genesis 19:26.
2. *a great Swamp*: A few miles northwest of the river crossing.

The Seventh Remove

1. *Squakeag*: The Indian name for the Northfield region, about eight miles north of the last stop.
2. *crickled*: Like *trickled,* but referring to granules rather than drops of liquid.
3. *Ground-nuts*: Edible wild tubers.
4. *"to the hungry Soul every bitter thing is sweet"*: Proverbs 27:7.

The Eighth Remove

1. *Naked came . . . the Lord*: Job 1:21.
2. *ashore*: Philip's encampment was on the site of Vernon, Vermont, on the west side of the Connecticut River just north of the Massachusetts line.

3. Sannup: Husband.
4. *Gossip*: Woman.
5. *the many weary steps*: She had now traveled close to ninety miles.

The Ninth Remove

1. *Here we abode a while*: In the valley of the Ashuelot River in New Hampshire, about five miles north of the border with Massachusetts and a little west of the Connecticut River.
2. *Naananto*: Better known as Canonchet, a Narragansett sachem and leading figure in the war; he was executed by Pequot allies of the English on April 3, 1676.

The Eleventh Remove

1. *the River*: The Ashuelot.
2. *hills*: The Pisgah Mountains.
3. *rest*: This leg of the journey ended at its farthest northern point, near present-day Chesterfield, New Hampshire. From this point onward the party traveled southward and eastward, essentially retracing the route of the first eleven removes.

The Twelfth Remove

1. Nux: Yes.
2. *Cut*: Style, make.

The Thirteenth Remove

1. *a mighty Thicket of Brush*: At or near the site of Hinsdale, New Hampshire.
2. *"Have pity . . . touched me"*: Job 19:21.
3. *" 'I will . . . from him"*: Judges 16:20.
4. *Hadley*: In central Massachusetts, just east of the Connecticut River.
5. *him who was a liar from the beginning*: Satan.
6. *the Mohawks*: Often at odds with the New England tribes to their east, the Mohawks sided with the English in King Philip's War.
7. *a flux*: Dysentery.
8. *Portsmouth*: In present-day New Hampshire.
9. *"For a . . . gather thee"*: Isaiah 54:7.

The Fourteenth Remove

1. *Reeking*: Giving off vapor.
2. *nice*: Finicky.

The Sixteenth Remove

1. *Wachusett*: A mountain about twenty miles north of the present city of Worcester.
2. *the Council*: The Governor's Council of Massachusetts Bay Colony.

The Seventeenth Remove

1. *Samp*: Corn meal.
2. *Rough or Ridding*: The discarded part.

The Nineteenth Remove

1. *Tom and Peter*: Christian Indians who were conducting the ransom negotiations.
2. *the master they served*: Satan, in Rowlandson's eyes.
3. *the General Court*: The name of the legislative body of Massachusetts Bay.
4. *Kab*: About three and a half pints.
5. *Sudbury-fight*: A battle with the English on April 21, 1676, only about twenty miles west of Boston.
6. Powwow: The word refers both to the ceremony and shaman who conducts it.
7. *black as the Devil*: With his face painted black, a sign of mourning.
8. *Pillowbere*: Pillowcase.

The Twentieth Remove

1. *the Governor*: John Leverett (1616–79), Governor of Massachusetts Bay Colony throughout King Philip's War.
2. *Charlestown*: A town just north of Boston, later included in that city.
3. *Mr. John Hoar*: A Concord lawyer, who acted for Rowlandson's husband.
4. *Matchit*: Bad.

5. *Kersey*: A coarse woolen cloth.

6. *James the Printer*: A Nipmuck who had been educated at the Indian Annex school of Harvard College and trained as a printer's
   apprentice; he assisted in the printing of John Eliot's Indian Bible
   (1661–63).

7. *"The bitterness of Death is past"*: 1 Samuel 15:32.

8. *"Help, Lord, or we perish"*: Matthew 8:25.

9. *Mr. William Hubbard*: Minister of Ipswich and historian of King
   Philip's War.

10. *Major Waldron's*: A unit commanded by Richard Waldron of
    Dover, New Hampshire.

11. *the Governor of Rhode Island*: William Coddington.

12. *Mr. Newman*: Noah Newman, minister of Rehoboth, Massachu-
    setts, about twelve miles from Providence; by Rhode Island, Row-
    landson refers not to the region making up the present state of that
    name but to the island of Aquidneck in Narragansett Bay, where
    the governor's seat at Newport was more than thirty miles from
    Providence.

13. *Dorchester*: About five miles south of Boston.

14. *"Money answers all things"*: Ecclesiastes 10:19.

15. *the finest . . . the rock*: Psalm 81:16.

Benjamin Church and Thomas Church,
Entertaining Passages Relating to
Philip's War

To the Reader

1. *Sakonnet . . . Little Compton*: Church refers to the projection of
   land that forms the eastern shore of the entrance to Narragansett
   Bay in what is now the state of Rhode Island, but which then belonged to Plymouth Colony. The name Sakonnet now belongs to
   a village at the southern tip of of the projection, while Little
   Compton is the name of both a village four miles north of
   Sakonnet and the township to which the two communities belong.

The Outbreak

1. *the Court*: The legislative body of Plymouth Colony.
2. *Rhode Island*: The name then referred only to the island of Aquidneck in Narragansett Bay to the west of Sakonnet, not to the area occupied by the present state of Rhode Island.
3. *Pocasset*: The region now encompassed by the township of Tiverton, Rhode Island, lying to the north of Sakonnet and Little Compton.
4. *purchase of . . . grant rights*: Parcels of land at Sakonnet were granted by the Plymouth Court to former indentured servants ("the Company"), who could sell their rights if they so wished.
5. *Philip, the great Mount Hope Sachem*: Philip, whose Native name was Metacom, was the son of Massasoit and heir to his father's authority over the Native peoples from the eastern shores of Narragansett Bay to Cape Cod, Martha's Vineyard and Nantucket; his headquarters were at Mount Hope, in the present town of Bristol, Rhode Island.
6. *Umpame*: The Native name for Plymouth.
7. *the River*: The Sakonnet River, a saltwater channel separating Rhode Island (Aquidneck) from the mainland.
8. *side*: Take sides.
9. *event*: Outcome.
10. *the Governor of Plymouth*: Josiah Winslow, son of Edward Winslow.
11. *the Queen of Pocasset*: Weetamoo, the widow of Philip's older brother.
12. *Sassamon's death, who was Murdered at Assawompsett Ponds*: Shortly after revealing Philip's war plans to the Plymouth authorities, Sassamon was found murdered, apparently on Philip's orders.
13. *Swansea*: A region that extended from Swansea, Massachusetts, to Barrington and Warren, Rhode Island.
14. *the Neck*: The land lying between Narragansett Bay and Mount Hope Bay, formerly known as Pokanoket.
15. *Major Bradford*: William Bradford, second son and namesake of the famous founder of Plymouth Colony.
16. *Massachusetts*: Massachusetts Bay Colony.
17. *Mattapoisett*: Site of the present village of South Swansea, Massachusetts.

18. *damp*: Daze or dejection.
19. *Captain Prentice's Troop*: A Massachusetts unit commanded by Thomas Prentice, who reputedly had served under Cromwell in the English Civil War.
20. *Furniture*: Equipment for riding.
21. *Pilot*: Guide.
22. *a buff Coat*: A jacket made of ox hide, used as body armor by soldiers.
23. *Kickemuit*: Just north of the present line between the towns of Warren and Bristol, Rhode Island.
24. *Mattapoisett River*: Now known as Lees River.
25. *Rehoboth*: About twelve miles east of Providence.
26. *Mr. Treasurer Southworth*: Constant Southworth, who was Church's father-in-law.
27. *Rusk*: Hard toast.

The Pease Field Fight

1. *Nannaquaket Neck*: A peninsula in the present town of Tiverton, Rhode Island.
2. *Punkatest Neck*: In the present village of Tiverton Four Corners, Rhode Island.
3. *Lake*: David Lake, a local landholder and probably the "pilot" mentioned earlier.
4. *charge*: Reload.
5. *Fogland*: A point projecting into the Sakonnet River from Punkatest Neck.
6. *B. Southworth*: Church's brother-in-law.
7. *meanness*: Short supply.

The Pursuit of Weetamoo and the Great Swamp Fight

1. *The next day*: July 9, 1675.
2. *Fall River*: Weetamoo's camp was near the site of the present city of Fall River, Massachusetts.
3. *Dartmouth's distresses*: The town, on the Apponagansett River a few miles southwest of the present city of New Bedford, was attacked in late July.
4. *improved*: Authorized (the violation of the promises).
5. *sold, and transported out of the Country*: To be slaves in Spain.

6. *Rehoboth Plain, and Patuxet River*: Now called the Seekonk Plain and the Blackstone River; Philip was fleeing northwest, past the head of Narragansett Bay.

7. *a Superior Officer*: Captain Daniel Henchman of Massachusetts Bay.

8. *chargeable*: Costly.

9. *the event soon discovered*: The outcome soon revealed.

10. *The United Colonies*: A league of all the New England colonies except Rhode Island.

11. *Reformado*: Individual volunteer.

12. *his Town*: At Shawomet, a point on the western shore of Narragansett Bay in present-day Warwick, Rhode Island.

13. *the evening*: Of December 11, 1675; Smith's garrison was a blockhouse at the entrance to Wickford Harbor.

14. *a Swamp*: The Great Swamp in the present town of South Kingston, Rhode Island, about sixteen miles from Smith's garrison.

15. *one of his Captains*: Generally thought to be Samuel Mosely, a Massachusetts Bay officer who was to become Church's chief rival in the performance of military exploits during the war.

16. *brusled*: Bustled.

The Vicissitudes of War

1. *the Nipmuck Country*: An inland region that took in northwestern Connecticut, northern Rhode Island, and central Massachusetts.

2. *Tents*: Rolls of soft, absorbent material, inserted into wounds to keep them open.

3. *bunts*: Butts.

4. *Netop's*: "Netop" means "friend" in the Narragansett language; the word came to be used by the English as a general term for any Native man.

5. *Schaghticoke*: About twelve miles north of Troy, New York.

6. *and drowned*: The battle took place on May 19, 1676 at the site of Turner's Falls, Massachusetts, and was less of a triumph for the English than Church indicates; they suffered heavy losses, including that of Turner himself, and were driven from the field.

7. *Wachusett hills*: North of present-day Worcester.

8. *Clark's Garrison*: Three miles southeast of Plymouth.

9. *destroyed by the Enemy*: On March 12, 1676.

10. *Saconnesset*: Falmouth, on Cape Cod.

11. *Pawtuxet*: A settlement a few miles south of Providence.

12. *those that had moved from Swansea, Dartmouth, etc*: That is, former inhabitants of Plymouth Colony.

13. *Elizabeth's*: The Elizabeth Islands, a chain of small islands extending southwest of Woods Hole.

14. *Occapeches*: Drams.

15. *supped*: Swallowed.

16. *the Pequots once made War with the English*: In 1637.

17. *Portsmouth*: With Newport, one of the two principal early settlements on Rhode Island.

18. *Sachueset Neck*: The southeasternmost point of Rhode Island (Aquidneck).

19. *the Neck*: Sakonnet Neck.

20. *The next Morning*: June 28, 1676.

21. *Nonquit*: The cove or pond that separates Punkatest Neck from the mainland of Tiverton (Pocasset).

22. *improve*: Employ.

23. *Sandwich*: On upper Cape Cod.

24. *Wepoiset*: At the entrance of the Kickemuit River, probably Touisset Neck in present Warren, Rhode Island.

25. *Agawam*: In the present town of Wareham, Massachusetts.

26. *Sippican River*: The river empties into Buzzards Bay midway between Wareham and Marion; Church's party is following the northwestern shore of the Bay towards the site of New Bedford.

27. *Firelock*: A flintlock musket, as distinct from the older and clumsier matchlock.

A New Commission

1. *got to Middleboro before day*: On July 12, 1676; the settlement at Middleboro lay some fifteen miles west-southwest of Plymouth.

2. *Monponsett Pond*: About ten miles northwest of Plymouth in the present town of Halifax.

3. *to receive to mercy*: To accept the surrender of enemies who put themselves at the mercy of the victors.

4. *Mr. Clark's Garrison*: William Clark's fortified house, three miles southeast of Plymouth, was attacked on March 12, 1676; eleven women and children were killed.

5. *Nemasket*: The Native name of Middleboro.

6. *Tuspaquin*: Known as the "Black Sachem," Tuspaquin, who was Philip's brother-in-law, had led a series of massive raids in southeastern Massachusetts during the preceding May.

7. *Assawompsett*: In Middleboro.

8. *the River side*: The bank of the Taunton River.

9. *cumber*: Encumbrance.

10. *Bridgewater*: About ten miles north-northwest of Middleboro; to go from Taunton to Plymouth by way of Bridgewater would add some eight miles to the direct route.

11. *Assawompsett Neck*: A stretch of land lying between a series of ponds in the present town of Lakeville, south of Middleboro.

12. *Acushnet*: A settlement just north of the present city of New Bedford, into whose harbor the Acushnet River empties.

13. *bating*: Stopping.

14. *Snapsacks*: Knapsacks.

15. *Russell's Orchard*: Southwest of the site of New Bedford.

16. *the great Cedar Swamp*: Acushnet Cedar Swamp, northwest of New Bedford.

17. *Quinnapin and the Narragansett-Sachem*: Quinnapin was a sachem of the Narragansetts who had married the widowed Weetamoo; the other Narragansett sachem may have been Pumham, who was killed at Dartmouth, Massachusetts, a few days later.

18. *Sconticut Neck*: A peninsula in the present town of Fair Haven that forms the eastern shore of the entrance to New Bedford Harbor.

19. *Mattapoisett River*: The river empties into Buzzards Bay midway between New Bedford and Marion; it is not to be confused with the stream in South Swansea to which Church gives the same name.

The Hunt for Philip and Totoson

1. *a Post came to Marshfield on the Lord's day Morning*: Governor Winslow resided in Marshfield, a settlement about twelve miles north of Plymouth; the news reached him there on July 30, 1676.

2. *the River*: The Taunton River.

3. *Philip's Wife and Son of about Nine Years Old*: Contrary to the advice of some of the colonial clergy, Wootonekanuske and her son were not executed but sold into slavery.

4. *quit*: Acquit.

5. *Totoson*: Leader of the attack on Clark's garrison in the preceding March.

6. *Pound*: An enclosure for stray cattle.

7. *arrived with all his Prisoners safe at Plymouth*: On August 4, 1676.

8. *Sam Barrow*: Reputedly Totoson's father.

Philip's End

1. *Sandy point over against Tripp's*: Tripp's ferry ran from Sandy Point in Bristol to Rhode Island (Aquidneck) across the narrows now spanned by the Mount Hope Bridge.
2. *beat up*: Surprise; flush, as in hunting.
3. *Petunk*: Pouch, or haversack.
4. *the last day of the Week*: August 12, 1676.

Annawon

1. *Prudence Island to Poppasquash Neck*: Prudence Island lies to the west of the northern end of Rhode Island in Narragansett Bay; Poppasquash Neck extends southward into the Bay from Bristol, forming the western shore of Bristol Harbor.
2. *Flankers*: Projections from the walls of a fortification from which a crossfire may be maintained.
3. *his Lieutenant*: Howland, who apparently had crossed over from Rhode Island with his men a day later.
4. *Squannakonk Swamp*: Just within the eastern side of the present boundaries of Rehoboth, Massachusetts.
5. *Asuhmequin*: Massasoit's other name.
6. *"Howok"*: "Who's there?"
7. *"Taubut"*: "Very well."

Last Campaigns

1. *Powow*: Shaman.
2. *Commissioners*: The officials of the United Colonies.
3. *the Honorable Governor Leverett*: John Leverett, who had served as governor of Massachusetts Bay Colony since 1673.
4. *he died within a Fortnight after*: Leverett in fact died in 1679, nearly two and a half years later.

FOR THE BEST IN PAPERBACKS, LOOK FOR THE

In every corner of the world, on every subject under the sun, Penguin represents quality and variety—the very best in publishing today.

For complete information about books available from Penguin—including Penguin Classics and Puffins—and how to order them, write to us at the appropriate address below. Please note that for copyright reasons the selection of books varies from country to country.

In the United States: Please write to *Penguin Group (USA), P.O. Box 12289 Dept. B, Newark, New Jersey 07101-5289* or call 1-800-788-6262.

In the United Kingdom: Please write to *Dept. EP, Penguin Books Ltd, Bath Road, Harmondsworth, West Drayton, Middlesex UB7 0DA.*

In Canada: Please write to *Penguin Books Canada Ltd, 90 Eglinton Avenue East, Suite 700, Toronto, Ontario M4P 2Y3.*

In Australia: Please write to *Penguin Books Australia Ltd, P.O. Box 257, Ringwood, Victoria 3134.*

In New Zealand: Please write to *Penguin Books (NZ) Ltd, Private Bag 102902, North Shore Mail Centre, Auckland 10.*

In India: Please write to *Penguin Books India Pvt Ltd, 11 Panchsheel Shopping Centre, Panchsheel Park, New Delhi 110 017.*

In the Netherlands: Please write to *Penguin Books Netherlands bv, Postbus 3507, NL-1001 AH Amsterdam.*

In Germany: Please write to *Penguin Books Deutschland GmbH, Metzlerstrasse 26, 60594 Frankfurt am Main.*

In Spain: Please write to *Penguin Books S. A., Bravo Murillo 19, 1° B, 28015 Madrid.*

In Italy: Please write to *Penguin Italia s.r.l., Via Benedetto Croce 2, 20094 Corsico, Milano.*

In France: Please write to *Penguin France, Le Carré Wilson, 62 rue Benjamin Baillaud, 31500 Toulouse.*

In Japan: Please write to *Penguin Books Japan Ltd, Kaneko Building, 2-3-25 Koraku, Bunkyo-Ku, Tokyo 112.*

In South Africa: Please write to *Penguin Books South Africa (Pty) Ltd, Private Bag X14, Parkview, 2122 Johannesburg.*